After Yugoslavia

Also by Robert Hudson

LAND AND IDENTITY (*edited with Neil Campbell and Christine Berberich, forthcoming April 2011*)

PEACE, CONFLICT AND IDENTITY: Multidisciplinary Approaches to Research (*edited with Francisco Ferrándiz and Wolfgang Benedek, 2009*)

DIFFERENT APPROACHES TO PEACE AND CONFLICT RESEARCH (*edited with Hans-Joachim Heintze, 2008*)

THE POLITICS OF IDENTITY: Migrants and Minorities in Multicultural States (*edited with Fred Réno, 2000*)

A HISTORICAL ATLAS OF ASIA (*edited with Ian Barnes, 1998*)

A HISTORICAL ATLAS OF EUROPE (*edited with Ian Barnes, 1998*)

THE PENGUIN HISTORICAL ATLAS OF RUSSIA (*edited with John Channon, 1995*)

Also by Glenn Bowman

SHARING THE SACRA: The Politics and Pragmatics of Inter-Communal Relations around Holy Places (*forthcoming 2011*)

COMMON GROUND: The Practice and Politics of 'Mixed Shrines' in Israel/ Palestine and Macedonia (*forthcoming*)

After Yugoslavia

Identities and Politics within the Successor States

Edited by

Robert Hudson
Professor in European History and Cultural Politics,
University of Derby, UK

and

Glenn Bowman
Senior Lecturer in Anthropology,
University of Kent at Canterbury, UK

First published 2012 by
PALGRAVE MACMILLAN

Palgrave Macmillan in the UK is an imprint of Macmillan Publishers Limited,
registered in England, company number 785998, of Houndmills, Basingstoke,
Hampshire RG21 6XS.

Palgrave Macmillan in the US is a division of St Martin's Press LLC,
175 Fifth Avenue, New York, NY 10010.

Palgrave Macmillan is the global academic imprint of the above companies
and has companies and representatives throughout the world.

Palgrave® and Macmillan® are registered trademarks in the United States,
the United Kingdom, Europe and other countries.

ISBN: 978–0–230–20131–6 hardback

This book is printed on paper suitable for recycling and made from fully
managed and sustained forest sources. Logging, pulping and manufacturing
processes are expected to conform to the environmental regulations of the
country of origin.

A catalogue record for this book is available from the British Library.

Library of Congress Cataloging-in-Publication Data

After Yugoslavia : identities and politics within the successor states /
edited by Robert Hudson, Glenn Bowman.
    p. cm.
Includes bibliographical references and index.
ISBN 978–0–230–20131–6 (hardback)
1. Former Yugoslav republics—Politics and government. 2. Post-
communism—Former Yugoslav republics. 3. Identity politics—Former
Yugoslav republics. 4. Ethnicity—Former Yugoslav republics. 5.
Nationalism—Former Yugoslav republics. 6. Social conflict—Former
Yugoslav republics. 7. Former Yugoslav republics—Social conditions.
8. Balkan Peninsula—Politics and government—1989– I. Hudson, Robert,
1955– II. Bowman, Glenn.

DR1318.A35 2011
949.703—dc22   2011007797

10 9 8 7 6 5 4 3 2 1
21 20 19 18 17 16 15 14 13 12

Printed and bound in Great Britain by
CPI Antony Rowe, Chippenham and Eastbourne

As always, Elizabeth
and with thanks to Maria for the two
most precious gifts in this world

For Robert-John, Emilie-Anne and Haris

May your generation be spared from some of the
terrible things experienced and witnessed
by your parents' generation.

Contents

Abbreviations and Acronyms

ASNOM   The Anti-Fascist Assembly for the People's Liberation
           of Macedonia (*Antifašističko sobranie na Narodnoto
           Osloboducanje na Makedonija*) – an independent
           Macedonian State formed between 1944 and 1994
CWWV   Centre for Women War Victims (in Zagreb)
DEMOS   Democratic Opposition of Slovenia (*Demokratična opozic-
           ija Slovenije*), coalition founded in 1989 and led by Jože
           Pučnik
DPA   Democratic Party of the Albanians (*Demokratska partija
           na Albancite/ Partia Demokratik Shqiptare*) in Macedonia,
           led by Mendu Thaçi
DS   Democratic Party (*Demokratska Stranka*) in the Republic
           of Serbia
DSS   Democratic Party of Serbia (*Demokratska Stranka Srbije*)
DUI   Democratic Union for Integration (*Demokratska unija za
           integracija*) Albanian movement in Macedonia, formed
           in 2001 and led by Ali Ahmati
FRY   Federal Republic of Yugoslavia (*Savezna Republika
           Yugoslavija – SRJ*) renamed the State Union of Serbia
           and Montenegro (*Državna Zajednica Srbija i Crna Gora*)
           between 2003 and 2006
FYROM   The Former Yugoslav Republic of Macedonia, i.e.
           Macedonia
HDZ   The Croatian Democratic Union (*Hrvatska Demokratska
           Zajednica*) originally led by Franjo Tuđman and now led
           by Jadranka Kosor, while the HDZ 1990 was a breakaway
           Bosnian Croat party, founded in 2006 and led by Boz
           Ljubić
IDP   Internally Displaced Person
KFOR   Kosovo Force
KLA/UÇK   Kosovo Liberation Army (*Ushtria Çlirimtare e Kosovës*)
LKÇK   National Liberation Movement of Kosova (*Levizja
           Kombetare per Çlirimine e Kosovës*)
LDK   Democratic League of Kosova (*Lidhja Demokratike e
           Kosovës*) founded in December 1989, led by Fatmir Sejdiu

LPK	Popular Movement for Kosova (*Levizja Popullore e Kosovës*), led by Emrush Xhemajli (2000–2008)
LPRK	Popular Movement for the Republic of Kosovo
MNT	Macedonian National Theatre (*Makedonski Naroden Teatar*)
NDH	The Independent State of Croatia, (*Nezavisna Država Hrvatske*) founded in April 1941 and existed until May 1945. Led by Ante Pavelić (1941–1943) and then by Nikola Mandić (1943–1945)
NGO	Non-Governmental Organisation
NLA	(Albanian) National Liberation Army in northern Macedonia (*Oslobiteljna Narodna Armija*) also known in Albania as UÇK (*Ushtria Çlirimtare e Kosovës*), founded in 1999 and led by KLA commander Ali Ahmeti
OECD	Organisation for Economic Cooperation and Development
OSCE	Organization for Security and Cooperation in Europe
OTPOR	Resistance (*otpor*) movement in Serbia
QIK	Kosova Information Center (*Qeendra për Informim e Kosovës*)
RS	*Republika Srpska* – the Bosnian Serb Republic
SANU	Serbian Academy of Arts and Sciences (*Srpska Akademia Nauka i Umjetnosti*)
SDP	Social Democratic Party in Croatia (*Socijaldemokratska partija Hrvatske*), originally led by Ivica Račan and now by Zoran Milanović
SDS	Serbian Democratic Party (*Srpska Demokratska Stranka*), originally led by Radovan Karadžić and now by Mladen Bosić
SDSM	Social Democratic Union of Macedonia (*Socijaldemokratski sojuz na Makedonija*), founded in 1990 and currently led by Branko Crvenkovski
SFRY	Socialist Federative Republic of Yugoslavia (SFRJ – *Socijalistička Federativna Republika Jugoslavija*)
SNSD	Alliance of Independent Social Democrats (*Savez Nezavisnih Socijaldemokrata*) – the Serbian party in Republika Srpska, led by Milorad Dodik
UNMIK	United Nations Mission in Kosovo
VRMO-DPNE	Internal Macedonian Revolutionary Party

Acknowledgements

The authors are very appreciative of the assistance provided for this project by the British Association for Central and Eastern Europe (Elizabeth Barker Fund); the Sarajevo Office of the British Council; Humanitariannet (the Thematic Network in Humanitarian Development Studies), and its offshoot EDEN (European Doctoral Enhancement Network in Peace and Conflict Studies); Research Analysts (Foreign and Commonwealth Office); and the University of Derby (Research Inspired Curriculum Fund). We would also like to thank Alexei Fedorov for his help with some of the editing, and Adem Repeša for his help with translating and his constant support and friendship over the years.

Contributors

John B. Allcock was head of the Research Unit in South East European Studies at the University of Bradford (1981–2001), where since 1996 he taught sociology, specialising in Yugoslavia and its successor states. He has published over 30 contributions in academic journals and books, most notably: *Black Lambs and Grey Falcons: Women Travellers in the Balkans* with Antonia T. Young (1991); *Yugoslavia in Transition* with Marko Miivojević and John Horton (1992); and, *Conflict in Yugoslavia: An Encyclopedia* with Marko Miivojević and John Horton (1998).

Neven Andjelić teaches Human Rights and International Relations at Birkbeck College, University of London, and the Bader International Studies Centre of the Queen's University (Canada) in the United Kingdom. He also works for CNN and contributes to the media in former Yugoslavia. Previously he has worked on research projects at the Universities of Sussex, Kent and Oxford and was a Fulbright Scholar at the University of California, Berkeley.

Glenn Bowman studied comparative literature, folklore and folk life, and critical theory in the United States before coming to Oxford in the late 1970s to work under Edwin Ardener and Michael Gilsenan at the Institute of Social Anthropology in Oxford. His doctoral field research was carried out on the topic of Christian pilgrimage in Jerusalem between 1983 and 1985 and gave rise to further regionally based interests in shrines, monumentalisation, tourism and – with reference to the Palestinian people – nationalism and conflict, diasporic and local identities, and secularist versus sectarian strategies of mobilisation. He has subsequently carried out a longitudinal study of the mixed Christian–Muslim town of Beit Sahour, near Bethlehem, which had played a substantial role in the Palestinian intifada (uprising). At present he is continuing his work in Beit Sahour, developing work on 'comparative walling', building on his study of the genealogy and impact of the Isreali 'separation barrier', and investigating historical and contemporary uses of shared shrines in Western Macedonia and Israel/Palestine. Bowman is Honorary Editor of the *Journal of the Royal Anthropological Institute* and is on the editorial boards of *Critique of Anthropology*, *Anthropological Theory* and *Focaal*.

Vojin Dimitrijević is Professor of Law at the Union University of Belgrade. He holds a Doctorate of Law from the University of Belgrade and also Dr iur. *honoris causa* from McGill University and the University of Kent at Canterbury. Dimitrijević is Director, Belgrade Centre for Human Rights; a member of the *Institut de Droit International*; and a member of the Permanent Court of Arbitration, Venice Commission for Democracy through Law. He has served as former vice-chairman of the UN Human Rights Committee. His latest book is *Transnational Terrorism, Organized Crime and Peace – Building Human Security in the Western Balkans* with Wolfgang Benedek, Charles Daase and Petrus van Duyne (eds,) (2010).

Ivan Dodovski is Dean of the School of Foreign Languages at the University American College Skopje. He holds a PhD in contemporary Balkan drama from the University of Nottingham, UK. He studied general and comparative literature with American Studies, and received his MA from the Ss. Cyril and Methodius University in Skopje, specialising in Macedonian literature and narratology. His publications include the study *Narrative Strategies in the Psychological Novel* (2004) and the edited volume *Multiculturalism in Macedonia: An Emerging Model* (2005), as well as three poetry books and a collection of short stories.

Slavko Gaber is Associate Professor in Sociology at the University of Ljubljana, Faculty of Education. His main teaching areas are the sociology of Education, Educational Policy Studies, and Power Relations in Education. His field of research, broadly speaking, concerns education in democratic societies. His recent publications cover a broad spectrum, from educational policy, comparative education, and equality in education, through to the reproduction on inequality in education.

Robert Hudson is Professor in European History and Cultural Politics at the University of Derby, and Director of the Identity, Conflict, and Representation Research Centre. A graduate of the School of Slavonic and East European Studies, University of London, he held a Yugoslav government scholarship as a Postgraduate Fellow at the University of Sarajevo. In the 1980s, he lectured at Exeter College of Art and Design and the University of Rennes (France). Hudson is a faculty member of the European Doctoral Enhancement Programme (EDEN) in Peace and Conflict Studies. He has revisited Yugoslavia and its successor states frequently since 1995 and during the 1990s participated on six missions with the OSCE (Organisation for Security and Cooperation in Europe) as an election supervisor. He co-edited *Politics of Identity: Migrants and Minorities in Multicultural States* (2000), *Different Approaches to Peace and*

Conflict Research (2008) and *Peace, Conflict and Identity: Multidisciplinary Approaches to Research* (2009). He is currently co-editing *Land and Identity* (to be published in April 2011).

Božidar Jezernik is Professor of Cultural Anthropology and a member of the Faculty of Arts at the University of Ljubljana. His research interests lie in the fields of the history and culture of the Balkans, the Perception and construction of 'Other', sex and gender studies, the history and politics of cultural heritage, globalisation, civilisations and terrorism, and extreme life conditions (concentration camps). Key books include *Urban Symbolism and Rituals* (1997); *The Words of Terror: The Media Image of Terror and Violence* (2002); and, *Wild Europe: The Balkans and the Gaze of Western Travellers* (2003).

Vesna Kesić is a journalist and a prominent Croatian feminist and anti-war activist. She has published many articles and has participated in many public debates in and outside Croatia, on issues of women and war. During the war in Croatia, she worked on the deconstruction of daily political rhetoric and popular culture. Today she is a freelance journalist and social researcher.

Shkëlzen Maliqi is an Albanian philosopher, art critic, political analyst, and leading intellectual in Kosovo. During the 1990s, Maliqi was also directly involved in politics as one of the founders of the Social Democratic Party of Kosovo, serving as its first president between 1991 and 1993. He also held leading positions in civil society organisations such as the Kosovo Civil Society Foundation (1995–2000) and the Kosovo Helsinki Committee (1990–1997). Maliqi has published several books on art and politics in Albanian, English, Italian, Spanish, and Serbian. Since the beginning of the 1980s, he has been a regular contributor to the most important media outlets in Kosovo and former Yugoslavia. He currently heads the 'Gani Bobi' Institute for Social Studies.

Vladimir Marković has a degree in Sociology from the Faculty of Philosophy, University of Belgrade in 2001. He was active in the student protest of 2006 and as a Marxist commentator and critic of his own society, he has written widely on social and political issues in Serbia over the last decade. His articles include 'Druga Srbija "u diskrepanciji"' (2001), 'Krox traziciju prilez teoriji privititacije' (2011) and 'Obrasci libralnog eksteremizima u Srbiji' (2011). The chapter which has been translated and published in this book was originally published in an earlier slightly different Internet version in September 2007 under www.protest.zbirka.net in support of the student protest movement, with reflections on the earlier protest of 1996.

Maja Muhić is Senior Assistant Lecturer at the SEE University in Tetovo, Macedonia. Her research is in the field of socio-anthropology where she has studied gender relations and behaviour within ethnic communities of the Balkan region. The bulk of her research is primarily focused on the construction of images, stereotypes, and the 'virtualisation' of different regions, particularly in the Balkans. She has conducted fieldwork among the Turkish community in Macedonia and has also conducted research into the literature used as a guide to the Balkans.

Ines Prica is Senior Researcher at the Institute of Ethnology and Folklore Research in Zagreb and Visiting Professor at the Zagreb Faculty of Humanities, teaching courses on the theory of cultural anthropology, the history of Croatian ethnology and the anthropology of transition. Her seminal work on Croatian ethnology (*Small European Ethnology*, 2001) is a basic textbook for ethnological university courses. Her current research is dedicated to theoretical issues of the anthropology of transition based on the epistemological tradition of Regional Studies and contributing to global cross-cultural comparativeness.

Renata Salecl is a Slovenian philosopher, sociologist, and legal theorist. She is Senior Researcher in Criminology at the Faculty of Law at the University of Ljubljana, and a leading scholar on the subject of Psychoanalysis and the Law. She was Centennial Professor at the Department of Law at the London School of Economics, UK and is now Visiting Professor at the LSE's BIOS Centre for the Study of Bioscience, Biomedicine, Biotechnology and Society, as well as Visiting Professor at the School of Law at Birkbeck College, London. In 2010, Renata Salecl was awarded the title of 'Slovenian woman scientist of the year'.

Irena Šumi is an anthropologist and Senior Scientific Associate. She is currently employed as Head of the Institute of Multicultural and Jewish Studies at the European Centre, Maribor, Slovenia. Her research interests and publishing include the anthropology of ethnicity, nationalism, and boundaries; post-socialism and post-colonialism (Native American Political History of the 20th century); and Holocaust and post-Holocaust studies. She has conducted fieldwork on the borders between Italy, Austria, and Slovenia, among asylum seekers in Slovenia and Holocaust survivors in Slovenia and Israel.

Nebojša Vladisavljević is LSE Fellow in Government at the London School of Economics and Political Science, UK. He teaches comparative politics and the regulation of ethno-national conflict in the Graduate School. He has also taught at the Faculty of Political Science at the University of Belgrade. His research interests are in the areas of authoritarianism and democratisation; social movements and policy opposition; nationalism and the regulation of national and ethnic conflict; constitutional design in new democracies and divided societies; and communism and post-communism. He is also the author of *Serbia's Antibureaucratic Revolution* (2008).

Introduction

Robert Hudson and Glenn Bowman

The dramatic disintegration of the Socialist Federal Republic of Yugoslavia in the early 1990s, which retrospectively seems to have been almost inevitable, caught both Yugoslav and international scholars and publics by surprise. While genocide ravaged Rwanda, Yugoslav, European and North American attention focused on the violent collapse of an at-least-nominally secular European federal state. To many, if not most, it was inconceivable that the SFRY, consolidated in 1944 by Marshall Tito out of the fragments of the earlier Kingdom of Serbs, Croats and Slovenes, could dissolve into fratricidal civil war. Yugoslav scholars encountered in Yugoslavia by one of the two editors of this volume in the early days of the war (24 June–4 July 1991) were nearly unanimous in their opposition to ethnic nationalism and their support for socialist federation; a year later, during a conference held in Canterbury in August 1992, the same academics had almost without exception sided passionately with their national constituencies.[1] Yugoslavia's transformations, although perhaps not exceptional when compared globally, are nonetheless exemplary in demonstrating to Western audiences the speed with which changes in politics, in social structures, in ideologies and in identities can occur under the conditions of modernity. The editors of this volume, one a historian with a long familiarity with the region and the other an anthropologist with an expertise in Israel/Palestine, were inspired by this mutability and by their involvement with the region to draw together a number of academics, journalists and politicians from Former Yugoslavia to reflect on those changes and their implications in the wake of the 'normalisation' that drew the wider world's attention away from Yugoslavia's 'successor states'.

After Yugoslavia constitutes a collection of post-Yugoslav voices reflecting recent developments and trends that have been wrought within the

Yugoslav successor states over the decade and a half since the signing of the Dayton Agreements in autumn 1995.[2] As such, this book offers a distinctive and desirable perspective on the seven successor states, their cultures, politics and identities by providing an internal perspective on the region and its developments through a multitude of views from scholars from across a region who, these days, are rarely brought into conjunction.

After Yugoslavia is interdisciplinary in its approach, and although an emphasis on contemporary politics provides focus to the book, the work draws together anthropologists, historians, sociologists, constitutional lawyers, political commentators and other scholars. *After Yugoslavia* particularly benefits from the insight provided by local academics and intellectuals, many of whom have international reputations and are highly regarded in their own disciplines. This book is most timely in its compilation and concentrates on current issues affecting the region. With the exception of one writer – himself with nearly forty years' academic and personal engagement with the region – all the contributors hail from the different successor states. Each of our contributors is an expert in his or her own field – either as a scholar/researcher or as a political participant – and each has the benefit of both local insight and academic or professional hindsight within their respective areas of expertise.

In putting this project together our contributors were asked to consider, as well as the implications of developments over the past fifteen years, possible trajectories that the successor states might follow in the future, assessing their implications not only for cultural, political, social and economic interactions in South Eastern Europe but also for academic work on and in the region. The authors have reflected upon the changes that the past fifteen years have had on their own thinking, 'from the inside out'.

The following key themes have been dealt with by our writers. First, Kosovar Albanian–Serb relations and the impact of the final resolution of the Kosovo question and the unilateral declaration of independence for Kosovo on the rest of the region, especially with regard to the security implications for northern Macedonia and southern Serbia (Preševo, Bujanavac and Medveđa). This is augmented by Kosovar Albanian perspectives on the different movements and factions in Kosovo, displaying their surprising compatibility with the perspectives on the situation displayed by the Serbian contributions to the book. This is especially timely as the role of internal forces in Kosovo is a topic that has been largely ignored by fellow academics. The book furthermore considers the road to full membership of the European Union being taken by the new states, highlighting Slovenia's current place in it. This movement contrasts with the need for truth and reconciliation in the Yugoslav successor states, and the lack of progress towards achieving it. Running as a leitmotiv throughout the book is the process and problematic of transition in each of the Yugoslav successor states, noticeably displayed in indigenous perspectives on civic society and citizenship in Bosnia and Herzegovina (BiH) in the decade and a half since Dayton. *After Yugoslavia* accounts for the role of gender in the formation of civil society as well as in processes of post-conflict reconstruction, rehabilitation and peace-building. Another important theme is the radical transformation that has taken place in Croatian cultural politics since the death of President Franjo Tudjman in December 1999. This change contrasts with the stabilising role of memory and forgetting, and with the ephemeral nature of political symbols representing the governing ideology of any given period. *After Yugoslavia* also considers the academic quest for objectivity and detachment in scholarship and research and the difficulties the region and its history pose for academics from a variety of disciplines.

In **Chapter 1**, 'Constitutional ethno-nationalism after fifteen years', the author, Vojin Dimitrijević, demonstrates how, through the experience of the break-up of Yugoslavia, our perceptions of nation and nation state have changed dramatically over the past two decades. He does this by an analytical survey of the constitutions of post-communist states in general and the Yugoslav successor states in particular, revealing a process gradually shifting towards the incorporation of liberal interpretations of the state based on the equality of citizens rather than on references to their ethnicity. The result has been that the most explicit versions of constitutional nationalism have been abandoned in recent years under the pressure of external actors and the concomitant development of more moderate nation states whose majority populations find themselves in a better position to work with minority representatives. Of significant importance here has been the compliance with intergovernmental organisations such as the EU and the Council of Europe. Ironically, in this process the constitution of Hungary, a country which in the early to mid-1990s had been interpreted by many commentators as a beacon for illuminating the concerns of ethnic minorities across the wider region, is today seen as being considerably more problematic than fifteen to twenty years ago.[3] Dimitrijević shows that Serbia, despite having missed the opportunity of radically changing its constitution after Milošević's overthrow in 2000 as a consequence the long-drawn-out dispute over the final resolution of Kosovo, has recently been playing catch-up in the constitutional shift from *ethnos* to *demos* as is evidenced in the changes made to the Serbian constitution in 2006.[4] Attitudes concerning the recognition of the February 2008 unilateral declaration of independence by Kosovo still hold Serbia back,[5] yet nonetheless the elections of May 2008 resulted in the defeat of premier Vojislav Koštunica, leader of the DSS Democratic Party of Serbia (*Demokratska Stranka Srbije*) and the re-election of President Boris Tadić, leader of the liberal DS Democratic Party (*Demokratska Stranka*) who has his eyes firmly fixed on Europe.[6]

The impact on Serbian attitudes towards Kosovo of the Kosovar constitutional framework for its provisional self-government, introduced on 15 May 2001 and authorised with the publication of the Constitution of Kosovo in 2008, is dealt with in **Chapter 2** which analyses it in considerable detail.[7] Here, Nebojša Vladisavljević analyses the situation in Kosovo and presents two dimensions of the contemporary Serb–Albanian conflict. He considers a number of alternative solutions to the Kosovo problem, while arguing that a multicultural state will not work. Ultimately, he advocates the partition of Kosovo along the lines of the con-sociational model introduced to Bosnia-Herzegovina by the Dayton Accords. His solution is the territorial separation of the national communities in Kosovo in a highly decentralised state based on power sharing. He uses an earlier plan that had been rejected by the Serbs as the foundation of his own plan.

The author argues that the dominant focus on the struggle between the Serbian government and the Kosovo Albanian leaders over the final status of the Kosovo Question reveals major flaws in research and policy proposals related to Kosovo. The conflict between Albanians and Serbs within the province, rather than the role of outside forces, has been largely ignored by previous scholarship. In the past two decades, there has been little interest in the grievances and behaviour of local actors, especially the Kosovar Serbs, nor in the changing political context in which they struggle and the consequences of their political actions. Academics and policymakers have consistently failed to distinguish the autonomous actions of various groups of Kosovar Serbs from those of political actors from Belgrade. In Vladisavljević's opinion, this failure to take seriously the internal sources of conflict in Kosovo has strongly contributed to the continuation of the conflict. He feels that it is essential to study the actions and aspirations of non-elite groups in Kosovo as well as those of the elites if one is ever to gain a proper understanding of the Albanian–Serb conflict in Kosovo. The author also demonstrates how the focus on actors outside Kosovo rather than on the internal sources of the conflict is one of the main reasons why the relevant international organisations have grossly underestimated obstacles to inter-ethnic peace in Kosovo and have developed a strategy towards the national communities that stands little chance of achieving success. Clearly integration has proved to be an elusive goal in Kosovo, since an integrated multi-ethnic society depends upon the creation of a common 'civic' identity above and in addition to existing national identities. The strategy of integration pursued by international organisations has failed badly in Kosovo, particularly when one considers the extent of violence meted out to Serbs since 1999 which has resulted in virtually no Serbs being left in Albanian-dominated areas. Kosovar Albanians and Serbs have differing views on the very existence of Kosovo as a political entity. For most Kosovar Albanians, the only legitimate unit is a Kosovo that is fully independent from Serbia; some even argue for union with Albania, although this is blocked by the 2008 constitution.[8] According to Vladisavljević, the majority of Serbs, by contrast, continue to consider Kosovo as little more than an autonomous region of Serbia.

Given that integration has failed, Vladisavljević proposes alternative strategies for bringing about a final settlement to the Kosovo Question, namely: partition or consociation. Partition has been more popular among Serbs than Albanians, though it has been totally rejected by radical Serb nationalists. Opponents to partition argue that it would create more problems than it would solve, triggering violence against remaining minorities and turning internal ethnic strife into inter-state conflict with knock-on effects throughout the immediate region (Southern Serbia, Preševo Valley, Sandjak and northern Macedonia) filtering further afield into Greece, Albania, Turkey and Bulgaria.[9] The alternative is a con-sociational model, which necessitates minority communities being granted a disproportionate stake in government. It involves power sharing between the majority and the minority, autonomy for the main segments of the divided society, proportional representation, and a minority veto. Ultimately, according to the author, what is required is a multilayered autonomy or a complex framework for self-rule at the provincial, municipal and sub-municipal levels that would depend upon the territorial concentration of national communities.

The Kosovar Albanian grassroots, non-violent resistance movement has been analysed and discussed by several scholars and analysts over the years as a model for the pacification of current and future conflict situations. Indeed there is little doubt that over nearly eight years the grassroots movement made a considerable contribution towards delaying the outbreak of armed conflict in Kosovo.

In **Chapter 3**, on why the peaceful resistance movement in Kosovo eventually failed, Shkëlzen Maliqi approaches two issues. First, he considers whether or not certain elements of the Kosovar non-violent resistance movement can serve as valid models for either avoiding or resolving inter-ethnic conflicts and other types of armed conflict. Second, he analyses and explains the circumstances and events that led to the eventual failure of the grassroots movement and argues that, contrary to received opinion, Ibrahim Rugova and the LDK (*Lidhja Demokratike e Kosovës* – Democratic League of Kosovo) in many ways contributed to the atrophy of the civil resistance movement. What Maliqi reveals is that Rugova's so-called 'philosophy of non-violence' was never clearly theoretically or philosophically articulated, but was instead a pragmatic political response improvised to meet each political event or crisis as it unfolded. The clearest exposition of his ideas was published in a book of conversations between Rugova and two French journalists, Marie-Françoise Allain and Xavier Galmiche, published in Paris in 1994.

Indeed we discover that the true movers and shakers in Kosovo in the first half of the 1990s were the so-called autonomists, members of the former communist *nomenklatura*, rather than Rugova and the LDK. Maliqi demonstrates that the continuation of Kosovo's autonomy era institutions, dating from the period 1974–1990 and maintained by the 'autonomists' rather than the LDK and Rugova, facilitated the political processes of the period 1990–1999 and ultimately gave rise to the creation of Kosovo's 'parallel institutions'. These parallel institutions were the real success story of the 1990s, drawing up the legal foundations for a true Kosovo state following the unilateral declaration of independence of 2 July 1992 and postponing armed conflict in Kosovo. For Maliqi the true heroes of the story are the autonomists.

Maliqi comments on relations between Rugova's rivals such as Adem Demaçi and Rexhep Qosja as well as on the growing inertia of the LDK before the demonstrations of Priština University students in October 1997 brought an abrupt end to Rugova's charismatic influence on the masses. Ironically, the normalisation of the educational system, signed separately by Rugova and Milošević, demonstrated the weaknesses of Rugova and the LDK. While it initially looked as though a successful model had been found for overcoming tensions between Serbs and Albanians, the school agreement became a source of problems for Rugova because it raised hopes that could not be fulfilled. At the end of 1997, the KLA emerged in the Drenica Valley. The subsequent insurgency in Kosovo against the Serbian government also represented a rebellion against the LDK leaders and Rugova. The grassroots movement was endangered both from within and, with the attack by the Serbian regime, without. At that point the KLA became the true alternative Albanian response to the growing crisis showing that armed resistance was the only way forward. Eventually the resolution of the crisis would become the responsibility of the international community.

Maliqi gets to the roots of Kosovar Albanian society and politics in the 1990s and exposes the social and ideological divisions within both Albanian society and the grassroots movement. His chapter provides detail that has not hitherto been published in English, updating earlier analyses by writers such as Noel Malcolm (1998) and Tim Judah (2000, 2008).

In **Chapter 4**, 'The paradox of the solution: The impact of the Kosovo Question on Macedonia', Maja Muhić politically and analytically explores the complex set of scenarios that could potentially have resulted from the final outcome negotiations regarding the status of Kosovo, especially as regards Macedonia. In so far as Albanians constitute the second largest ethnic group (approximately 25 per cent) of Macedonia's multi-ethnic population, the resolution of the Kosovo status negotiations risked bringing Macedonian and Albanian parties into open confrontation. Although at least notionally this chapter has been overtaken by events (the unilateral Declaration of Independence of Kosovo was announced in February of 2008) it provides more than a historiographical perspective in so far as many of the tensions it delineates continue to exist and could, with any shift in the current situation, burst into open conflict.

Muhić analyses four potential scenarios and trajectories following alternative 'solutions' to the Kosovo Question, as it was seen in late 2007. Her first scenario considers the possibility of independent status being granted to Kosovo without partitioning and without the consent of Belgrade. She balances the idea of Macedonia recognising the independent status of Kosovo against the alternative idea of Macedonia delaying recognition of Kosovo for strategic purposes. Her position is that it would be extremely unlikely that, were Kosovo to gain independence without partitioning, Macedonia would take a proactive role on the Kosovo Question and asserts that under no circumstances would Macedonia be the first country to recognise Kosovo's independence. As events have since shown, it would not be until 9 October 2008 that Macedonia would eventually recognise the independence of Kosovo, with full diplomatic relations being established nine days later.[10]

Indeed, of the four countries that border Kosovo (Albania, Macedonia, Montenegro and Serbia) only Serbia refuses to recognise the independence of Kosovo.[11]

Muhić then considers the possibility of an independent status for Kosovo that would include the partitioning of Kosovo's territory with the consent of Belgrade. This would impact upon the situation in Southern Serbia's Preševo Valley (Preševo, Bujanovac and Medveđa) and trigger Albanian nationalist sentiments both there and in northwestern Macedonia thus signalling a return to events which had previously come to a head in the period 2000 to 2001 when the KLA armed Albanian insurgents in the Preševo Valley and armed and officered the NLA (National Liberation Army) in northern Macedonia.[12] This article helps us understand the Macedonian mindset and its political positioning on the cusp of Kosovo's unilateral declaration of independence.

Muhić's third scenario is that of Macedonia respecting the territorial integrity and sovereignty of Serbia with Kosovo remaining, at least in a formal sense, an integral part of Serbia. Her last scenario considers what would happen were Kosovo's final status to remain frozen until 2020, as was mooted by some commentators at the time. Muhić concludes that the most probable outcome is that set out in her first scenario with Macedonia recognising a Kosovar independence declared without Belgrade's consent. She argues that this case would offer the greatest source of stability for the region with the others potentially more threatening to Macedonia.

As she draws her chapter to a close, she considers the implications of the final status of Kosovo on academic scholarship both on and in the region; a theme that will be taken up by John Alcock in the concluding chapter of our book.

Less has been written on Macedonia (officially known as FYROM – The Former Yugoslav Republic of Macedonia) in the English language than on any of the other states that broke away from Yugoslavia. Possibly this is because, despite its mix of peoples, it was the only republic, with the exception of the almost mono-ethnic Slovenia, to break away peacefully from the Socialist Federal Republic of Yugoslavia in the early 1990s.[13] The country remained peaceful, at least from a Western perspective, until the inter-ethnic conflict that erupted in 2001. In *After Yugoslavia*, the voice of Macedonian identity is given to Ivan Dodovski in **Chapter 5**, 'Pride and perplexities: Identity politics in Macedonia and its theatrical refractions', where he provides the reader with an analysis of identity and violence in the Balkans. It opens with a brief historical overview of the situation confronting Macedonia in the early 1990s, before embarking on the main body of his text which demonstrates how contemporary Macedonian theatre represents significant aspects of the politics of national identity in a period of political and social transition. With reference to works by Ernest Gellner (1994), Benedict Anderson (1991), Ger Duijzings (2000) and Shkëlzen Maliqi (1998), Dodovski demonstrates that Sarkanjac's contention that postmodern discourse on national identity cannot be a prerequisite to but instead a consequence of mutual recognition (Sarkanjac 2005) clearly applies to Macedonia, particularly with reference to the representation of relations between the majority Macedonian community and the 'non-majority' Albanian community. Although Dodovski acknowledges in his opening paragraph that film and television are normally considered to be the dominant media of social construction in the contemporary world, it is his contention that in Macedonia it is theatre that has captured significant aspects of the politics of national identity in what, for Macedonia, has been a period of considerable social transition.

Reflecting on issues raised in the first chapter by Vojin Dimitrijević, Dodovski comments on attempts to move Macedonia towards a new type of nation-building based on multicultural values and civil loyalty which posits a political nation founded citizenship rather than ethnic background. This trend towards nationhood founded on citizenship is countered by another trend that seeks legitimacy by appealing to the concept of cultural pluralism but which reflects the fact that public space is now dominated by the cultural nationalism of the two dominant ethnic communities. 'Multiculturalism' in practice seems to translate into a bicultural cleavage between Macedonians and Albanians wherein identity is expressed as ethnicity.

Meanwhile, in the autumn of 2006, students of the Belgrade universities took a decisive first step in organising themselves against the neoliberal reformation of higher education taking place in Serbia. By doing so they joined in a struggle putting them in line with their student peers in France, Greece and other European countries. This was part of a trend rejecting the treatment of education and knowledge as mere commercial products, a leitmotiv of the student protest of 2006. It is interesting to consider some of the vocabulary and slogans used at the time on posters and banners displayed in the student demonstrations:

Rektor kaže:
Ko ima u glavi imaće u žepu;
Da li to znači, Ko nema u žepu,
Neće imati ni u glavi

(The Rector says: S/he who has it in the head will have it in the pocket; does that mean that S/he who does not have it in the pocket, will not have it in the head?)

This theme is taken up by Vladimir Marković, in **Chapter 6**, 'A re-examination of the position of the student movement in Serbia'. This is a polemical text which began life as a political pamphlet and was then published on the Internet under a different title (*Istorijska pozicija studenskog protesta 2006*)[14] before being offered to the editors of this book for translation from Serbian into English. The editors feel that the polemical nature of Marković's work is very much in keeping with several other voices in this book which also veer towards the polemical in providing snapshots of current thinking and discourse in the successor states. Some more extreme left-wing terminology used in this text bears witness to Marković's polemical voice; for example, expressions such as *potlačeni* or 'oppressed masses'. While solutions to some of the social and political problems extant in present-day Serbia will not be found in this text, generic links and references may be made with the anti-globalisation movement. Above all, this chapter serves as a primary source document for the current state of affairs in Serbia. What it demonstrates is that Serbia is at last returning to a state of normalcy given that the students' real grief is economic rather than political and that the students' organisation of 2006 was self-organised rather than originating in the well-established official students' union, long mistrusted as an organ of the regime. The most significant things to note about the student protest of 2006 is, first, the participants' insistence upon direct participation and democratic decision-making, and second the independent nature of the protest, unaffiliated either to any political party or to traditional, established and formal student organisations. Its character suggests that life in Serbia has greatly changed for the better, certainly in comparison to the situation faced by the OTPOR (resistance) movement of 1996.

The most important problem for the students was student fees. They demanded a reduction of 30 per cent, as fees had increased under the Koštunica government by 70 per cent globally and up to 180 per cent in faculties such as that of architecture. The second complaint was directed at the Bologna Process which had been introduced to Serbia so that its higher education institutions could join the European family of universities. Bologna's introduction involved limiting the standard Bachelor's degree course to three years (six semesters) whereas Serbian university courses had normally lasted for four years (eight semesters). Students demanded that the Serbian university diploma should equate with the Master's in the European system, and that graduates who already held a four-year degree should be upgraded to a Master's. The Serbian government and university authorities, while agreeing, insisted that an administrative fee should be paid by the individuals concerned rather than simply authorising it.

From student protests in Serbia, we move to the complex issue of identity in Bosnia and Herzegovina, where there is no Bosnian nation as such but only a territorial identity that is Bosnia. Today, two communities, Serb and Croats, find themselves situated involuntarily in the state of Bosnia and Herzegovina, while the third, the Bosniaks, can hardly be described as being happy with the present constitutional order and with intra-state relations between the ethnic groups. In **Chapter 7**, Neven Andjelić addresses the competing roles of citizenship and nationality in Bosnia and Herzegovina, noting that a single national identity is absent and arguing that existing identities have been cast in a religio-cultural mould. While each community speaks a similar language, if not indeed the same language, each names its language after its own ethnic group, believing that 'our language is our morality...our spirituality and our refuge' (Isaković 1993: 7). On an everyday level, this enters into the realms of the ridiculous with different expressions – *Bosanska kafa, Hrvatska kafa* and *Srpska kafa* – used to refer to coffee in the different parts of Bosnia and Herzegovina. One must bear in mind in the days of the SFRJ all traditional coffee was simply referred to as *Turska kafa* anyway![15]

Amila Buturović, in her seminal work *Stone Speaker: Medieval Tombs and Bosnian Identity in the Poetry of Mak Dizdar*,[16] points out that 'Bosnia and Hercegovina is not a nation at all, but home to three nationalities' (2002: 2). For Buturović Bosnian identity is a paradox in that territorially one can be Bosnian, but nationally one can be non-Bosnian. While in terms of land, 'homeland' and territorial integrity, Bosnian identity appears to be constant and uninterrupted since the central Middle Ages, for over 50 per cent of the population of Bosnian territorial space there is no sense of Bosnian national identity whatsoever. Nonetheless, the region continues to play a salient role in the construction of identity, and even in the wake of the tensions and conflicts of the 1990s and 'amidst the extreme nationalist plans to carve pieces of Bosnia into Greater Serbia and Greater Croatia, the cultural differences between the Serbs and Croats of Bosnia from those of Serbia and Croatia become more prominent and their regional sentiments more enhanced' (2002: 3).

There is, in Bosnia and Herzegovina, no universal political mobilisation on the level of the entire state; mobilisation is carried out in opposition to the other two ethnic groups as well as, in the Bosniak case, in opposition to the neighbouring countries of Serbia and Croatia.

The identification of two of the three constituent ethnic groups, the Serbs and the Croats, with the country's neighbouring states inevitably leads the Bosniaks, who themselves have no nation state to identify with, to identify with the state of Bosnia and Herzegovina. This pronounced identification of Bosniaks with the state of Bosnia and Herzegovina repels Serbs and Croats from the idea of a Bosnian and Herzegovinian state, and directs them ever more towards identification with the matrix nation states of the Serbs and Croats, respectively.

Andjelić considers Switzerland and Belgium as potential role models for Bosnia and Herzegovina with regard to the relationship between nationality and citizenship. He compares the *Republika Srpska* with Umberto Bossi's *Padania*, in northern Italy, noting that these are artificially created identities with no historical precedent as contrasted with other nations without states such as Catalonia, Scotland or Wales which have all been independent entities at one time or another in the past.

According to Andjelić, if the external supervisory powers hold off much longer in bringing about cross-communal agreement on the nature of the state, local nationalist elites are likely to prepare again for a violent solution. In order to prevent this, it might be advisable, as Michael Ignatieff advised in his argument on nation-building, 'to force responsibility onto local elites' (Ignatieff 2003: 126). Is it possible that a real new nation of Bosnia and Herzegovina will be born out of this process or that instead three practically new national para-states will be created in the Balkans? At the end of the day, Andjelić suggests, it may be that forging a Bosnian identity needs to be taken out of the hands of local politicians and parties and given to cultural and intellectual groups and activities in this area.

The pre-eminence of culture in the formation of national identity in Yugoslav and post-Yugoslav Studies has long been recognised – see Čolović (1994), Ramet (1999), Smith (2009) and Wachtel (1998), inter alia. In her groundbreaking and extremely timely contribution, **Chapter 8**, 'Singing the politics of the Croatian transition', Ines Prica analyses a complete and radical change in Croatia from the cultural politics of the 1990s to a politics grounded in irony that could be called 'postmodern' (with a hilarious reference to the Croatian, Russian-sounding, expression *pas materna* replacing *posmoderna*!). Against the backdrop of the politicisation of show business and the transnational spread of 'turbo-folk' from Serbia to Croatia, she refers to the transition through the use of sex appeal and celebrity status from the wholehearted patriotism of the Croatia of the 1990s to the seemingly political indifference of the present. She uses as the icon of Croatian female transition the controversial Croatian pop-star, Severina, who has transmogrified from the village girl next door to today's almost divine and emotionally untouchable icon of the 'Croatian metropolis'. This chapter's study of the interplay between culture and politics and its impact and relevance to the 'Balkans' shows that Croatia has entered its own postmodern stage in the post-conflict era of its 'second transition' where post-socialism reveals itself as an aspect of post-colonialism. This chapter penetrates into the *heart of darkness* of the European East (Verdery 1996).

In **Chapter 9**, 'The gender dimension of conflict and reconciliation: Ten years after: Women reconstructing memory', Vesna Kesić writes from the premise that, in the aftermath of the conflicts across the former Yugoslavia when nation state consolidation has become a priority, the role of women's groups in resisting war and nationalism has been largely marginalised and forgotten. The author's hypothesis is that, from the late 1970s, women's groups played a formative and crucial role in the reconstruction of civil society in the former Yugoslavia and that, in the late 1990s, they became the most organised actors against war and nationalism by networking across the newly imposed borders. Her chapter opens with a consideration of the role of the Centre for Women War Victims, founded in 1992 in Zagreb. It comments on how this organisation sought to empower women in general by enhancing women's human rights against the backdrop of gendered nationalism which had silenced and de-politicised women. CWWV worked with thousands of refugee and displaced women through the organisation of self-help groups in refugee camps and the distribution of humanitarian aid. The Centre also organised psychological and legal counselling and, by opposing warmongering, nationalism and hate speech, militated against all forms of sexual abuse of women. In considering the contribution of women's groups to post-conflict reconstruction, rehabilitation and peace-building, the chapter focuses on the role of women's groups in reconstructing memory in the face of the expropriation of the collective memory by nationalist governments in post-socialist and post-conflict societies. For Vesna Kesić there is a critical need to recreate the gender dimension of public memory and the role of women in peace-building because if women are excluded from recent memory they are also excluded from contemporary social and political processes.

In her polemical **Chapter 10** on the debate on the national self in post-socialist Slovenia, Irena Šumi sets out to explain what sort of state Slovenia has become over the past two decades. She asks whether or not Slovenia's period of transition has come to an end, and, given that Slovenia is now a fully fledged member of the United Nations, NATO and the European Union, whether or not Slovenia has become a truly Western democracy. Noting that Slovenia has been a cleft society since the time of the Second World War, Šumi believes a cleavage lies at the heart of the debate on national identity and reconciliation in Slovenia. She demonstrates this by analysing the debate on national reconciliation rooted in a left–right and confessional cleavage which originated in the Partisan-Home Guard controversy of the Second World War. Šumi unveils a widespread perception of a dying autochthonous nation held by the right-wing with its strong affiliation with the Catholic Church. This bloc believes that Slovenian primordialist national identity, posited upon the Slovenian language and culture as well as upon pseudo-biological concepts of blood and belonging, is endangered and can only be saved by increasing the nation's fertility and by raising national pride and awareness with the assistance of the Catholic Church. The author provides us with some of the absurdities of what is considered autochthonic in everyday practice.

With regard to democracy and transition (which in practice entails the re-introduction of capitalism) Šumi makes reference to Žižek's writings on China (2008) and asks the question: What if capitalism can exist and prosper in virtually any social system? If Western-style democracy should prove to be an obstacle to economic progress rather than its agent, what impact would this have upon Slovenia, and indeed upon all post-communist, transitional and post-transitional societies? This is a theme taken up later in the volume by Renata Salecl.

It can be said that symbols speak for and represent the governing ideology of the time, reflecting ideological changes. In **Chapter 11**, 'No monuments, no history, no past: Monuments and memory', Božidar Jezernik investigates the political machinations lying behind the building of monuments and their subsequent removal. This is a chapter about memory and forgetting, and the ephemerality of monuments, which are dependent upon the ebb and flow of history. Marble or bronze give a false sense of continuity; in the Slovenian case, monuments that were erected to last 'until the end of human history' only survived a mere half-century.

Public monuments in Slovenia in the late nineteenth century were instrumental in the formation of Slovene national identity and were meant to serve as material expressions and encouragement of the nation's self-confidence, self-esteem and sense of its own excellence. After the Second World War, an increase in memorial sculpture took place, with an extensive new programme of monument-building celebrating the national liberation struggle and the socialist revolution. After Slovenia became an independent republic the new authorities, without much ado, got rid of Tito's monuments. Today, according to the author, the capital of independent Slovenia appears as if its history has been ideologically cleansed as not a single public monument has been left standing testifying to Ljubljana's links with former regimes. According to Jezernik, 'public memory is more a reflection of present political and social relations than a true reconstruction of the past, which is why, after a revolutionary coup [or major political transition – eds] certain monuments no longer fit the new historical and ideological context of a society'. Successive political changes throughout the twentieth century have meant that today's Slovenes have been deprived of and denied access to representations of centuries of shared Austrian, Austro-Hungarian and Yugoslav history. This situation may be found in other South East European states after socialism, with changes in street names and names of buildings as well as the systematic destruction of monuments.[17]

In **Chapter 12** on Slovenia's entry into the European Union, Slavko Gaber returns to many of the themes raised by Vojin Dimitrijević from the perspective of constitutional law and foreign policy in Slovenia. In 'Belgrade-Ljubljana-Brussels' Gaber demonstrates how Slovenia's 2003 vote for accession to the European Union was the culmination of a fifteen-year process in the course of which Slovenia moved from a decision on independence and the reassertion of a previously surrendered sovereignty to once again transferring an important part of its sovereignty to a 'higher power'. This chapter demonstrates that a commitment to democracy and to standing up for national sovereignty drove both the decision to obtain independence and the decision to transfer part of its sovereignty to the European Union. Gaber's thesis is that Slovenia demonstrates that the coexistence of 'national' and democratic forces is possible, and that it is even possible for one to strengthen the other. After discussing the impact of nationalism on the break-up of the former Yugoslavia, the author shows that fear of nationalism can drive commentators to oppose 'national' and 'democratic' processes, despite the fact that the forming of nation states can often strengthen democracy. With reference to Touraine (1994), Gaber notes that just as it is rightly said that democracy has often been a victim of nationalism, it is also true that modern democracy has been closely connected with the nation state. Noting, like Dimitrijević, the inner tensions within the nation state between *'ethnos'* and *'demos'*, Gaber argues that a re-conceptualisation of citizenship rights towards differentiated citizenship rights is required if we are to understand what has been happening in Europe since the 1990s.

How can the successor states to Yugoslavia come to terms with the postmodern world generated by the marketing and branding of image and lifestyle by big, globalised corporations? In **Chapter 13**, Renata Salecl seeks to address this question by positing hypercapitalism as the replacement of old nationalist fears. How after Socialist Yugoslavia can its successors come to terms with new fears, analogous to those which have haunted the West over the past three decades, generated by the decline of older systems of authority and the ephemeral nature of identities and relationships? This encounter is made all the more threatening by all-pervasive feelings of Balkan in adequacy. This is a challenging article about the impact of hypercapitalism seen from a post-Yugoslav perspective. In many ways, Salecl's chapter reminds the reader of some of the reflective inquiries into society and identity by earlier post-Yugoslav writers, such as Slavenka Drakulić and Dubravka Ugrešić writing at the beginning of the 1990s. The difference is that Salecl is representing a totally different Yugoslavia coming to terms, after its own conflictual break-up, with a very different world. Renata Salecl's work goes beyond considering identity, life and attitudes in the Yugoslav successor states as, with reference to Freud and Lacan, she analyses the contemporary collective condition as seen from her post-Yugoslav perspective.

In this chapter, we see how the present condition – post-conflict and post transition – is now shared by both Eastern and Western Europe. Salecl addresses issues of globalism and the psychology of capitalism, with its concomitant freedoms and tyrannies of choice. She considers how the Yugoslav successor states, along with the rest of the post-socialist world, are rapidly transforming themselves into the kind of consumerist societies that predominate in the Western world, as is evidenced today by the rise of shopping malls on the outskirts of Former Yugoslav towns and cities. Salecl looks at how the search for money and profit are overcoming nationalist divides, noting for instance that Slovenian firms continue to profit from the South, particularly Serbia and BiH, just as they had in the 'former' Federal Yugoslavia. These transnational developments suggest, at least at first sight, that capitalism might well present much more than a mere cure for communism.

In the final contribution, **Chapter 14**, John Allcock revisits Yugoslavia as an object of scholarship.[18] He points out that concomitant with the fine array of scholarship produced by academics in the early 1990s, there was also, unfortunately, a plethora of hysterical writing reflecting some very partisan positions. Here he confronts the problem that we all had (and still have) as scholars and academics of South Eastern Europe in maintaining objectivity when our chosen area of study has been engulfed by conflict. Allcock, with reference to Robert Hayden's comment 'if truth is the first journalistic casualty of war, objectivity is the first scholarly one' (Hayden 2000: 18–19) asks 'who amongst us is not in some sense and to some extent partisan in relation to one or another of the peoples or regions of the former-Yugoslavia?' Using Norbert Elias to confront this dilemma, Allcock contrasts early 1990s British research with French scholarship on the Balkans before attempting to analyse his own 'Yugophile' position. Different disciplines employ different methods, and Allcock contrasts his discipline, sociology, with those of history and law to show that, whereas the historian demands hindsight or comparability, the sociologist requires methodology. Although Allcock obviously cannot speak for all British scholars of the former Yugoslavia and its successor states, his chapter powerfully brings our book to a conclusion by calling on readers to reflect upon their own interpretations and representation before, during and after the conflicts. It is only by achieving that distance on their own positions that readers will be able to understand the positions that others – including those from very different backgrounds brought together in this book – have taken in responding to the collapse and transformation of the Yugoslavia which shaped them.

Notes

1. See 'Antagonism and Identity in Former Yugoslavia', Special Issue of *Journal of Area Studies*, 3, autumn 1993, ed. Glenn Bowman.
2. The seven successor states now include the Republics of Slovenia, Croatia, Bosnia and Herzegovina, Serbia, Montenegro, Kosovo and Macedonia.
3. For example, see Martyn Rady, 'Minorities and Minority protection in Eastern Europe', in Robert Hudson and Fred Réno (eds), *Politics of Identity: Migrants and Minorities in Multicultural States* (Palgrave, 2000), pp. 205–222.
4. See *Ustav Republike Srbije*, Službeni List, Belgrade, 2006.
5. A snapshot of Serbian public opinion was presented in a vox pop survey on the BBC Serbian website, on Monday 7 July 2008. The survey reflected Serbian and Albanian opinion in Kosovo, following the announcement of a new Constitution for Kosovo on Sunday 15 June. Here is a sample of some of the comments made: 'Mi samo želimo mir i tišinu' (*We only want peace and quiet*); 'Samo želimo da živimo normalno' (*We just want to live normally*); 'Ne zanima nas ko će dolaziti na Kosovo. Svejedno nam je.' (*It doesn't matter to us what happens in Kosovo. It's all the same for us*); 'Velike sile su odlučile kakav će biti ishod svega ovoga – ne mi, obični ljudi' (*The big powers have decided what will be the result of all this – not us, the ordinary people*); 'Ne mislim da

ćemo mi Srbi poštovati ovaj Ustav – mi ne priznajemu država Kosova' (*I don't think that we Serbs will respect this Constitution – we don't recognise the state of Kosovo*); and 'Naravno, Srbi su protiv tog dokumenta a niko ne zna šta će dalje biti. Mi ovde, na neki način, živimo paralelnim životom' (*Naturally, Serbs are against this document and no one knows how it will turn out. We, here, in a certain way, are living parallel lives*). The upshot is one of resignation generally and a refusal to accept the fait accompli of the existence of Kosovo as an independent state in particular.

6. It was Tadić who took over the leadership of the DS after the assassination of President Zoran Đinđić in March 2003.

7. Particularly note the use of terminology, whereby reference is made to 'peoples' and 'inhabitants' of Kosovo in this document rather than the 'nations' or 'nationalities' of the 1974 Constitution of Yugoslavia.

8. Section 3 of Article 1 [Definition of State] in Chapter 1 (Basic Provisions) of the Constitution of the Republic of Kosovo (2008): 'The Republic of Kosovo shall have no territorial claims against, and shall seek no union with, any State or part of any State.'

9. See also Robert Hudson, 'Federal "Balkania", "Kosovka Republika" or Balkan meltdown?' in David Turton and Julia González (eds), *Cultural Identities and Ethnic Minorities in Europe* (Bilbao, Spain: Humanitari Net, Universidad de Deusto, 1999), pp. 71–79.

10. 'Kosovo and FYR of Macedonia Establish Diplomatic Relations', New Kosova Report, 18 October 2009, www.newkosovareport.com/200910182035/Politics/Kosovo-and-FYR-of-Macedonia-establish-diplomatic-relations.html, last accessed 20 January 2010.

11. At the time of writing (January 2010) some 63 countries out of 129 United Nations member states had recognised the independence of Kosovo. They include the United States and 22 out of the 27 member states of the European Union. However, more than 100 countries, including Russia and China (two of the five members on the UN Security Council) have not recognised the independence of Kosovo. The five countries in the European Union who do not recognise Kosovo as an independent state are Greece, Romania, Slovakia, Spain and Cyprus. Of all the Yugoslav successor states, the only other state, apart from Serbia, that still has not recognised the independence of Kosovo is Bosnia and Herzegovina. BiH is deeply divided because it is made up of two entities: the Bosniak-Croat Federation and the Republika Srpska (Bosnian Serb Republic). In February 2008, the Republika Srpska adopted a resolution denouncing and refusing to recognise the unilateral declaration of independence of Kosovo from Serbia, while nonetheless adding that the parliament of the Bosnian Serb Republic sees the secession of Kosovo from Serbia as a precedent legitimating its own intended referendum on Republika Srpska's constitutional status within Bosnia and Herzegovina. Future developments around Kosovo's independence and its international recognition will continue to impact on the region and provide exciting topics for future academic work.

12. Although Macedonia had been spared the inter-ethnic violence that had broken out in Croatia and Bosnia and Herzegovina following the break-up of Yugoslavia in the early 1990s, the country came close to civil war ten years later, in February 2001. Rebels, led by the Albanian NLA, staged an

uprising in the name of greater rights for ethnic Albanians. Months of skirmishes followed in an insurgency which generated a wave of refugees before the president of Macedonia, Boris Trajkovski, was able to strike a peace deal with the ethnic Albanian leadership. Under the Ohrid agreement, the NLA insurgents laid down their weapons in return for greater ethnic-Albanian recognition within a unitary state.

13. A small list to which we may since add Montenegro, which broke away peacefully from Serbia in May 2006.
14. This translates as 'The Historical Position of the Student Protest of 2006'. See also protest.zbirka.net/node/991, last accessed 22 December 2008.
15. After the war the editors in their travels encountered three different languages where previously only one (*Srpsko-hrvatski*) had existed. In conversation individuals were emphatic that they were speaking *Hrvatski*, *Srpski*, or *Bosanski*.
16. This book draws on the wonderful translations of Dizdar's work that are provided by Francis Jones. See also: Mak Dizdar, *Kameni spavač-stone sleeper*, prijevod/translation – Francis Jones; *pogovor*/afterword – Rusmir Mahmutćehajić, Sarajevo, 1999.
17. Robert Hudson well remembers his own musings on the ephemeral nature of symbols at the sight of rusting, forlorn and flagless SFRJ flagpoles at the tomb of the unknown warrior and that of Marshal Tito, at Avala, just outside Belgrade on a cold and bitter winter's day, in November 1997.
18. See his 'Involvement and Detachment: Yugoslavia as an Object of Scholarship' in 'Antagonism and Identity in Former Yugoslavia', Special Issue of *Journal of Area Studies*, 3, autumn 1993, ed. Glenn Bowman: 144–160.

1
Constitutional Ethno-Nationalism after Fifteen Years

Vojin Dimitrijević

During the first phase of the crisis in the former Yugoslavia and at a moment when it was felt that the conflicts in the territory of that state would have tragic consequences, though there was still hope that some of the worst consequences could be avoided, I presented a paper, at a conference organised at the University of Kent, Canterbury, entitled 'Ethnic nationalism and the Constitutions: the apotheosis of the nation state'.[1] It later transpired that I had been dealing independently with a phenomenon which had also been observed by the American scholar Robert Hayden. We had both concentrated, more or less, on the written phases of the post-communist nation-building process and the revival of the nation state after the collective rule of the Communist Party.

There was a tendency at that time to define the constitutional set-up of post-communist countries as that of states 'belonging' primarily to an ethnic group, to the *ethnos*, and not the *demos*.[2] To put it more simply, post-communist states and their constitutions were seen as classical nation states created by history and the will of the majority, as these states were considered to be heavily coloured and dominated by an ethnic majority. Nevertheless, in some cases, such ethnic marking was not convincing, due to the presence of so many ethnically diverse citizens. Nonetheless, multinational states were mostly regarded as vestiges of the communist period and in some cases as a result of military occupation by others, predominantly by the Soviets in countries which had been forced to join in with the Soviet Union. People who were ethnically different were generally, and with few exceptions, treated as 'historical guests' with ethnical links to other countries, their kin-states, whose protection they could enjoy, and to which in the worst-case scenario they could return. These assumptions could be observed in the operational part of the constitutions or in their preambles, where the state was defined as the state of a given nation and where members of other nations were, if listed at all, referred to only as secondary citizens who did not belong to the true national corpus. These provisos would of course involve disadvantages for them should the constitution be interpreted in an illiberal and unfavourable manner.

Groups that in the communist period had been recognised as nations were to be regarded as the artificial 'children of communism'. The situation of those without a kin state, especially the Roma, was difficult, as they were in effect stripped of 'national rights'.[3]

Reading the text of this paper fifteen years later certainly provides an interesting experience. It allows the author to reconsider his initial position and to observe the later course of events, producing a need to establish what has changed and to understand the reasons for such developments.

One of the possible conclusions is that in most subsequent constitutions there has been a tendency to avoid direct constitutional statements indicating the primacy of the majority nation and to relegate such references to the historical preamble sections. In these sections it is generally maintained that efforts of self-determination which led to the creation of the state had been the result of historical developments; the preambles often describe the difficult path followed by the dominant nation in establishing a state where it could attain the full enjoyment of its citizens' right to self-determination.

Let us first deal with those states that have reduced emphasis in their constitutions on their primarily belonging to a single nation[4] and have introduced some elements of a liberal understanding of the state resting on the equality of all citizens without regard to their ethnicity. The Constitution of Lithuania of 1992 was amended for this purpose in 1996 and in 1998. The Constitution of Latvia, which essentially is a revival of the 1922 constitution, was amended in 1991 and 1998, and now includes a chapter guaranteeing the use of four languages. A similar case may be provided with the Constitution of Estonia of 1992.

The Constitution of Macedonia of 1991 was amended both in 1992 and in 2001. It still lists the peoples who, in addition to those of the Macedonian nation, are recognised as bearers of state sovereignty, but it has corrected the often criticised absence of the Serbs, who are now mentioned together with Albanians, Turks, Wallachians, Bosniaks and others. It is well known that the latest amendments followed a crisis when the Macedonian Albanians, the second most populous people in the country, militantly insisted on a larger say in running the affairs of the state.

The attempt to define Montenegro as an ethnic state in its new 2007 constitution has failed (Article 1). Many inhabitants of Montenegro do not accept that there is a Montenegrin nation, considering this to be a 'Communist invention' and recalling that the concept of Montenegrin identity was developed after 1945, primarily by communist politicians, often of Montenegrin origin, such as Milovan Djilas. The Serbian List, a political group believing that all Montenegrins are Serbs, has argued that Article 1 should state that: 'Montenegro is the state of the Montenegrin and Serbian people and of all equal citizens, regardless of their national or ethnic background, language and religion'. The alternative of the Bosniak Party for Article 1 was: 'Montenegro is the state of Montenegrin, Serbian, Bosniak and other nations and all the citizens residing therein'.[5]

The liberal and the ethnically neutral constitution of the Czech Republic of 1992 only makes reference to its traditions, such as the legacy of the Crown of Bohemia, in its preamble. The same goes for the constitution of Albania, amended in 1998, where the role of the Albanian nation is expounded in the preamble. The constitution of Belarus, amended in 1996 for other reasons, is similar, as are the constitutions of Estonia (1992) and the multiply revised post-communist constitution of Hungary (amended in 1990, 1994, 1997 and 1998). The constitution of Bulgaria of 1999 was not only free of pronouncements of the dominance of the Bulgarians, but had also got rid of a dubious provision favouring the Eastern Orthodox Church, which had been declared the 'traditional' church of Bulgaria without clarification of what was meant by this.

In spite of amendments, adopted by a referendum in 1993, the constitution of Romania remains as mysterious as before. At first sight, it is ethnically neutral, but the meaning of the 'Romanian people', mentioned in Articles 1(3), 2(1) and 4(1) remains unclear.[6] As in 1992, Article 7 is still puzzling: 'The State shall support the strengthening of links with Romanians living abroad and shall act accordingly for the preservation, development and expression of their ethnic, cultural, linguistic and religious identity with the observance of the legislation of the State whose citizens they are.' Does this apply to members of non-Romanian ethnic groups?

The constitution of Croatia of 1990, while amended in 1997, 2000 and 2001, still contains a long historical introduction relying heavily on the efforts of the Croatian people to establish an independent state. This conveniently omits the period of the Independent Croatian State, between 1941 and 1945, an omission which imposes on those teaching the history of Croatia a duty to interpret historical events in the light of that text and thus to ignore the implications of an extremely violent period of Nazi collaboration. Croatia was 'relieved' in 1995 of the majority of individuals belonging to non-Croat groups, most eminently the Serbian minority, and can now afford a more liberal view of the so-called 'autochthonous' minorities, free of the sense of the danger of 'others within' which permeated the 1990 constitution.

Slovenia also belongs to the family of those states that have constitutions that are at first sight 'nationally neutral'. Nonetheless it asserts in its historical introduction the right to self-determination of the Slovenians and still favours Slovenes and their descendants when discussing naturalisation. Slovenia recognises small 'autochthonous' national minorities (the Italians and Hungarians), but has not found a way to deal with the larger minorities which settled in Slovenia in the time of the former Yugoslavia, when Slovenia was Yugoslavia's most prosperous republic. Many of these come from Bosnia and Herzegovina, the majority of them being Muslims who have asked for the free exercise of their religion, including the building of mosques. At present a solution to this problem has not been found.

The only regression, compared to the 1992 situation, can be observed in Serbia. Its 1990 constitution, adopted to serve the regime of the since-deposed leader Slobodan Milošević, had many inconsistencies and was heavily criticised, but it was on the face of it a modern constitution relying on the sovereignty of the people, irrespective of their national belonging. The opportunity to change that constitution, which among other things had reduced the power and competencies of the autonomous provinces (Vojvodina and especially Kosovo), was missed after Milošević was defeated in 2000, so that the new constitution was quickly and without sufficient preparation adopted in late 2006.[7] The most visible defect of this constitution is a preamble paragraph imposing on all decision-makers the duty to act on behalf of the preservation of Kosovo as a constituent part of Serbia. This provision has caused many international problems, but we are more concerned here with the introduction of the ethnic principle in the constitution. After long debate, Serbia's liberals were defeated by nationalists and Serbia is now defined in the first article of the constitution as the state of Serbs and 'other citizens' of Serbia. The effects of such a differentiation have yet to be seen but this is a historical setback compared to the old constitution.

The reasons for the general weakening of ethnic rhetoric, which can be described as the toning down of constitutional nationalism, can be explained by the influence of several factors. One of them has been coming from 'outside'. All the countries in question share their wish to be admitted to the European Union, and one of the conditions for admission remains the implementation of the OECD Copenhagen principles of 1995. This impact was especially noticeable on the Baltic countries who had previously attempted to obviate their large Russian minorities which had been viewed in the early 1990s as a subversive instrument undermining the independence and sovereignty of the Baltic states and serving as vehicles for their reintegration into the Soviet Union. Membership of the Council of Europe, into which all post-communist countries (except Belarus) were admitted after 1989, also played an important role. This was effected through a number of judgements of the European Court of Human Rights, which was very sensitive to discrimination against members of the Russian minority, especially those using as a pretext the Russians' purported inadequate command of the local language.

Similar remarks can be made regarding other new members of the European Union, such as Hungary, Bulgaria and Romania, where their new membership was also instrumental in reducing their ambitions to protect co-nationals abroad, although this, in the Hungarian case, remains equivocal.

Ironically, Slovenia, which has already achieved successful membership of the European Union, was not required to remove from its constitution provisions smacking of constitutional nationalism, and as a result the position of non-autochthonous minorities remains much the same.

Croatia is also aspiring to membership of the European Union[8] and is apparently exposed to pressures to reduce the ethnic component of the state in its constitution. The reference to constitutive nationalism in the preamble of the constitution can be understood as an attempt to gain constitutional legitimacy while playing down the apparent lack of practical consequences. However, as has already been said, the strongest and most troublesome Serb minority has, through the expulsion of many predominantly rural Krajina Serbs in 1995, been deprived of its subversive potential, so Croatia can now afford to deal more rationally and in a more amenable manner with the remnants of that minority. It is working to involve them in the affairs of state through electoral laws providing for a guaranteed number of seats in parliament and through practical political alliances, such as the coalition of the Serbian Democratic Forum with the right-wing and nationalist Croatian Democratic Community, which provide the representatives of that Serbian party with some influence in the executive branch.

In conclusion, it can be said that the most explicit versions of constitutional nationalism have been abandoned in recent years under the pressure of external actors and as a result of the practical reduction of minorities to manageable sizes. Because of the latter development, the majority finds itself in a better position to deal with minority representatives within the framework of a moderately liberal nation state. This does not, however, essentially change the strong drive towards national states which remains an impetus still perceptible in the majority of former communist countries.

Notes

1. V. Dimitrijević, 'Ethnonationalism and the Constitutions: The Apotheosis of the Nation State', *Journal of Area Studies*, 3 (1993): 50–56.
2. Similar conclusions were reached by Nenad Dimitrijević, in *Ustavna demokratija shvaćena kontekstualno* (Belgrade: Fabrika knjiga, 2007: 159 ff.).
3. See V. Dimitrijević, *The Insecurity of Human Rights after Communism* (Oslo: Norwegian Institute of Human Rights, 1993: 24 f.).
4. All constitutions referred to in this text, except those of Montenegro, Romania and Serbia, have been translated in: *Constitutions of Europe. Texts Collected by the Council of Europe Venice Commission* (Leiden-Boston: Martinus Nijhoff, 2004).
5. Document of the European Commission for Democracy through Law (Venice Commission) CDL (2007) 053.
6. The English text of the Romanian Constitution is available at www.cdep.ro/pls/dic/site.page?den=act2_2&par1=1.
7. *Ustav Republike Srbije* (Javno preduzeće Belgrade, *Službeni list*, 2006).
8. By the spring of 2003, Croatia had made sufficient progress to allow it to apply for EU membership, though the accession talks were postponed because of the Croatian government's failure to detain General Ante Gotovina, who was wanted by the International War Crimes Tribunal (ICTY), in The Hague. In October 2005, Croatia got the green light to recommence EU membership talks and Gotovina was arrested in Spain shortly afterwards. It is anticipated that Croatia will become a member of the EU by 2011. At the time of finalising the editing of this book (April 2009) Croatia had just become a member of NATO in the year of that organisation's sixtieth anniversary [RH].

2
Kosovo and Two Dimensions of the Contemporary Serb–Albanian Conflict

Nebojša Vladisavljević

In debates over the Kosovo conflict,[1] scholars and policy-makers have focused largely on broadly conceived Serb–Albanian relations, centred on: the conflicting nationalist ideologies of Serbs and Albanians; the status of Kosovo; and relations between Belgrade and Priština (or Priština/Tirana). Yet such a focus can be misleading. Another, equally important, dimension of the Kosovo conflict is the Albanian–Serb conflict within the province. Yet over the past two decades scholars and policy-makers have not taken into account the grievances and behaviour of local actors, particularly those of the Kosovo Serbs, within the climate of the changing political context within which they have struggled. The failure of local and external political actors – before, during and after the rule of Milošević, including that of representatives of the international organisations involved in the post-war reconstruction and institution building – has strongly contributed to the atmosphere of intractability that threatens to undermine a major opportunity to reach a fair and sustainable solution.

Kosovo Serbs or the Serbian government?

A major source of the failure to grasp the internal dimension of this conflict over national self-determination, in other words, the Albanian–Serb conflict inside Kosovo, has been brought about by confusion over the autonomous action of various groups of Kosovo Serbs and that of Belgrade-based political actors. By and large, Kosovo Serbs have either been ignored or regarded as little more than proxies of the Serbian government.[2] In this respect, nothing much has changed since the early

1980s, regardless of whether Ivan Stambolić, Slobodan Milošević or, since October 2000, democratic governments have been in power in Belgrade.

Scholars and policy-makers tend to regard demands cast by various groups of Kosovo Serbs, and their networks and political activity, as inspired and articulated, organised and funded and, at least in part, implemented by political actors from Belgrade, who aim at the reduction of the autonomy of Kosovo and its full integration into Serbia at the expense of Kosovo Albanians.

However, little evidence exists to support these views. The mobilisation of various groups of Kosovo Serbs pre-dated the rise to power of Milošević and, despite interaction and cooperation with various political actors, they remained an autonomous and influential political factor between 1985 and 1988, that is, both before and after Milošević's rise to power. Influential Kosovo Serbs started lobbying party-state officials in both Serbia and Yugoslavia to take their grievances seriously in the early 1980s, and a full-blown social movement emerged with their popular protests in 1986. They demanded that the authorities prevent inter-ethnic inequalities and insisted on closer links with Serbia.[3]

After Milošević took over the main levers of power in September 1987, following the removal of Ivan Stambolić (Serbia's president and his former political mentor), leaders of the social movement began to cooperate with Serbia's new strongman. They supported him publicly, while taking decisions about protest events autonomously, including those which triggered the anti-bureaucratic revolution, that is, the wave of popular unrest that took place in Serbia and Montenegro in 1988–1989. That the collective action of the protest groups from the Kosovo Serb community was largely autonomous is revealed by an analysis of their protest networks, demands and protest strategies as well as their links with the dissident intellectuals and high officials of Yugoslavia, Serbia and Kosovo.[4] After the counter-mobilisation of Kosovo Albanians, the leaders of the anti-bureaucratic revolution gradually lost their political influence, and by the winter of 1988–1989 the anti-bureaucratic revolution hardly mattered any more, as Serbia and Montenegro fell into a state of turmoil. Moreover, as popular support for Milošević skyrocketed on the wave of discontent with the old political establishment, Milošević was able to sideline all actual and potential rivals in Serbia.

The anti-bureaucratic revolution resulted in major changes in power relations in Yugoslavia and Serbia, and Milošević faced few constraints with respect to his policy towards Kosovo. The constitutional reform of March 1989 and, especially, the new constitution of Serbia of July 1990 reduced the autonomy of Kosovo considerably, while Milošević acquired full control over its political life and the public sector. Serbia's government responded to the resistance of the Kosovo Albanians to constitutional reforms by introducing a range of decrees that amounted to gross violations of their individual and collective rights. It disbanded Kosovo's Assembly, fired thousands of Kosovo Albanians from the public sector and replaced them with Serbs. There were numerous reports about arbitrary arrests, detention without trial and even torture occurring in response to popular protests.

The initial disorientation of Kosovo Albanians after the crackdown gave way to non-violent resistance. By rejecting Serbia's political authority over Kosovo and through the creation of parallel institutions, principally in education, Ibrahim Rugova's Democratic League of Kosovo (LDK), became widely accepted as the voice of the Kosovo Albanian community which aimed at the secession of Kosovo.[5] The regime largely tolerated the development of a parallel system. Since Kosovo Albanians refused to be co-opted to a new power structure, and the costs of the full imposition of compliance remained high during the conflicts in Croatia and Bosnia, the regime settled for control of the provincial political institutions and the public sector in exchange for the quiescence of the majority population. Already in 1989 and 1990 Milošević filled political offices in the province with local Serb apparatchiks, mainly those who had little connection with earlier grass-roots mobilisation. Unsurprisingly, these officials were little more than Milošević's proxies. Obscure officials of an increasingly personalistic regime however should not be confused with Kosovo Serbs in general.

Constitutional reform and greater involvement of the Serbian government in the affairs of Kosovo, especially with respect to the protection of the rights and property of the Kosovo Serbs, met their main pre-1989 demands. At the same time, the Kosovo Serbs realised that the standoff between the Serbian government and the majority community in Kosovo was only a temporary arrangement, convenient to the regime, but the one that exacerbated conflict and offered little assurance to the Kosovo Serbs in the long run.

With respect to the Kosovo Serbs, the regime ruled through a mixture of patronage and selective repression. Supporters were granted lucrative jobs in the government-controlled organisations, while opponents suffered harassment by the regime.[6] Those among the Kosovo Serbs who opposed the regime's strategies towards Kosovo could hardly expect much from approaching the Kosovo Albanian leaders. Despite the non-violent character of the movement, demands for secession remained at the forefront and there was little interest in taking the concerns of the Kosovo Serbs seriously.

The insurgency of the Kosovo Liberation Army (KLA) in 1997–1998, and the harsh counter-insurgency response by the Serbian government, followed in 1999 by the NATO bombing of the Federal Republic of Yugoslavia, resulted in radical changes in power relations between Albanians and Serbs in Kosovo. While UN Security Council Resolution 1244 from 10 June 1999 stated that Kosovo remained part of the Federal Republic of Yugoslavia (Serbia and Montenegro), the province effectively became an international protectorate, initially guarded by 40,000 NATO soldiers (KFOR – *Kosovo Force*). Several hundred thousand Kosovo Albanians, who had been expelled during the war by Yugoslav paramilitaries and regular forces, returned to Kosovo, while well over half of the Kosovo Serbs left the province in a new wave of ethnic expulsions. The remaining Serbs, showing determination to remain in Kosovo and attract the world's attention to their predicament, initiated various protests, including petitions, delegations, protest marches, demonstrations and road blockades, targeted principally at the officials of the UN Interim Administration (UNMIK) and less at the Serbian government.

Despite apparent local initiatives, activists of the emerging movement and their leaders have been regarded by Kosovo Albanian political parties and most UNMIK officials as being the proxies of the Serbian government. This especially applies to Serb leaders in northern Kosovo. Serbs who live north of the river Ibar, that is, in and around the northern part of Mitrovica, constitute the largest and most compact group of Serbs, probably over 60,000, in a territory that is contiguous with central Serbia (Serbia proper). They were therefore able to resist the advance of Kosovo Albanians headed by the KLA in the immediate aftermath of the war and have ever since boldly demanded that their rights should be taken seriously, even at times coming into conflict with Kosovo Albanians from southern parts of Mitrovica, the UNMIK officials and KFOR soldiers. By contrast, Serbs who live in enclaves south of the Ibar, numbering several tens of thousands, have not been in a position to test the commitment of UNMIK and KFOR and have often been under pressure to forfeit their rights for mere physical security and basic supplies.[7]

The main implication of the view that confuses political actors among Kosovo Serbs with those in Belgrade is that the conflict is misleadingly regarded as imported from outside Kosovo. The struggle of various groups among the Kosovo Serbs to have their legitimate interests and concerns taken seriously was equated mistakenly with the policy of the Milošević regime aimed at diminishing Kosovo's autonomy at the expense of the Kosovo Albanians. The same erroneous conclusions were drawn from the action of the Kosovo Serbs in the mid-1980s, during the rule of Ivan Stambolić, and have been drawn since late 2000, despite the establishment of democracy in Serbia. While actors outside Kosovo have often played an important role in internal political developments, they have not invented conflict out of thin air but have only contributed to its intensity. The focus on actors outside Kosovo and not on the internal sources of the conflict partly explains why the UN, EU, OSCE and other international organisations, as well as Western governments, grossly underestimated the obstacles to peace in Kosovo and have developed policies towards its national groups that stand little chance of achieving success.

Kosovo as an integrated multi-ethnic society? The strategy of integration and its consequences

Recent attempts to address the internal sources of conflict in Kosovo by the eradication of national diversity through expulsions serve as a powerful reminder about the ruthlessness of some of the key political actors involved and of the profound moral unacceptability of such strategies. The expulsion of Kosovo Albanians by the Yugoslav paramilitaries and regular forces in response to the 1999 NATO bombing of the Federal Republic of Yugoslavia was unprecedented even in the violent recent history of the region in terms of the sheer scale and systematic character given to it by the involvement of the state. The expulsion of Kosovo Serbs in the aftermath of the war, however, was hardly less repulsive, not least because victims included well over half of all members of this community.[8] While justifications provided by the perpetrators differed, from the 'occupation' of their homeland, threats to the state of security and revenge for past or recent suffering, consequences of ethnic expulsions for their victims were always the same. These horrific acts also testify to the destructive consequences of expulsions in general. In contrast to claims of the perpetrators, ethnic expulsions do not end but often merely displace and exacerbate conflict, and amplify the prospects of prolonged political instability, authoritarianism and economic underdevelopment.

Kosovo's new constitutional engineers from the international organisations involved in post-war reconstruction and institution-building probably had this legacy in mind when they set out to address the conflict through a democratic framework. Elements of the new conflict regulation strategy, based on UN Security Council Resolution 1244, are provided in the Constitutional Framework for Provisional Self-Government in Kosovo (15 May 2001) and in the recurring statements and reports of the relevant international organisations. Resolution 1244 provides a broad framework for both an interim administration for Kosovo and a political process leading to the final settlement. The Resolution provides for: 'substantial autonomy and meaningful self-administration for Kosovo', while recognising the sovereignty and territorial integrity of the Federal Republic of Yugoslavia.[9] It also refers to 'the people' and 'inhabitants' of Kosovo rather than to 'nations'. Likewise, the Constitutional Framework refers to the 'people of Kosovo' (preamble) and designates Kosovo as 'an undivided territory' (Article 1.2).

The Constitutional Framework, nevertheless, explicitly accepts the existence of different 'national communities' and provides a list of rights to which their members are entitled, including the recognition and institutional protection of their languages, symbols and tradition, equal access to employment in the public sector, education and health care (Chapter 4). Some institutional mechanisms aimed at achieving the fair treatment of minority communities are also included, such as a reserved authority for the Special Representative of the UN Secretary-General, that is, a head of UNMIK, to ensure the protection of their rights, proportional representation or over-representation of non-Albanian communities in the provisional institutions and special procedures in the legislative process.[10]

Representatives of the relevant international organisations have repeatedly stressed that their main goal is the creation of an 'integrated multi-ethnic society' in Kosovo. As the Head of the Security Council Mission explained in Priština on 14 December 2002, 'members of minorities must integrate into Kosovo society. Parallel institutions have no future; integration is the only way forward'.[11] Likewise, the statement by the president of the Security Council from 6 February 2003 asserts: 'the Security Council further reaffirms its commitment to the objective of a multi-ethnic and democratic Kosovo and calls upon all communities to work towards this goal and actively participate in the public institutions as well as the decision-making process, and integrate into society'.[12] The reference to the parallel structures relates to the institutions and organisations in the Serb majority areas, principally for health and educational services, which were either inherited from the period before the war and maintained since or created in the aftermath of the war to protect their rights, such as the 'unions of municipalities'. The parallel structures are by and large seen as a 'detrimental factor for the integration and interaction of minorities with the majority population'.[13]

The strategy of inter-ethnic integration pursued by the UN and other international organisations has failed badly in Kosovo. The violence against non-Albanian communities, especially Serbs, has been a persistent feature of political life in spite of the substantial presence of international security forces. Killings, harassment, intimidation, abduction, house-burnings and arbitrary arrests have produced a continuous exodus of Kosovo Serbs to Serbia, Montenegro and the few remaining Serb enclaves within Kosovo. The violence occurred on a large scale in the first two years following the 1999 Kosovo War and has since declined, principally because there are virtually no Serbs left in the Albanian-dominated areas. Those Serbs who still remain in the enclaves south of Mitrovica are often denied any freedom of movement and depend upon physical protection by international security forces. Concomitant with the absence of any freedom of movement, their access to public services, health care, education and employment has been extremely difficult and often impossible. Serbs are often denied the right to the use of their language and alphabet in law courts, agencies and other public bodies, while the destruction of their cultural and religious heritage has proceeded apace. The implications for the life-chances of the affected are enormous, which in turn facilitates the further exodus of Serbs and other minority groups.[14]

These realities have proved to be an insurmountable obstacle to the return of internally displaced persons (IDPs) from Serbia and Montenegro to their homes in the province. The returns so far have been insignificant and to be counted in hundreds against the backdrop of well over 100,000 Serbs expelled from Kosovo after the war. While the 'unfixing' of static checkpoints and the reduction of escorts by the international security forces for those living in the enclaves were introduced with the aim of increasing inter-ethnic interaction, the main consequence of this policy was an increase in the physical insecurity of minority communities, especially the Serbs. The members of these communities face an additional problem – they are in many cases denied use of their property. Without major improvements in physical security, freedom of movement and access to public services and private property, the return of IDPs is unlikely.[15]

Kosovo Serbs have largely avoided participating in elections and provisional institutions at both provincial and municipal levels. Although the electoral system provides for the representation of minorities through the positive discrimination of their parties and coalitions, there is a widespread feeling among the Kosovo Serbs that the provisional institutions do not provide effective mechanisms for the protection of their rights and interests, and that they can do little more than voice their opposition to the policies of the dominant community. The over-representation of non-Albanian communities in the provisional institutions and special procedures in the legislative process provide no guarantees that draft legislation incompatible with the fair treatment of minority communities will not ultimately become the law. The reserved powers of the Special Representative to block policy decisions that violate the rights of minority communities are also inadequate since too much is left to the discretion of the official whose success in office largely depends upon the cooperation of leaders of the majority community.

Dismal initial results in the integration process led to the introduction of the 'standards before status' policy in an attempt to provide incentives to representatives of the Kosovo Albanians to protect the rights of minority communities. The policy stated that a political process leading to the final settlement for Kosovo would not start before major improvements had been made in the functioning of democratic institutions, the rule of law, freedom of movement, returns and reintegration, economy, property rights, and dialogue with Belgrade and the Kosovo Protection Corps. For each of these areas benchmarks were set to monitor progress. The policy did not last long, partly due to the failure to reach improvements and partly because Western governments became concerned that Kosovo Albanians might turn against UNMIK and KFOR because their goal of the independence of Kosovo was being postponed. The large-scale violence of March 2004 appears to have played an important role in this respect.

On 17–18 March 2004 a pogrom-like event occurred in Kosovo, triggered by hate propaganda broadcast by Kosovo's main television channel and other media. Thousands of Albanians attacked Serbs, their property and sacred sites throughout Kosovo. Eight Serbs were murdered and many injured, over 700 Serb homes were destroyed or damaged as well as over thirty Serbian Orthodox churches, monasteries and other religious and cultural sites, some from the fourteenth century. Several thousand Serbs and members of other minority groups, especially the Roma, were forced to leave the Albanian-dominated areas. Eleven Kosovo Albanians were killed in clashes with KFOR and UNMIK police. Several dozen KFOR and UNMIK officers were injured and the property of these two organisations was also destroyed or damaged. Most Kosovo Albanian politicians tacitly approved the events or half-heartedly condemned the violence.[16]

In the wake of the events, little hope remained for an 'integrated multi-ethnic society' in Kosovo, not least because those Serbs who were most integrated into society, that is, those who lived in Albanian majority areas, suffered the most.[17] The question is why integration has proved to be so elusive in Kosovo. After all, this strategy aimed at a noble goal of bringing different national communities together in a democratic framework and was built upon the correct observation that various authoritarian solutions from previous decades had failed to alleviate the conflict. Integration implies the creation of a common 'civic' national or patriotic identity above and in addition to existing national identities. Liberals support integration as a way of treating all citizens as equal, regardless of their ethnic, racial, religious or linguistic characteristics, and of preventing discrimination on these grounds. Historically, integration was successful when different groups willingly accepted it as a way of opposing common enemies or in the case of voluntary migrants who were ready to modify their ethnic identity. Immigrants typically wish to integrate into the larger society in order to take advantage of opportunities available to its full members, and their demands are largely limited to some accommodation of cultural differences. In contrast, historical communities who live in their national homelands wish to maintain themselves as distinct societies. They demand autonomy and self-government to ensure their survival as such. In these states attempts at integration are generally seen by members of various national groups as a threat to their national identity and are vigorously resisted. If imposed, integration is likely to exacerbate conflict.[18]

Keeping in mind Serb–Albanian relations since the second half of the nineteenth century, the patterns of their political mobilisation and the extreme nature and scale of the violence of the past decade, Kosovo was an unlikely candidate for successful inter-ethnic integration. For the greater part of its modern history Kosovo has been a deeply divided society, polarised by conflict between Albanians and Serbs. At the local level Albanians and Serbs have lived largely separate lives in settlements in which one or the other group dominated. In some periods, polarisation turned into open confrontation and violence, which further exacerbated inter-group tensions. In addition to a dominant division in the region, initially based on linguistic, ethnic and religious loyalties and subsequently on national identity, other cleavages in the population mattered, such as those between urban and rural populations, between various clans and tribes, between religious groups (especially among the Albanians), as well as between political and ideological groups or factions.[19] Without doubt, these divisions have considerably amplified the complexity of Kosovo's political problems. However, their effect was principally to divide the Albanian and Serb communities internally rather than to serve as a foundation for the development of stable affiliations that would cut across the main line of cleavage and thus effectively alleviate Albanian–Serb antagonisms.[20]

Political mobilisation among Albanians and Serbs developed principally along national lines. Even during the communist period, the claims about the solution to the national question through the Marxist-Leninist strategy largely concealed the domination of one or the other group. In the late 1980s political mobilisation once again became overtly synonymous with the national mobilisation of Kosovo Albanians and Serbs. Since 1999, despite persistent attempts by the officials of an interim administration and various NGOs to develop 'civic' as opposed to 'nationalist' politics, all relevant political groupings in Kosovo today have been based exclusively on national lines. Moreover, the extreme nature and scale of violence in recent times, which followed a prolonged low-intensity conflict, has hardened the identities of Kosovo Albanians and Serbs to a point where reconciliation between the two groups is unlikely in the near future, let alone the creation of a common identity. In these conditions, policies aimed at inter-ethnic integration do not simply further inflame conflict, but, by encouraging the outflow of the remaining Serbs, facilitate the accomplishment of maximalist nationalist goals, that is, the creation of an Albanian, mono-national polity.

Kosovo's final status: Proposals and alternative solutions

The June 2005 report by Kai Eide, Special Envoy of the UN Secretary-General, acknowledged the failure to meet standards, especially with regard to the protection and rights of non-Albanian communities.[21] The report nonetheless suggested that a new policy should be introduced, which should aim simultaneously at meeting standards – the list of which had already been substantially reduced after the March 2004 violence – and reaching final status for the province. In late 2005, Finland's former President Martti Ahtisaari was appointed Special Envoy of the UN Secretary-General for the future status process for Kosovo. In February 2007, Ahtisaari produced a proposal for the future status[22] which was applauded by the Kosovo Albanians and rejected by the Kosovo Serbs and the Serbian government. The proposal offered a somewhat modified institutional framework for Kosovo, with enhanced municipal autonomy for Kosovo Serbs, as well as greater protection of their religious and cultural heritage, but was still aimed implicitly at inter-ethnic integration. The main novelty was that Kosovo should be granted 'conditional independence', that is, statehood during a transitional period with government powers somewhat circumscribed and supervised by representatives of international organisations.

It remains unclear, however, how a slightly modified strategy of integration, of managing national diversity in a unitary state/political entity, would now work in a scenario of thinly veiled majoritarianism. Previous attempts by UNMIK at managing such a policy had already failed, and in the new climate supervision by the international organisations would be even lighter than before. The proposal by and large ignored the internal dimension of the Kosovo conflict, that is, the extreme polarisation between Albanians and Serbs in a severely divided society which gave rise to the acute vulnerability of Kosovo Serbs. It pushed aside their key concerns and demands for meaningful political – as opposed to administrative – autonomy for their majority areas while offering no more than a limited devolution of powers to the municipalities. It did not provide effective protection against the imposition by the majority community of decisions considered detrimental to the interests of the Kosovo Serbs, making their veto on such decisions in the Kosovo Assembly conditional on the support of representatives of other national communities. This, in light of the fact that the latter are extremely vulnerable to pressure from the Kosovo Albanian parties, was clearly insufficient. The proposal even included a substantial reduction of the existing over-representation of national minorities in the Assembly. Links with Serbia's government were limited and, like the acceptance of financial support from Serbia, conditional on the agreement of Kosovo Albanian ministers or international supervisors.

Ahtisaari's proposal essentially provided legitimisation for the secession of Kosovo from Serbia, satisfying the claims of the Kosovo Albanians to national self-determination, while denying the analogous claims of the Serbs. Members of the two groups have contrasting views on Kosovo's very existence as a political entity. For the majority of Kosovo Albanians, Kosovo is the only legitimate political unit. For some, the end point of the political process is Kosovo's union with Albania. Nearly all agree that they do not want to have anything to do with Serbia. By contrast, most Serbs, in and outside Kosovo, consider the province as little more than an autonomous region of Serbia. While these nationalist aspirations cannot be satisfied simultaneously, attempts to impose the maximalist claims of one group on the other are likely to lead not only to further ethnic violence in the province, but also to the further emigration of Kosovo Serbs. This will lead not only to the creation of an Albanian mono-ethnic polity but as well to prolonged instability in the wider region, caused in part by the creation of a powerful revisionist bloc in Serbia.

One proposal that arguably tackles both the internal and external dimensions of this nationalist conflict arrived on the agenda too late to be seriously considered by the Kosovo Albanian leaders, who now would settle for nothing less than independence. The Serbian government's preferred solution is a condition 'more than autonomy, less than independence' (also referred to, equally poetically, as the 'one country, two systems' plan). The plan proposes that Serbia should retain formal sovereignty over Kosovo in exchange for forfeiting any say in the rule over the province's majority population. Kosovo would therefore enjoy full executive, legislative and judicial autonomy and, apart from not having a seat in the United Nations, would function as an independent state. The plan also outlines territorial autonomy for the Kosovo Serbs in the areas where they are in majority and links between their institutions and Serbia's government. It was the timing of the proposal rather than its actual content that barred its acceptance.

Two other ethnic conflict regulation strategies, which have not been seriously taken into account by policymakers,[23] arguably address both the internal and external dimensions of the Kosovo conflict. One is the partition of Kosovo between Albanians and Serbs and the other involves the secession of Kosovo, radical federalisation and power-sharing between predominantly Albanian and Serb self-governing units, and confederal links of the Serb unit with Serbia. Partition would involve the creation of a new state, consisting of the bulk of Kosovo's territory (roughly 85 per cent) in which Albanians constitute a majority, and the accession of the province around northern Mitrovica, which has a Serb majority, to Serbia proper.

Partition may be appropriate in cases in which alternative conflict management strategies, such as integration or territorial autonomy in a multinational state, have repeatedly failed to alleviate conflict and where members of different national communities manifestly do not want to live together, as reflected in recurrent mutual hostilities and extreme inter-ethnic violence. In principle, partition is not incompatible with liberal democracy; while continuous group conflict and violence in a multinational state often facilitate authoritarianism, the separation of hostile populations may remove obstacles to democracy in newly separated territories or states. The same argument could be made for the prospects of economic development after partition. In contrast, critics argue that partitions create more problems than they resolve; that is, that they encourage expulsions and breakdowns or political order, create more violence than would have otherwise occurred, and turn internal into more menacing inter-state conflict. There are no fair or just partitions that would fully satisfy the interests of all parties in conflict and 'clean' cuts are by and large not feasible, partly because, barring expulsions, no new border would fully separate hostile groups and partly because any agreement on the borders among warring parties is unlikely.[24]

The formal territorial separation of national communities in Kosovo would hardly increase conflict because a degree of informal separation has already been created on the ground through expulsions and extreme violence during and after the 1999 Kosovo War. One obstacle to the partition of Kosovo may be that only around half of the remaining Kosovo Serbs live in the northern part of the province, which is territorially contiguous with Serbia proper, while the other half remains in enclaves situated deeply within Albanian-populated areas, mainly in central and eastern Kosovo. However, experience from comparable cases, such as the Turkish Cypriot enclaves in Cyprus in the years before the 1974 de facto partition, as well as the March 2004 pogrom-like violence against Serbs in Kosovo, suggests that ethnic enclaves within hostile surroundings are extremely vulnerable and probably unsustainable in the long run.

It is unclear what the alternative may be in Kosovo to the formalisation of the borders 'drawn in blood'. Any attempt at the reversal of de facto partition and the forced remixing of Albanians and Serbs in a 'multi-ethnic society' is virtually certain to increase hostilities and the suffering of minorities, and to result in the creation of an Albanian-only polity and instability in the wider region. The formal recognition of Kosovo by the United States and large European states and the continuation of the de facto partition would only turn the conflict into a frozen one, on the model of Cyprus, which would hardly be beneficial either to the parties involved or to the broader region as a whole. In contrast, partition would arguably take into account important, though not the maximalist, interests of both the Kosovo Albanians and Serbs. As a result, Serbia and the newly created state of Kosovo need not be hostile to each other and few obstacles would remain to economic and other forms of cooperation. This solution is also unlikely to have more adverse consequences for the broader region than its alternatives. The secession of the whole territory of Kosovo would arguably create more instability by leaving many Serbs on the 'wrong' side of the border and provoking revisionist policies by present and future Serbian governments.

Another alternative to inter-ethnic integration and Ahtisaari's proposal that has not been considered so far would, like partition, build upon the existing informal separation of national communities on the ground. It would largely satisfy the nationalist aspirations of Kosovo Albanians by way of the secession of the whole territory of Kosovo from Serbia, but also take into account some interests of the Kosovo Serbs by granting them self-rule in a highly autonomous territorial unit which would include both northern Kosovo and existing enclaves south of Mitrovica. This alternative would entail power-sharing between Albanian and Serb political units, as well as the establishment of confederal links between the Serb 'entity' and Serbia. There is already a moderately successful precedent in the region. The 1995 Dayton Peace Agreement established Bosnia and Herzegovina as a highly decentralised state consisting of Republika Srpska and the Bosniak-Croat federation. This was based on power-sharing between representatives of three nations and of the two 'entities', and entailed the units' confederal links with neighbouring Serbia and Croatia respectively. Based on the recognition of segments of a divided society, it includes all elements of consociational democracy – executive power sharing between national groups, segmental (here also territorial) autonomy, proportional/parity representation and mutual veto rights.[25] It also recognises the fundamental disagreement of parties over the legitimacy of Bosnia and Herzegovina as a political unit – supported unequivocally only by Bosniaks, while the majority of Serbs and Croats prefer joining their neighbouring kin states – by establishing confederal links of the two entities with Serbia and Croatia.[26] Similar external links with a kin state, with the aim of addressing intractable national self-determination problems, were established between Northern Ireland, the United Kingdom and the Republic of Ireland by the 1997 Good Friday Agreement.[27]

Conclusion

Recent policies and proposals for dealing with the Kosovo conflict largely ignore its complexity. They fail to recognise its two, equally important, dimensions; that is, polarisation and conflict between Albanians and Serbs within Kosovo, and the broader Serb–Albanian nationalist conflict centred on relations between Belgrade and Priština. The policy of integration, conducted under the auspices of UNMIK, did not simply fail to achieve its widely proclaimed goal of an 'integrated multi-ethnic society' in Kosovo, but also increased the insecurity and suffering of non-Albanian communities, especially the Serbs. A modified, now implicit, version of the same project in Ahtisaari's proposal is only slightly less inadequate in its address to the internal dimension of the Kosovo conflict. It threatens to create further instability in the wider region because the secession of Kosovo and minor concessions to Kosovo Serbs fail to address both the Kosovan Serbs' concerns and the interests of Serbia's government. In contrast, the alternative proposals outlined above would arguably address both the internal and external dimensions of the Kosovo conflict. The partition of Kosovo between Albanians and Serbs, and the package of Kosovo's secession and 'soft' partition, coupled with self-rule for, and power-sharing between, Albanian and Serb 'entities' with confederal links to Serbia, seem to deserve serious consideration. Partition, as a simpler and largely self-enforcing option, stands more chance of putting an end to the conflict than do the solutions put forth by the international community.

Notes

1. The term Kosovo (Kosova in Albanian) is widely accepted in the West. Serbs normally use the term Kosovo-Metohija.
2. See, for example, *The Kosovo Report* by the Independent International Commission on Kosovo (Oxford: Oxford University Press, 2000).
3. Nebojša Vladisavljević, *Serbia's Antibureaucratic Revolution: Milošević, the Fall of Communism and Nationalist Mobilization* (London: Palgrave Macmillan, 2008), chapter 3 and Vladisavljević, 'Grass Roots Groups, Milošević or Dissident Intellectuals? A Controversy over the Origins and Dynamics of Mobilization of Kosovo Serbs in the 1980s', *Nationalities Papers*, 32, 4 (2004): 781–796.
4. Vladisavljević, *Serbia's Antibureaucratic Revolution*, chapters 3 and 4. See also Darko Hudelist, *Kosovo: bitka bez iluzija* (Zagreb: Centar za informacije i publicitet, 1989) and Sava Kerčov, Jovo Radoš and Aleksandar Raič, *Mitinzi u Vojvodini 1988. godine: radjanje političkog pluralizma* (Novi Sad: Dnevnik, 1990).
5. Denisa Kostovicova, *Kosovo: The Politics of Identity and Space* (London: Routledge, 2005); Besnik Pula, 'The Emergence of the Kosovo "Parallel State", 1988–1992', *Nationalities Papers*, 32, 4, 2004: 797–826; Paulin Kola, *The Search for Greater Albania* (London: Hurst, 2003); and Howard Clark, *Civil Resistance in Kosovo* (London: Pluto Press, 2000).
6. See for example Mario Brudar, *Politički život Srba na Kosovu i Metohiji, 1987–1999* (Belgrade: Nova srpska politička misao, 2003).
7. The Serbs in these enclaves were dependent upon UNMIK/KFOR for their security because these enclaves were largely isolated from each other and had no direct access to Serbia. Travel outside the enclaves was restricted to military convoys. This often led to human rights abuses against Serbs and other ethnic minorities committed by Kosovar Albanians whereby, for example, access to Albanian-run Kosovo hospitals was restricted for Serbs and other minority groups, such as the Roma, Gorani, Ashkali and

Egiptiani, who were accused of having colluded with the Serbs during the period of the KLA-led insurgency. While minor ailments and injuries could be treated in local KFOR field hospitals, more serious cases had to be air-ambulanced to Belgrade, which technically was situated in another country [RH].

8. For details see the OSCE reports *Human Rights in Kosovo: As Seen, As Told*, Volume I, October 1998–June 1999 and *Human Rights in Kosovo: As Seen, As Told*, Volume II, 14 June–31 October 1999.

9. The federation changed its name to Serbia and Montenegro in 2002. Four years later, Montenegro separated from Serbia after a majority voted for independence in a referendum. The Constitutional Charter of the State Union of Serbia and Montenegro stated that, should Montenegro break away from the union, all international instruments pertaining to the common state, particularly the UN SC Resolution 1244, would concern and apply in their entirety to Serbia as the successor (Article 60).

10. Articles 8.1 (a), 9.1 (3, 12–13, 22, 39–42) and 9.3.5.

11. *Report of the Security Council Mission to Kosovo and Belgrade, Federal Republic of Yugoslavia, 14–17 December 2002* (S/2002/1376), Annex I: 16.

12. S/PRST/2003/1, p. 1.

13. See, for example, *Tenth Assessment of the Situation of Ethnic Minorities in Kosovo* (period covering May 2002 to December 2002), OSCE Mission in Kosovo, UNHCR, March 2003: 5.

14. The extent of the human rights violations has been well documented. See, for example, the OSCE report *Human Rights in Kosovo: As Seen, As Told*, Volume II, 14 June–31 October 1999; subsequent OSCE reports – *Assessments of the Situation of Ethnic Minorities in Kosovo*; and a detailed first-hand account by two high-ranked UNMIK officials, Ian King and Whit Mason, *Peace at any Price: How the World Failed Kosovo* (London: Hurst, 2006), part I.

15. See the Comprehensive Review of the Situation in Kosovo, United Nations, Security Council, S/2005/635, Annex: 15–16.

16. Report of the Security-General on the UNMIK, United Nations, Security Council, S/2004/348. For a detailed account of the March 2004 events see King and Mason, *Peace at Any Price*: 5–20.

17. King and Mason, *Peace at Any Price*: 13.

18. John McGarry and Brendan O'Leary, *The Politics of Ethnic Conflict Regulation: Case Studies of Protracted Ethnic Conflicts* (London: Routledge, 1993): 17–20. See also Donald Horowitz, *Ethnic Groups in Conflict* (Berkeley: University of California Press, 1985): 567–568 and Will Kymlicka, *Multicultural Citizenship: A Liberal Theory of Minority Rights* (Oxford: Clarendon Press, 1995): 11–26.

19. See Ger Duijzings, *Religion and the Politics of Identity in Kosovo* (New York: Columbia University Press, 2000): 12–13.

20. Vladisavljević, *Serbia's Antibureaucratic Revolution*, chapter 3.

21. Comprehensive Review of the Situation in Kosovo.

22. Comprehensive Proposal for the Kosovo Status Settlement, United Nations, Security Council, S/2007/168/Add. 1.

23. The final version of this paper was submitted in December 2007.

24. Sumantra Bose, *Bosnia after Dayton: Nationalist Partition and International Intervention* (London: Hurst, 2002), chapter 2 and Brendan O'Leary, *Debating*

Partition: Justifications and Critiques, Mapping Frontiers, Plotting Pathways Working Paper 28, 2006.

25. Arend Lijphart, *Democracy in Plural Societies: A Comparative Exploration* (New Haven, CT: Yale University Press, 1977): 25.

26. Bose, *Bosnia After Dayton*.

27. Brendan O'Leary, 'The Nature of the British–Irish Agreement', *New Left Review*, 233 (1999): 66–96.

3
Why the Peaceful Resistance Movement in Kosovo Failed

Shkëlzen Maliqi

Kosovo and the disintegration of Yugoslavia

It is generally accepted by most scholars of the Western Balkans that at the end of the 1980s and the beginning of the 1990s the crisis of the former Yugoslav federation revolved around the Kosovo question.[1] Of course the real cause of the federation's disintegration lay not in Kosovo itself, but rather in a complex process that was rooted in inherited antagonisms. Yugoslavia, since its creation in 1918, had always been a 'fragile state' because of the 'contradictions between the Serbian and the Croatian understanding of the term Yugoslavia',[2] and throughout the 1980s Kosovo served as a 'catalyst' and generator of Serbian irredentism (Maliqi 1989: 69, 178).[3]

Although analysts were predicting that war would erupt in Kosovo first (The Kosova Report: 42–44), the war actually started in Slovenia,[4] and then spread into Croatia and Bosnia and Herzegovina. The aim of the wars was not the defence of the federation, but the realisation of a Greater Serbian state based on the platform of the so-called Memorandum of the Serbian Academy of Sciences and Arts (SANU 1986).[5] The aim of the wars was: 'to remove populations of the "wrong ethnicity" en masse from the territories considered to belong to the Serbs' (*Rat u Hrvatskoj i BiH*: 161–175 and Maliqi 1998: 128–132).

The sudden shift of the crisis from the margins (Kosovo) to the centre (the Serbian–Croatian conflict) did not result solely from the manoeuvres of the Serbian regime, as the Albanian political movement, which had emerged at the end of the 1990s under the leadership of Ibrahim Rugova, took the path of non-violent resistance, by not responding to force in kind. The main goal of the Kosovar Albanian movement was the independence of Kosovo, but its methods were carefully chosen and it sought support from the international community. Albanian self-restraint made it possible to maintain the status quo, so that Kosovo experienced neither war nor peace for the time being (Maliqi 1998: 185).

The Kosovar 'parallel society' functioned successfully until the Dayton Peace Conference, which ended the war in Bosnia. Dayton caused disappointment among the Kosovars because it overlooked the Kosovo question. Militant circles in the Albanian movement considered that the non-violent resistance had failed. In the meantime, they prepared for rebellion, through the auspices of the Kosovo Liberation Army (KLA), which emerged in 1997. Milošević's regime, which had been shaken by the loss of the local elections in the Federal Republic of Yugoslavia and the 100-day demonstrations that took place between November 1996 and January 1997, took up the challenge posed by the KLA. The Serbian regime finally had its *casus belli*, but it was not satisfied with just conducting actions against the KLA, and Milošević consequently opted for a so-called 'final solution' of the Kosovo question. The Serbs began by employing a 'scorched earth' strategy that included reprisals against the civilian population, and the destruction and burning of villages and other settlements, in what effectively seemed to be the same kind of policy that had been conducted in previous wars in Croatia and Bosnia and Herzegovina.[6]

The international community, which had learned from mistakes made from its late response in Bosnia and its prior recognition of the results of a fait accompli and of the so-called 'ethnic cleansing of territories', acted quickly and more decisively in Kosovo to prevent a new genocide.[7]

The development of civil resistance in Kosovo

The Albanian movement in Kosovo in the late 1980s arose as a reaction to Serbian hegemony. As in other parts of Yugoslavia, Kosovo also entered a phase of total 'ethnic homogenisation' of the political disposition of its citizens. The first mass rebellion erupted in November 1988 against the changing of the provincial leadership.[8] After these demonstrations, Kosovar Albanians gained in self-confidence, which was initially aimed at the defence of Kosovo's autonomy.[9] In February 1989, 215 Albanian intellectuals signed a petition against the curtailment of Kosovo's autonomy (Clark 2000: 50; Maliqi 1990: 273). On 20 February, the miners of Trepça rebelled, which turned into a seven-day general strike. Serbia responded by imprisoning the communist leader

Azem Vlasi, and the leadership of the Trepça mine, and by imposing martial law (Clark 2000: 47; Maliqi 1998: 81–95). The pro-Western federal government of Ante Marković was weak or compromised in the belief that it could stop Milošević by political and economic measures (pluralism and the introduction of the free market economy).[10] Around 400 Kosovar intellectuals were imprisoned during the first days of March. Their 'isolation' was also intended to convey a threatening message just before the meeting of the Kosovo Assembly,[11] which was held on 26 March 1989 under the state of emergency, and which was intimidated into accepting the changes of Kosovo's constitution.[12]

Through 1989, Kosovo was held under the pressure of a tyrannical regime. While in other parts of Yugoslavia opposition parties and organisations were forming, in Kosovo all public meetings were banned. Only by the end of 1989 were the first opposition meetings held in Kosovo.[13]

When the Congress of the Communist League of Yugoslavia was interrupted on 25 January, Milošević's regime through Kosovo's puppet leadership tried to provoke a rebellion in the province, so that it could gain a pretext for imposing martial law thereby ensuring Serbian control over developments, which were leading towards the disintegration of the federation. However, in that critical period between the end of January and the middle of February 1990, the Albanian movement unexpectedly passed from a phase of anarchistic rebellion into a phase of self-discipline.[14] This was assisted by the rapidly increasing membership of the LDK (Democratic League of Kosova) and the popularity of its leader, Dr Ibrahim Rugova.[15] On the evening of 2 February 1989, Rugova made an appeal on local television for the demonstrations to stop, and the following day the unrest came to an end. Kosovo's grass-roots movement suddenly gained structure and a hierarchy. The movement's spiritual power was based on an almost fanatical belief in democracy and peaceful protest, as the most effective means of resisting the communist regime and Serbian nationalism (Maliqi 1998: 97–105). The democratic revolutions in Eastern Europe, where communism was collapsing like a house of cards, created the certainty among Kosovars that in Kosovo, too, it would unavoidably lead to a turn towards democracy. On the brink of a war and concomitant chaos, the idea of free elections pacified Albanian ambitions.

On the popular side, the Serbian political and intellectual elite formed a broad nationalist and populist coalition (Magas 1993: 200; Popov 1993; Vujacić 1995), which all supported the idea that prior to the elections the autonomy of Kosovo should either be curtailed or completely abolished.[16] A race against time began as Albanians opted for democracy, while Serbs opted for political or military dictatorship, in order to: 'save Serbian territories'. Both anti-communists and liberal democrats in Serbia accepted Milošević's formula that for the Serbs' national interests, democracy is less of a priority than the protection of the Serbian state and national interests in Yugoslavia.[17]

In Kosovo, the struggle was being played out between Kosovo's weakened institutions and Serbia's powerful state apparatus. Until June 1990, Kosovo's provincial institutions were still functioning,[18] but the political mood of the masses was controlled by a new centre of power, the LDK and its leader Rugova. The LDK's charisma and also that of Rugova grew enormously after a fifteen-person delegation of Albanians spoke at a hearing in the US Congress, on 24 April 1990. In a hearing that was held in front of the Congressional Commission on Human Rights, the Kosovar delegation faced the Serbian delegation, which was led by Dobrica Ćošić.[19] The Albanian-American Civic League succeeded in obtaining special protection for Rugova.[20] After the hearings, Rugova was portrayed in the Kosovar public as 'America's chosen man', who received the type of escort that is normally only reserved for statesmen of the highest rank. In the Kosovo media, the visit was interpreted as indirect support for Rugova and the movement for the independence of Kosovo.

By the end of June, Kosovo's provincial institutions, at least the Albanian portion of these, stimulated by the mood of the masses, tried to cause a change in the situation by preparing the ground for proclaiming the Republic of Kosovo. The President of the Assembly, a Serb, obstructed the attempt of the Albanian delegates and interrupted the meeting of the Assembly on 25 June, after a 'verbal incident'.[21] The following day, 117 Assembly delegates gathered in front of the Assembly building, which was guarded by the police. Since they were prevented from entering, they held the meeting in front of the gates, where they proclaimed the Declaration of Independence of Kosovo. Three days later, Serbia replied by approving a law which 'temporarily' suspended the powers of all of Kosovo's provincial institutions. Then a series of laws followed, that placed all public institutions and economic resources under the control of the Serbian state.[22] Milošević had achieved his goal of a 'united Serbia'.[23] In Kosovo, Milošević's regime instituted an apartheid system, in which Albanians were excluded even from cultural and sports associations.[24]

The Albanian delegates of Kosovo's formally disbanded Assembly considered Belgrade's measures as unconstitutional and illegal, and on

7 September 1990 held a secret meeting in the small town of Kačanik, where they proclaimed the Republic of Kosovo.[25] The Albanians maintained control of the print media; private properties and small businesses; as well as those segments of 'organised society', such as: the trade unions; schools; political and humanitarian organisations, professional associations and citizens' associations; and segments of the health-care system. Organs of local self-management that were forcibly disbanded, and the leadership of firms, continued to present themselves as 'the legal institutions of Kosovo', but without the possibility of realising any administrative and economic functions. The government in exile now had a symbolic function, by adopting regulations that could not be wholly applied.

The real centre of political and moral power among the Albanians was the LDK, which governed the so-called 'parallel institutions', most of which were inherited from the period of autonomy.[26] In a way, the Serbian regime handed over control of Albanian society to the LDK and Ibrahim Rugova, in order to dedicate itself to solving the Serbian question in other parts of Yugoslavia. The temporary pacification of Kosovo suited Belgrade well, because at the time, it was preparing for the 'defence' of Serbian territories in the other Yugoslav republics, namely the third of the Serbian nation who lived outside the actual borders of the Republic of Serbia.

Kosovo's non-violent resistance as a grass-roots movement

Non-violent resistance and the organisation of the 'parallel society' and 'parallel institutions' as an answer to repression and as a way of solving the inter-ethnic conflict presented a very specific experience, by contrast with those that brought conflict and wars to other parts of Yugoslavia. In a certain period, 1990–1997, the Albanian grass-roots movement was considered by many as one that was unique and that could serve as a model for the pacification of conflict situations. Indeed, despite predictions that war was unavoidable and expectations that it would happen before those that took place in Croatia and Bosnia and Herzegovina, Kosovo's grass-roots movement contributed enormously in delaying the war for a certain period of time. The aim of the grass-roots movement had been to avoid war, although in the long run it did not succeed in this goal, as war broke out in 1998. The reasons for this failure can be found in the general, unbefitting circumstances, and in the weaknesses within the movement. This analysis of Kosovo's grass-roots resistance movement will focus on the following crucial question: Can we find elements in the Kosovar non-violent resistance movement for developing a specific model for either avoiding or resolving inter-ethnic conflicts; elements that might be valid in other conflict situations?

Why did this grass-roots movement fail?

As a model, according to many analysts, the Kosovar movement represented a unique social and political experiment, and as such it merits careful attention and analysis. However, although as a form of civil resistance and a political movement it has been pragmatically evaluated as a positive development, neither its protagonists nor external factors and analysts reflected on its real potential and effects in a timely manner. Contextually, the non-violent resistance was judged to be relative to the regional crisis. Kosovo was seen as a kind of 'oasis of good behaviour' by comparison with other crisis areas, where allegedly 'irreconcilable' ethnic interests had led to bloodshed and exceptionally cruel wars. Kosovo's response to the crisis, which in essence had the same radical and conflicting 'ethnic' character, was in many ways much idealised both within Kosovo and by external actors. That idealisation was based on a sort of blind illusion of ostensible stability in Kosovo. In reality, Kosovo's relative peace provided a situation for maintaining the status quo and a balance of fear, which rested on very weak and unstable premises and compromises.

The international community, although aware of the difficulty of the situation, did not have the effective tools for preventive intervention. Economic and political sanctions, neither in their severe nor in their soft phases, had no effective influence on Milošević's regime, nor on the general political mood within Serbia, where the idea that Kosovo was both Serbia's and Yugoslavia's 'internal issue' prevailed. In fact, the international community, with regard to this issue, in principle supported the idea of Serbian sovereignty over Kosovo. It condemned only Serbia's radical repressive measures and the massive violation of human rights in Kosovo. Although the general goal of the movement was the independence of Kosovo, the Albanian movement created the illusion – which was motivated by political pragmatism – that the conflict over sovereignty and the control of the territory could be resolved by a compromise, whereby Kosovo's grass-roots movement would delay the war until the democratisation of Serbia had taken place, namely, after the fall of Milošević's bellicose regime. Thus, the main premise of international policy with regard to the problem of Kosovo became the postponement of the conflict.

The postponement of the conflict was also the main premise of the Albanian movement. Rugova and the LDK, in the period between 1990 and 1992, accepted the strategy of resistance which was based on the principles of a non-violent, political struggle for achieving the goals of the Albanian movement. Although the movement was not based on a deep philosophical belief and was not articulated in a systematic and theoretical manner, it created the impression of a deeply grounded, highly motivated and well-organised social movement, which some authors portrayed as the 'miracle of Kosovo', a movement that was 'unique in political history'.[27] The Independent International Committee on Kosovo also concluded that: 'The LDK, under the leadership of Rugova, set about developing a historically unique parallel state apparatus' (*The Kosovo Report* 2000: 45). The evaluations of the Albanian grass-roots movement were indeed quite euphoric. A French lawyer and human rights activist claimed that: 'The nation, which was, without any doubt, the most oppressed in former Yugoslavia, has created the most free man' (Rugova 1994: 101). Similar high opinions about the Albanian non-violent resistance were expressed by several Serbian and Slovenian authors.[28] Recent studies, such as the one by Howard Clark, very positively estimate the early phase of civil resistance in Kosovo, commenting that: 'Kosovar Albanians organized themselves impressively during 1990–92';[29] but they are reserved about the later phases, when the movement began to show its internal weaknesses. A similar opinion is expressed by Tim Judah, who in speaking of the non-violent movement states: 'It was an extraordinary experiment and it failed' (Judah 2000: 59).

The failure of Kosovo's experiment can certainly be explained by the influence of factors external to it. We already mentioned the absence of any legal means for preventive intervention, and the international community policy of postponing the conflict until the democratisation of Serbia/Yugoslavia. However, the democratisation of Serbia was from the very beginning of the crisis tied in an intricate knot over the Kosovo question. The problem was, in a way, being laid out backwards. The solution of the Kosovo question did not depend upon the democratisation of Serbia, but the democratisation of Serbia depended very much on the solution of the Kosovo question. Milošević's regime came to power first by opening and then brutally placing the lid on the Kosovo question, and he remained in power through a raft of political and electoral manipulations in Kosovo. Milošević governed Serbia and Yugoslavia through Kosovo, and through Kosovo he constantly maintained the threat of war, as a means of prolonging his power. The war in Kosovo can partly be explained as Milošević's answer to the crisis of his regime at the end of 1996 and the beginning of 1997.

However, although Milošević certainly was the main person responsible for the war in Kosovo – since he had provoked conflict and had accelerated it in the direction of a 'final solution', he would probably have faced more difficulties in starting a war had he not found an opponent that not only accepted the challenge of conflict, but also provoked it. The Albanian movement had already lost its earlier homogeneity, high-level organisation and self-control. Furthermore, the doctrine and practice of non-violent resistance was seriously undermined within the Albanian grass-roots movement, within which – initially as a marginal force but decisive in its action – there emerged the KLA. The public appearance of the KLA with armed formations, however small in number, provided Milošević with his *casus belli*.

Rugova's non-violent resistance

The idea and the movement for non-violence are linked to its leader, Ibrahim Rugova. Although a man of letters, Rugova was always terse in articulating his political views. His 'philosophy of non-violence', which brought him fame, was never clearly articulated in his articles and speeches. Essentially, his politics were more pragmatic than theoretically and philosophically based. His views on non-violence as a method of political struggle can be found in a systematic form in the book by Marie-Françoise Allain and Xavier Galmiche, *Ibrahim Rugova: La Question de Kosovo*, which is in fact a book of conversations that these authors had with Rugova.[30]

Rugova's answers give the impression that his 'philosophy of non-violence' is more of a kind of improvisation than a theoretically and practically well-thought-out policy. Considering himself: 'a realist and not a man of fantasy' (Rugova 1994: 176), Rugova saw the politics of non-violence as the only alternative that the Kosovar Albanians had, given the circumstances that Kosovar Albanian society found itself in and the balance of power in Yugoslavia. Rugova considered the situation as being dramatic, since he believed that: 'the situation is worse than a state of war' (1994: 169). After the removal of autonomy, Kosovo was under a serious 'threat of ethnic cleansing' (1994: 117) that was 'even more tragic than the one in Bosnia and Croatia' (1994: 169). Rugova did not hide his apprehension that 'things could get out of control' (1994: 118), which he thought would amount to a 'prologue to a catastrophe' (1994: 123).

In such circumstances he thought that the best political response was self-control – a decision which found ready support among the Albanian masses. According to Rugova: 'Self-control was imposed on us because of the terror' (1994: 9, 41), and he added that: 'The aim of our policy is to avoid a tragedy' (1994: 170), namely, to prevent a genocide against the Kosovar Albanians (1994: 123).

So as not to leave an impression of total defeatism resulting from his fear of Serb power, in his other responses, Rugova stressed the liberating effects of abstaining from violence. He stressed 'the tradition of endurance' (1994: 128) and the 'culture of solidarity' (1994: 62) among the Albanians as an explanation for the high level of self-control, and the feeling of 'moral authority' and 'moral victory' of the Albanian movement (1994: 55). 'They have the power, we have the authority' (1994: 42). 'Our activity is not directed towards war, but has another aim; we have our internal and psychological freedom, and these are the first steps towards achieving physical and collective freedom' (1994: 44). Aware that it is a risky and uncertain project, for which the Albanians are 'paying dearly', he is nonetheless convinced 'that the people can be saved by the methods of democratic governance' (1994: 109). At the time, Rugova's main goal was to avoid a war, but he was also hoping 'that in the long term a victory can be achieved' (1994: 42). The French authors of the book quote the Serb historian and leader of the opposition Ivan Djurić, who, like Rugova, thought that: 'every day that passes is a victory for the Albanians' (1994: 149).

In other contexts Rugova has opaquely stated that: 'the Albanian aspirations are concrete' or even that: 'in Kosovo ours is the only system that functions' (1994: 128).

Rugova, however, did not have a clear idea of how a victory could be achieved in the long term, because he favoured not only a non-violent policy, but also a passive politics of waiting, and was against any risky activity. Because of this he rightly concluded that the Albanian 'resistance is not Gandhian' (1994: 62), which he knew called for active resistance and constant demonstrations and protests against the repressive regime.[31] 'In these circumstances we cannot even organize peaceful, public demonstrations, because it has become extremely dangerous to even venture out into the streets', says Rugova (1994: 141). The very 'danger for life' (1994: 124) imposes the strategy of waiting (1994: 142), 'because it is the only way, with no alternative' (1994: 141).

Rugova's strategy of waiting was not completely without substance. It sustained itself on the belief that Kosovo was under a special form of surveillance by the international community. The main goal of Rugova's

LDK was the internationalisation of the Kosovo question. The Kosovo question must be 'affirmed in the international arena' (1994: 128). Rugova had an almost 'unlimited belief in the international institutions' (1994: 58), even though he sometimes expressed a grain of doubt, which was traditional among the Albanians, that 'Europe is deaf' about the fact that Kosovo had become 'a big prison and concentration camp' (1994: 60). But that is why he believed in the support and positive influence of the United States, as a leading world power, and the idea that sooner or later the US and other international players would have to 'award the politics of non-violence and peace' (1994: 178).

As for his vision of a political solution to the Kosovo problem, Rugova displayed rather deficient and generalised ideas, which he repeated almost on a weekly basis at his press conferences, held every Friday at 11.00 am in the LDK headquarters. His 'democratic nationalism' (1994: 179) was based on the idea that: 'Kosovo would be a neutral country open towards Serbia and Albania, as well as Montenegro and Macedonia' (1994: 47, 180). The importance of Kosovo, as an open country, would be achieved: 'through an international protectorate', for which he thought there was a 'legal basis' (1994: 172).

Rugova also had a very rudimentary vision of the Balkans as a: 'community of small and equal nations' (1994: 48), and believed accordingly that the Albanians in Kosovo have 'a state-building culture' and 'enormous internal power' (1994: 186, 87). On the other hand, Rugova considered that: 'the Serbs are aware that they cannot continue to keep Kosovo by force' (1994: 94), a fact that he believed supported the solution that he had proposed.

The ideas expressed here are not merely a simplified summary of Rugova's concept of non-violent resistance. In essence, his ideas can be – without doing any disservice to them – summarised in three pages, and are ones that he stuck to from the beginning. However, this scantiness of ideas and argumentation did not have a significant impact on his popularity and influence. In strengthening his position as a leader, it was not his personal capacities, the depth and power of his thought, nor even his leadership and political skills that counted; of the greatest significance for Rugova's political position and authority among the masses was the support that he gained, from the very moment that he stepped onto the political scene, from international factors, primarily from the US and European powers. That support enormously increased his domestic charisma.

However, the correlation of charisma and influence was in fact bi-directional. In his contacts with foreign statesmen, diplomats, experts and journalists, Rugova was very impressive with his moderate ideas about a political and democratic solution of the Kosovo question. However, the support that he enjoyed in the world was conditioned by the way he controlled Kosovo. World policy, which was caught out by the Yugoslav crisis and did not have a right answer for it, wanted peace in Kosovo at any price. In contrast with the wars in Croatia and Bosnia, which were treated as 'internal' and local wars without significant international repercussions (ethnic cleansing in Bosnia was for the international community above all a moral and not a geostrategic problem)[32] an eventual war in Kosovo or in Macedonia was seen through the lens of a so-called 'domino effect', namely, a war that would spread in a chain reaction and grow into a dangerous regional and perhaps even wider European war, which would endanger world peace and stability. For this reason, US President George Bush proclaimed, in 1991, his famous 'red line' doctrine – that it would be a transgression of US and NATO interests if the war spread into the south of Yugoslavia, in other words, into Macedonia and Kosovo.[33]

Even though many of Rugova's domestic and international conversationalists realised that, as Tim Judah would later say, he was 'extraordinarily dull' (Judah 2000: 61), in certain circumstances, this was simply not relevant, or was dismissed as Rugova's own kind of mimicry or pretence.

The symbiotic character of the Albanian movement

Kosovo's civil resistance movement had its strong sides, which had made it possible to attain a high and impressive level of self-organisation and self-discipline, but it also had its weaknesses, which over time became more apparent and brought the non-violent resistance closer to disaster and confusion, and then into war. This thesis can be phrased in the form of a paradox. Namely, the main weakness of the movement lay in what seemed to be its very power, in other words, its manner of organisation and leadership. However, further analysis will show that it had nothing to do with a paradox, but rather with the specific historical and social situation that enabled exceptionally bad leadership, and, in essence, improvisations at linking with a strong social and national movement, which in its key elements had been structured and organised earlier, so that it did not require great efforts to build a parallel society and parallel structures, despite Serbia's measures of repression and annexation.

In almost all analyses of social and political processes in Kosovo at the end of the 1980s and in the early 1990s, which deal with the emergence of 'two systems of parallel institutions'[34] in Kosovo, it is neglected or even overlooked that: 'the parallel institutions in Kosovo had in fact existed before as institutions of Kosovo's exceptionally enhanced autonomy'.[35] In fact, Kosovo had been an organised society that performed many autonomous functions, since 1968, if not even since 1945. By 1989, Kosovo had had almost two decades of experience as a state, because Kosovo's autonomous status included state structures that were identical to those of the other Yugoslav republics. In July 1990, Serbia took over these state institutions, which had earlier been controlled by the Kosovars, and above all the Albanians, themselves. As such the Serbs never succeeded in completely annulling all the autonomy-era institutions. Serbia took the course of selectively crushing Kosovo's classical state functions (government, territorial defence, police, economic planning and so forth) not because it did not want more, but because it did not have the military and repressive potential to crush all of Kosovo's institutions at the same time. Indeed, Serbia did try to cancel or substantially scale down the Albanian school system,[36] but when the Albanians decided that the system should continue to function outside occupied school buildings, Serbia did not command the resources necessary to prevent nearly 400,000 students and teachers from continuing their work in 'parallel institutions'. The same occurred with the media, partly with the health institutions and the cultural and sports organisations. Only the pluralistic forms of political and trade union organisation were a novelty.

The second reason that Serbia did not take a course of total repression and impede the work of parallel institutions was the war in Croatia and in Bosnia and Herzegovina. Belgrade did not want a premature opening of 'a southern front' in Kosovo. If Serbia's repression was total, it would have provoked a different Albanian reaction. In that case the Albanians would have no illusions about the prospects of defending themselves with non-violence.

Finally, the third reason was Belgrade's ever-worsening international position. Although Milošević led an intransigent international policy, he nonetheless knew that his behaviour was being constantly monitored by many governmental and non-governmental organisations, which were accusing Serbia of 'massively violating the human rights of the Albanians'.[37]

The relatively 'selective repression' had in some cases a propagandistic function. For example, Serbia placed under its control strategically important electronic media, but it allowed a free press and books to be printed in the Albanian language, without any strict censorship, as a way of showing the world that the Albanians had the right to express themselves freely, but that they were abusing this right for separatist purposes. The Serbian propaganda machinery, emanating from both the regime and the opposition, maintained that the problems in Kosovo had nothing to do with the humanitarian and national rights violations of the Albanians, but with measures that were aimed at restraining the separatist ambitions of a 'Greater Albania movement'.[38]

The thesis that Kosovo's 'parallel institutions' were in essence a continuation of the legal institutions of the autonomy era, and that the new leadership basically attached itself to them as a parasite, can be illustrated by the evidence which indicates the crucial role of the autonomy-era institutions in spearheading the self-organisation that emerged under the circumstances of increased repression, and that it was those institutions, and not the LDK and Rugova, that facilitated the political processes of 1990–1992 which led to the rise of Kosovo's 'parallel institutions'.

The behind-the-scenes ideologues and leaders of that process were some of the major political leaders of Kosovo's former 'communist nomenclature'. Although they had been publicly ostracised as 'autonomists' and pro-Yugoslavs, they thought out and drew up the moves that laid out the legal foundations of the Kosovar state. Published in 1995, the book, *Vitet e humbura* ('The lost years'), written by of one of the LDK's founders, Mehmet Kraja, categorically affirms that Ibrahim Rugova and the LDK leadership did not make one single decision regarding the creation of the 'parallel' institutions and a 'parallel' government in Kosovo. Kraja writes that: 'the LDK did not operate independently, but there were other centres making decisions'.[39] According to Kraja, the LDK Presidium was unaware of the efforts being made to prepare a Declaration of Independence on 2 July 1992.[40] The Presidium did not know about the proclamation of the Republic of Kosovo made at Kačanik on 7 September 1990, and they did not have their assent to the general strike that started on 3 September that same year. The LDK played a relatively marginal role in the reconstruction of Kosova's government-in-exile in the summer of 1991 and only a partial role in scheduling the referendum for independence in September 1991 and the 'parallel' elections, held on 24 May 1992.

In the background of the construction of Kosova's parallel institutions there was an ongoing conflict between legalists and anti-legalists. The legalists thought that the independence of Kosovo could be built on the basis of the strong position that Kosovo had held in the Yugoslav federation. The constitution of 1974 had granted Kosovo the status of an equal member of the federation. Although it was not a republic in name, Kosovo had all the functions of a republic and the right of veto at the federal level. Anti-legalists, on the other hand, claimed that Kosovar Albanians, as part of a forcibly separated Albanian nation, should not be tied to the legacy of the Yugoslav federation, but that they should enjoy the fundamental right to national self-determination. According to the anti-legalists, the legalist solution could only result in Kosovo remaining within the framework of a new Yugoslavia or Serbia, while, by contrast, the exercise of the fundamental right to self-determination, which the anti-legalists advocated, would lead directly to the independence of Kosovo and probably even to a desirable unification of Kosovo with Albania.[41]

The key figure that served as an intermediary in the development of strategy and in the making of decisions was not Ibrahim Rugova, as president of the LDK, but its vice-president, Fehmi Agani. He was one of the intellectual ideologues of the demand for the republican status of Kosovo, going back to the demonstrations of 1968, who later maintained contacts with a group of communist leaders that led a realistic policy and accepted Tito's compromising formula of a double status for Kosovo as an equal unit of the federation and, simultaneously, a part of Serbia. While Rugova played the role of a big leader and became embroiled with his historical mission, Agani was leading a pragmatic policy and managed the active part of the legalistic policy, balancing the tensions between the governing structures of the movement and the centres of power, that is, the parliament and government of Kosovo.

However, although the active part of politics was formulated and conducted by circles of experienced politicians, as well as by ambitious young leaders, such as Veton Surroi or Blerim Shala, after the elections of May 1992, which coincided with the outbreak of war in Bosnia, the LDK and its leader Rugova took the grass-roots movement under their control and opted for a complete abstention from all active resistance while maintaining the already established political structures. The crucial moment that shifted the centre of power was the control of the funds that began to be collected from Kosovo's diaspora in the Western countries, as well as in Kosovo. To maintain the existence of the parallel structures in Kosovo, above all the schooling system, it was necessary to maintain a constant flow of money for teachers' salaries and the maintenance of buildings. The LDK and the government-in-exile, headed by Bujar Bukoshi, a close Rugova associate since 1990 (who would later denounce him in 1995 at the time of the Dayton Peace Agreement) used the national fund to secure dominant positions in the parallel system, and created a special monopoly, especially on information. Although there were several independent weekly magazines published in Kosovo, the LDK controlled public opinion through the only daily newspaper, *Bujku*, which was a substitute for the banned *Rilindja*, and the QIK news agency (Kosova Information Center).[42]

Dr Rugova's authoritarianism

Kosovo's grass-roots movement contributed, without any doubt, to avoiding direct inter-ethnic tensions and conflict. The Kosovar leaders even publicly emphasised that they were in conflict with the Serbian state apparatus and not with the Serbian people. The making of parallel institutions and the politics of apartheid led to a physical distancing in communications between the two national communities. Serbs kept the main institutions and symbolically occupied the important buildings and the centres of towns, while the Albanians were expelled from institutions and withdrew to the margins, into the suburbs and the parts of settlements where they held the majority and felt safer. Also, cultural life went underground as exhibitions were organised at restaurants or theatrical performances were held in improvised spaces.

The reduction of physical contact between the two communities basically reduced the contacts and incidents among them. This created the illusion that the conflict was not inter-ethnic, that it was not a conflict between citizens of different nationalities, but that in between them had been interposed the Serbian administration and police, which artificially and repressively maintained the distance between them. Sometimes, even from the Albanian side, there were statements that the state's repression was directed not just against the Albanians, but also against the Serbs who wanted to maintain normal contact with their Albanian neighbours.

Nevertheless, although there were indeed no direct conflicts and incidents, the divide between the two communities was tectonic, and was not just between the Albanian population and the actual Serbian regime. Indeed, the Serbian population actively supported the regime, and proportionally much more so than the regime was supported in Serbia itself. Meanwhile, Albanians were indiscriminate in their support for Rugova and the LDK, and were not only against the Serbian regime and police, but also against the Kosovar Serbs, who had accepted the privileges of an apartheid regime. The Albanian movement did not even try to decrease the distance between the two communities. Albanians decided for a boycott of Serbian institutions, as well as for the boycott of almost all connections with the local Serbian population, except the most basic which were necessary for survival.

Just as with the Serbs in Serbia itself, Milošević was the 'saviour of Kosovo's Serbs', while for the Albanians, Rugova was their 'saviour'. This made inter-ethnic relations totally dependent on the authority of each nation's 'leader'. Two communities looked up to their leaders as gods, and their relation to the crisis determined the character of inter-ethnic relations, as an anomaly of the status quo, whereby the Serbian leader controlled though coercion, while the Albanian leader asked his community to remain passive, patient and non-violent.

Such an anomalous status quo certainly suited the privileged side more than the other side which was objectively losing. Milošević manipulated the Kosovar Serbs by giving them concrete power and privileges, while Rugova offered his followers only empty promises that 'someday it would be better'. For this reason, Rugova's authority was much more vulnerable than that of Milošević. And it was expected that things would gradually crumble and melt away, because a number of Albanians could not believe that the daily repression and disparagement could last for ever.

However, Kosovo's grass-roots movement of non-violent resistance did not become weak just because of Rugova's objectively anomalous position of authority, but also because of the subjective and personal weaknesses of Rugova's leadership.

One of the main reasons for the degeneration of the Albanian peaceful movement should be sought in the structural distinction of Rugova's position of leadership, and his unparalleled position of authority. After he received 99 per cent of the votes in the presidential elections of 1992, Rugova received enormous power and an unrivalled position in the movement. Although his speeches gave the impression of a modest and gentle politician, in essence he created a system of authoritarian personal power, based on a variant of the cult of personality. He became the distinct and peerless leader of the rest of the 'parallel' structures on which Kosovar Albanian society depended. Mehmet Kraja sees the party and movement's fundamental weakness as lying in the fact: 'The LDK is identified with Rugova' (Kraja: 208). Rugova became a self-contained figure of the movement, almost completely ignoring the LDK leadership when making (or blocking) decisions. Rugova blocked all political initiatives that could possibly endanger his own position within the movement. For example, he did not allow the elected parliament of Kosovo of May 1992 to be constituted. Even though, soon after the elections, on 23 June, a constitutive meeting had been scheduled, it was thwarted by the Serbian police. After this, all endeavours and pressures to constitute the parliament and have it start its work – and thereby complete the structure of the parallel system, were blocked by Rugova.[43] The party itself, with its monopoly, became Rugova's captive. Its founder, Kraja called it: 'a leaderistic party based on Rugova's charisma' (Kraja: 209), and in this he saw one of the main reasons for the 'internal erosion' not of the party itself, but of the whole grass-roots movement in general (Kraja: 212).

The dominant authoritarian structure of Albanian society in Kosovo and the institutional vacuum suited the movement's monopolisation. The communist system had also created a mentality of passivity, which not only hindered individual political initiatives but also crippled the collective will. Political decisions were not made on the basis of social consensus or by consulting with different streams of thought within the movement; instead, they were made by the political elite or by the leader himself. Between the collective and the leader there was a relationship similar to that between a shepherd and his flock, in which the leader/shepherd not only represented but also articulated the collective will. The leader/shepherd persona was the dynamic part of the movement, while the people followed him, seeing their will in him.

The LDK monopoly was gradually reduced down to Rugova's personal monopoly. The Kosova Presidential Council was favoured above all other party and institutional structures, through the appointment of Rugova's personal advisers and close friends, or like-minded persons and yes-men, to whom he delegated the management of all the sectors of the parallel society, in the function of continuing his autocracy. In essence, Rugova was advised by a very small circle of people, who, through the media, were able to control and maintain his cult of personality, and attack all those who expressed different points of view or criticised his policy as enemies and traitors. Rugova, himself, never personally responded to any attacks, and was thus able to give the impression that he was a gentle politician who avoided all conflicts and quarrels.[44] He left such matters to his media and party officers.[45]

The ideological split within the movement

The Kosovo grass-roots movement not only appeared as a new social movement, but also arose from the matrix of a certain inherited mentality in the community, and the clash of ideas which had existed prior to that community. In Kosovo, Albanian society was not homogenous; it had been ideologically divided from a much earlier period.

The homogeneity displayed to the outside world was forced upon the Albanians by Serbian aggression, and the need for the community to defend itself against that aggression. Yet, this failed to destroy the internal heterogeneous matrices of social and ideological divisions within Albanian society. From the outside, the movement seemed unique but within it there was a struggle for control going on between different groups with different ideological leanings.

One of the reasons why Rugova marginalised the party and favoured informal groups of advisers must be sought in the internal ideological clash, which existed from the beginning in the leading force of the movement, within the LDK. The LDK was, in essence, more of a movement than a party. Within the LDK there were different groups who worked with tendencies, which ideologically were closer to classical ideology, namely that of the communist left, centre or populist right. Rugova himself, as a representative of 'democratic nationalism' (1994: 179) leaned towards populism and to some kind of schematic anti-communism and, in essence, to the extreme right. He and his closest collaborators understood democracy as the reverse of the communist scheme of the 'clash of the classes'. Because of this, Rugova and his close collaborators, such as the writer and critic Dr Sabri Hamiti, came into conflict with members of the so-called Marxist-Leninist or Enverist groups, which from the 1960s, when Adem Demaçi had been arrested and sentenced for the first time, created the active core of an underground Albanian liberation movement in Kosovo. After the demonstrations of 1981, this movement was permanently recruiting new forces since many thousands of 'nationalists' or 'irredentists', as Serbian propaganda used to call them then, were arrested and sentenced to long-term imprisonment. These former prisoners in 1989 and 1990, when communism failed and the new Kosovar political elite was being created, quickly became 'out of fashion' and found themselves in a state of confusion (Maliqi 1998: 21–23). A segment of these former prisoners remained very distrustful of pluralism and the realistic course of the new political forces in Kosovo, especially towards the idea of non-violent resistance, continuing to operate, in any case, illegally. The strongest group was the LPRK (Popular Movement for the Republic of Kosova), which was divided in 1993 into two factions: the LPK (Popular Movement for Kosova) and the LKÇK (National Liberation Movement of Kosovo) (Judah 2000: 115–120).

In 1990, a part of the membership of these illegal leftist-nationalist groups joined the newly formed parties, above all the LDK. Since the LDK practically represented the whole of the Albanian people's aspirations, they thought they ought to be with the people, and by operating within the LDK, as a legal and registered party, they could realise those aims for which they had previously fought illegally. From the start, a number of these new members formulated the idea that Rugova, Agani and other LDK leaders could temporarily be at the head of the movement, though they could be replaced at a later date by those who had sacrificed the most, and had done more and had gained more merit with regard to the emancipation and liberation movement of the Albanians. Some of them thought that the illusion of liberating Kosovo through democratic and non-violent means would soon consume itself, and because of that they prepared the ground for taking over the positions of leadership in the movement, when their turn would eventually come. Some of them did not hide their ambitions about 'conquering the castle from the inside', through an infiltration of the membership and the leading structure of the LDK.[46]

These groups succeeded in gaining an overwhelming majority on the Main Council and on the presidency of the LDK at the LDK Congress held in 1994. Subsequently, Agani was removed from his post, along with some of the moderate leaders, such as Edita Tahari. Rugova, fearing a split and the domination of the party by former prisoners, known as the 'red faction', immediately prevented the internal surge of the 'revolutionaries'. He issued a decree to turn the situation around and restored the 'Agani group'. Fearing an early split, the leftists settled on a compromise over their control of the LDK Main Council and the division of power in the presidency. However, this turned out to be a Pyrrhic victory, because it gave Rugova an additional reason for ignoring the part leadership, the presidency and the Main Council, in favour of his own personal authority, whereby he became accountable to no one.

The final split with the party's leftists occurred at the next Party Congress in February 1998, shortly before the war. By this time, it was too late for the leftist dissidents to take over power inside the LDK, so they joined one of the political wings of the KLA.

Denying Rugova and non-violent resistance

Rugova's strategy of non-violent resistance was widely accepted among the masses until the students' demonstrations of 1997 and the beginning of the insurgency in March 1998, when it came to an open split in the movement. Indeed, Rugova had been confronted with some severe criticism from the beginning, but this had little effect on changing the mood of the masses.

The first to criticise Rugova and the LDK was the academic Rexhep Qosja, who in the 1980s held the reputation of being the 'father of Albanian nationalism'. When the LDK was founded, Qosa was seen by many as being its president. The founders of the party offered him the position of leader, but he rejected it. Later, Qosja argued that he was not satisfied with the confused programme and aims of the LDK, but it is quite probable that, at the time, he had not really taken into account the situation and had misjudged the mood of the masses. Qosja was, however, one of the main ideologues of the solution of the Albanian question. Since the LDK, in its early days, opted for a 'realistic autonomy (as had been stated initially in the first programme of the party, which had been written, at the time, with a view to being accepted by the Yugoslav authorities), which meant a determination for the Republic of Kosovo, as a federal unit within Yugoslavia. From the beginning, Qosja harshly attacked the LDK and its leader Rugova, because the party's goals had been set too low and they were not taking advantage of the historical circumstances that had opened up the Albanian question 'as a whole' (Qosja 1998: 185). Qosja and a group of like-minded intellectuals founded the Forum of Albanian Intellectuals, which fought against the 'segmentation' of the Albanian movement, and especially against the monopoly of the LDK. In the unique historical situation and under the regime of Serbian occupation, Rugova and other leaders were playing with democracy and pluralism, instead of creating a unique front in the leadership. Qosja was in favour of the 'creation of a National Council, which would organize the people' and work against the further splitting up of the Albanian territories, in other words: 'the tragic partition of the Albanian people' (Qosja 1994: 13–24). After the failure of the project to establish a National Council,[47] Qosja began to seriously campaign against Rugova and the LDK, accusing them of conducting a policy that had become nothing more than 'a democratic decoration for the Milošević regime', in other words, that Rugova and the LDK were 'collaborating with Serbia' and were committing 'high treason' (Petrović 2006: 109).

Adem Demaçi, Kosovo's Mandela, who spent 28 years of his life in the prisons of Yugoslavia, also became a severe critic of Rugova and the LDK. When Demaçi was released from prison in the summer of 1990, the LDK was already dominant and had a charismatic leader. Although he enjoyed high moral and political authority Demaçi remained on side.[48] Demaçi and Rugova did not have any close collaboration, but in the early days there was no open enmity between them.

Demaçi began a campaign against Rugova and the LDK after the faction of former prisoners had failed to take over the 'castle from the inside', in 1994. This became even more pressing in the autumn of 1995, when the Dayton peace process completely ignored the Kosovo question. Like Qosja, Demaçi thought that the organisation of the Albanian movement in Kosovo was not fit for purpose (Petrović: 272), because its bureaucracy and policies which lacked any innovation were the result of exceptionally bad management. According to Demaçi, there was a 'false intelligentsia at the head of the movement', which was not ready 'to sacrifice itself' (Petrović: 268). Put another way, he felt that the leaders were mere 'political amateurs' (Petrović: 272), which resulted in a lack of development within the movement (Petrović: 268), something which Tim Judah would later describe as a 'grotesque symbiosis between Belgrade and Priština' (Judah 2000: 74), because the LDK and Rugova had 'effectively pacified the province, which was exactly what the [Serbian] authorities wanted' (Judah 2000: 84).

Instead of passive resistance, Demaçi advocated active resistance of a Ghandian type, which meant putting permanent pressure on the Serbian regime and a readiness to sacrifice oneself in order to achieve its goals (Judah 2000: 270–271). Demaçi believed that active resistance did not entail having to go to war, but rather something that he referred to as: 'neither war, nor capitulation'. But the main problem for both Demaçi and Qosja was that their talk of active resistance was more of a theoretical than a practical nature. A hunger strike organised in June 1993 for the defence of the Albanian media was the only form of resistance that Demaçi resorted to.

Meanwhile, the LDK was criticised for merely being prepared to speak out without actually doing anything and while its leaders were accused of not only being sluggish, but, to quote Judah (2000: 269), they were using 'deception and narcosis' to influence the masses, who were badly led and this led to the inertia and atrophy of the movement and the blocking of all initiatives. Bardhyl Mahmuti, a spokesman of the LPK, who would later be a spokesman for the KLA, explained the blockade phenomenon as follows:

> Rugova applies totalitarian politics aimed at preventing any resistance to the Serbs. He gave the illusion that the international community would resolve the crisis and that independence would come as a gift. The LPK always tried to persuade people that this illusion was dangerous and that no one would come and liberate us and that we would have to pay the price. But, our message only got through very slowly. We had no media and he has television, dailies, weeklies all giving the same message. (Judah 2000: 126)

Mahmuti complained that: 'the LDK controlled the people's imagination' and that it was necessary for the Dayton agreement to happen, whereby Kosovo was completely avoided and forgotten about, and a space was created for different and active politics of resistance to develop. In other words: 'Our room for manoeuvre [had] opened up' (Judah 2000: 126).

What led to conflict and the defeat of the grass-roots movement?

Radical streams in the Albanian movement, from the beginning, were sceptical of the non-violent resistance. They thought that Kosovo could be liberated only through active resistance, which meant armed resistance and rebellion. Radical groups, especially those in Western Europe (the LPK and LKÇK), began the preparations for a rebellion. Kosovo's government-in-exile was also involved in those preparations. They handled important funds collected from the Albanian diaspora, and soon came into open conflict with Rugova and the LDK.

In November 1995, the Peace Conference on Bosnia and Herzegovina was held at Dayton, Ohio. Kosovar expectations that the Kosovo question would be discussed remained unfulfilled. Kosovo was not even mentioned in any of the documents. The grass-roots policy of non-violent resistance, from that moment on, began suddenly to lose all credibility. Rugova's rivals, especially Qosja, stated publicly that Dayton represented the 'end of the illusions that the international community would heed Kosovo's call for independence' (Clark 2000: 123). Rugova and the LDK continued with the politics of doing nothing and the paralysis of the movement, still counting on internationalisation and the help of the international community.[49] But after Dayton, it seemed that the international community had in a way rehabilitated Milošević and his regime, because he had gained the role of a guarantor of the Bosnia agreement. Only the US was openly suspicious of Serbia, or more precisely, the Milošević regime, and insisted on holding the so-called outer wall of sanctions on Belgrade until the Kosovo question had been solved.

International factors, including the United Nations, in essence had neither the responsibility nor the effective instruments to resolve the inter-ethnic tensions in Kosovo, nor any instruments for the prevention of an eventual war. Yugoslavia – or, more precisely, Serbia – was completely non-cooperative and expelled from all international organisations. Temporary crisis monitoring, above all, the practice of monitoring the violations of human rights and freedoms, as well as many critical reports and notes sent to the government in Belgrade from international institutions and associations for the protection of human rights, hardly had any influence on Belgrade's policy. In fact, from May 1993, when a pact of the Great Powers was signed in Washington on the principles of solving the Yugoslav crisis,[50] which had settled upon the idea the Bosnia and Herzegovina must remain a union, that the integrity of Macedonia could not be endangered and that Kosovo should get back its high level of autonomy within Yugoslavia, and that the Milošević regime should renounce its irredentist policy to the Serbian part of Bosnia with the discontinuation of all institutional forms of international monitoring of the situation in Kosovo. Belgrade broke off the talks on Kosovo that had been established by the special group for Kosovo at the Geneva Peace Conference on Yugoslavia and revoked the credentials of the OSCE Permanent Mission in Kosovo. By calling on the principle of the inviolability of the borders of the 'former' Yugoslavia, which had been insisted upon by the Contact Group of Great Powers, Belgrade, had, from May 1993, treated Kosovo exceptionally as an 'internal question' of Serbia.

The Kosovo grass-roots movement was in a way left to its own devices, with respect to the politics of inertia. The role of an intermediary in solving concrete problems, such as the issue of normalising the work of the school system, for which the Belgrade government was showing a readiness to talk, was taken up by non-governmental humanitarian organisations. On 1 September 1996, the Santo Eggidio humanitarian organisation from the Vatican, following secret talks held between representatives of the Serbian government and Kosovo's negotiating team, headed by Fehmi Agani, achieved an agreement on the normalisation of the school system. The agreement was signed separately by Milošević and Rugova.

At that moment in time it seemed that a model had been found for overcoming all tensions through a step-by-step approach, which on the one side provided certain concrete satisfaction for the grass-roots movement and at the same time ensured the cooperation of the Serbian regime. But the problem with this agreement was that its implementation remained blocked because neither side could agree on concrete measures and the dynamics of implantation.

Instead of being helpful to Rugova's politics, the school agreement became a source of problems for him, because it raised high hopes which could not be fulfilled. The students of Priština University were especially disappointed, because they had studied under the most

difficult conditions. In December 1996, the students drew up a petition to Rugova – in which they had collected 500 signatures – and they
presented Rugova and the LDK with an ultimatum to realise the agreement whereby the occupied university building should be given back to
the students and that the Albanian university should be granted complete freedom to work. A year later, on 1 October 1997, the students'
union was no longer willing to listen to the empty promises of Rugova
and his collaborators. The control of the students' union allied with
the radical streams in the Albanian movement, who accused Rugova of
treason and collaboration with the Serbian regime. On 1 October 1997,
students and teachers organised peaceful demonstrations, which were
forcibly crushed by the police. It was this event that flagged up the end
of Rugova's revered charisma and his influence upon the masses.

By the end of November that year, at the funeral of a victim of Serbian
repression, the as yet mysterious KLA appeared for the very first time
at a meeting held in Drenica, a traditionally rebellious region. Here
the KLA was welcomed with frenetic applause and cheering. Rugova
and the LDK had neither the reply nor the strategy to effectively resist
the rebellion. In February 1998, some weeks before the massacres of
civilians that the Serbian police carried out in the villages of Drenica,
Likosan, Qirez and Prekaz, by which the Serbs, in reality, sparked off the
conflict, the LDK was split into militant and pacifist wings.

The KLA not only started an insurgency against the Serbian government in Kosovo, but also represented the rebellion against the 'internal
regime' and parallel government which had been organised by Rugova
and the LDK leadership. This meant that the Kosovo grass-roots movement was endangered from within as well as being attacked by the
Serbian regime. During the insurgency, the grass-roots movement of
civil resistance became disoriented and failed to understand the need
to accept the reality that the KLA had become the alternative Albanian
response to the crisis. Rugova never recognised the KLA as the authentic
force of resistance and claimed that it was a 'Serbian conspiracy' or that
they were 'hirelings who were instructed by the Serbian secret police'.

Our analysis has shown that Rugova and the LDK had, in many ways,
contributed to the immobilisation and atrophy of the civil resistance
movement, leading to feelings of complete despair and hopelessness
with regard to reaching a peaceful and democratic resolution of the
Kosovo crisis. The success of this large and unique grass-roots movement depended on its ability to control critical situations, which could
lead to armed conflict. Before 1997, there were certain mechanisms in
the movement for controlling the mood of the masses that prevented

them from starting an open rebellion. At the end of 1997, this had become impossible, not only because of Serbian provocations, which had been present for some time, but also because of the leadership's myopia and blundering. Then, in fact, it became clear that the weaknesses of the movement's organisational leadership, which had had high goals, namely the independence of Kosovo, without employing any serious instruments for their realisation and which wanted to avoid war by resorting to a 'strategy' of inertia, by waiting and doing nothing, in a way numbed and disabled its own system of sensing the danger of war. The basic weakness of Kosovo's civil resistance movement was that because it had taken on the functions of a 'fire brigade' it had forgotten to fill its tanks with enough water necessary to quench a fire, even in the station where they were on duty.

Resolving the crisis thus became the responsibility of the international community. In March 1998, it reacted decisively, trying to prevent war and achieve a political agreement based on the principles agreed on by the Contact Group in May 1993. The Great Powers – the USA, the EU and Russia – imposed on Belgrade the acceptance of a negotiation process, threatening that it would use force against the superior and aggressive party in the conflict.

In the spring of 1998, the Kosovo grass-roots movement of non-violent resistance experienced its failure. The Serbian regime understood only the language of force. Nevertheless, the non-violent resistance was not completely futile. They provided international actors involved in the crisis with the political and moral arguments for justifying military intervention against Serbian aggression and genocidal policy.[51]

Conclusion

The insurgency and NATO's intervention in Kosovo set in motion a wide international debate about the most vital issues of what was colloquially referred to as the 'new world order'. How should the international community respond to conflicts and crises such as the one posed by Kosovo? In Kosovo, the lives of millions of people were endangered by 'internal aggression'. The state that considered itself sovereign in terms of international law defined that sovereignty as the law of the ethnic majority, the Serbs, despite the fact that the structure of the state's population was multi-ethnic. Indeed, the Albanians of Kosovo made up nearly 90 per cent of the population and had enjoyed broad political autonomy. Albanians did not hide their own aspirations for self-determination and independence from Serbia, on the same principle of the ethnic right of statehood, on which the Serbs were insisting. The Serbian state used its military power first to suspend the political autonomy of Kosovo, then to try to completely physically eliminate a part of its own 'citizens'. The Serbs were interested in territory and the idea of Kosovo as their 'holy land', but not in the principle of cohabitation with the Albanian population.

For Kosovar Albanians, Yugoslavia as a Federation, which guaranteed their particular political, national, cultural and religious rights, was acceptable as the lesser evil, even though in their midst there was also a strong movement that thought that for Kosovo it would be better to be in a community, not with a Southern Slavonic people, especially not with the Serbs, but with Albania. For Kosovar Albanians it would be inconceivable to remain in Serbia, in a Serbian ethnic state, under repressive conditions, whose final goal was genocide. Kosovo's inter-ethnic conflict was going on under the conditions of a so-called 'borderline situation', as a struggle for exclusive ethnic rights on a territory. As in other parts of the former Yugoslav federation, the basic conditions for political and ethnic compromise were absent.

Kosovo's grass-roots movement of non-violent resistance arose from the matrix of Yugoslav ethnic exclusiveness and fragmentation. Even though it chose non-violent methods, it was not 'pacifist' in the strict sense of the word. It was about a liberation and it was a state-building movement. Such situations usually end in rebellions and armed conflict. In the end, Kosovo could not avoid liberation, rebellion and war. However, at the level of the conflict of people's will and confronting the aggression of the superior side, Kosovo's grass-roots movement of non-violent resistance probably created a model of behaviour that is valid for other, similar crisis situations. First of all, it enabled the transfer of conflict, although only temporarily, from the premises of war, into political and democratic premises. Instead of open conflict it demonstrated opportunities for a 'peaceful' rebellion and non-violence, continued with the organisation of a boycott against the repressive measures of a 'sovereign' country, by which it clearly showed the limits of that sovereignty and the discriminatory character of that country. Kosovo's movement was more than just a form of civil disobedience, because at the same time it worked on organising a parallel society and parallel virtual state, which, although called a 'farce' and a 'phantom state' (Judah 2000), had nevertheless affirmed – as a kind of continued referendum – the continuous will to the right to self-determination of Kosovo's citizens. Nearly 2 million people demanded respect for their will and demonstrated that there is no power that can subdue that will.

People can be expelled and killed, which is what Serbia did, but their will and their desire for justice and freedom cannot be daunted.

On the other hand, the Albanian movement, which knew that militarily it was inferior, decided on a kind of saving of resources and potentials, by making transparent Serbia's tyranny and aggression. Pushed into building a kind of colonial government and an apartheid system, Serbia lost all credibility in its claims of being a modern state that does not discriminate against its citizens. Thus, the total Albanian boycott also impeded Serbia's colonial exploitation of Kosovo's economic resources. Keeping Kosovo under its control cost Serbia enormously. This contributed decisively in weakening its economic resources, which had already been seriously damaged after the wars in Croatia and Bosnia and Herzegovina that had resulted in the imposition of economic sanctions by the international community. The Serbian regime and elite were aware that time was on the side of the Albanians, which is why in a critical moment, when it came to a split in the Albanian movement, it took the risky war option, so that it could free itself from the burden of disobedient Albanians and the burden of Kosovo, because it had become too costly for Serbia. The Serbian regime did not limit itself to repulsing the KLA, but fought against civilians instead. In the summer of 1998 it was clear that the Serbian option was to expel and destroy, and to inflict genocide upon the Albanians, who were punished for their will to self-determination and independence.

Of course, there exists a certain sense of consensus between international actors and most UN member states in that in cases of so-called 'borderline' situations, described in Chapter VII of the Charter of the United Nations as genocide, the intervention of the international community is desirable, if not necessary. In Kosovo there was a precedent of the first international humanitarian intervention. Kosovo's grassroots movement gained an additional reason for satisfaction, because for years it was pressing for the establishment of a UN protectorate as a possible interim solution for the conflict of wills and the right to self-determination of peoples at risk. The intervention did not lessen the tensions between Serbs and Albanians, but it lessened the tensions in the region, which is now in the phase of stabilisation, imposed by the presence of international forces in the Bosnian Federation and in Kosovo, and a preventive force in Macedonia. The intervention in Kosovo, to some extent also enabled the change of regime and the beginning of the development of democratic processes in Serbia proper.

However, the intervention in Kosovo is still not 'capitalised' in international law, as a model for resolving inter-ethnic and armed conflicts.

In Kosovo an ad hoc instrument of intervention was applied, based more on the momentary security and political interests of the member states of the Western Alliance, among which there does not exist a full consensus on the purpose and model of intervention. The international security system remains imperfect and incomplete. That is also reflected in the relatively unstable status of the UN, as an organisation that should be the most responsible for global security, stability and cooperation.

In Kosovo's case, the UN, practically on the very day that the peace agreement was signed at Kumanovo, was informed that it must send its peacekeeping mission (UNMIK), whose function was not only peacekeeping but also peace-building and the active administration of the territory in the interim period. That is, if it is not the most extensive, as it is, of course, the most difficult mission that the UN has carried out in its history. UNMIK has functions that no earlier UN missions ever had – above all, the function of acting as a protector, which had to be built hastily on the basis of a limited and compromised mandate which came from Security Council Resolution 1244.

UNMIK is a complex mechanism, which must cooperate with the OSCE mission and KFOR, with the purpose of creating local self-governing institutions in Kosovo, on whose construction and maintenance the Kosovo grass-roots movement was involved during the 1990s. And, just as the Kosovo grass-roots movement was involved throughout the 1990s, as in the case of BiH, the foreign interventionist factor is obliged to manage the situation of extreme division and distrust among the ethnic communities, which insist on their own territorial rights, and at the end of the day, on the rights of unlimited self-determination. The existence of a third, neutral, power, certainly creates more possibilities for controlling the crisis than the situation of one side's ethnic domination against another, weaker side, which led to war. Just as no long-term model had been found for resolving the inter-ethnic conflict in Cyprus, one could not expect an easy and quick solution for Kosovo.

However, a more active position of the UN and other international actors in Kosovo, compared to earlier interventions whose purpose was to physically divide the parties in conflict and create conditions for dialogue and negotiations, can have positive effects not only in the sense of the prevention of new conflicts, but also in creating the preconditions for overcoming the crisis and creating a new model of stability. However, we cannot expect the UN mission in Kosovo to simply eliminate the essential matrix of inter-ethnic conflict, namely, that it can play the role of reconciling the party while promoting a new type of multi-ethnic community, where the different ethnic communities would live in harmony. That is only an interventionist and missionary illusion, mainly with counterproductive effects, as the experience in BiH has shown, which constantly disappoints missionaries, because in its elections the constant winners are the nationalist parties.

For the UN mission in Kosovo, as in Bosnia, I believe that a more productive path would be a variant of scepticism and a pragmatic attitude to the problem of aspirations in conflict. The active position of a UN protector should be the building of systems, based on political, social and economic pre-conditions for the genuine democratisation of Kosovo and the region. Certainly, this more active role would be significantly easier if in the meantime the parties in conflict came to an agreement, or if the Great Powers or the Security Council succeeded in cutting the Gordian knot of the question of sovereignty in Kosovo, which was formulated as a compromise in Resolution 1244; formally Kosovo was to remain under Yugoslav sovereignty, but in practice all sovereign functions were given to UNMIK. In the meantime, following the split up of the Federal Republic of Yugoslavia into the separate states of Serbia and Montenegro after the referendum on independence (May 2005), the UN Security Council should have drawn the logical conclusion that UNMIK was only temporarily sovereign in Kosovo, and that there is no higher jurisdiction, as a subject of international law, and that members of the UN, which could claim rights in Kosovo. Kosovo's problem in that case should be resolved on the principles of the basic right of a territory under an international protectorate to realise self-determination.

Notes

1. 'Without any exaggeration it can be said that Yugoslavia really was overthrown in Kosovo' (Pesić: 35). 'Yugoslavia was effectively destroyed on 5 July 1990 when the Kosovo Assembly was dispersed ... The Federal Assembly could no longer legally and validly function, since one of its constituent elements, with the right of veto, had be forcibly abolished ... The action of 5 July 1990 was, therefore, effectively a *coup d'état*, which started Yugoslavia's descent into chaos' (Maliqi 1996: 150).
2. 'Different understandings of the Serbian and Croatian national question' provided the main lever, which was pushing both sides into the extreme position of the critical years of the 1990s' (Pesić: 28).
3. On Serbian irredentist war aims, see: Pesić: 58. M. Kraja shares the opinion that: 'Serbia used Kosovo for its national revival; Kosovo was not the target, but rather the first hurdle towards this aim' (Kraja: 150).
4. The axis of Yugoslav antagonism was additionally accelerated by Slovenian separatism, which used the crisis for 'catapulting' Slovenia into

independence(26 June 1991). But there is evidence that Serbia had expelled Slovenia from Yugoslavia (Mesić: 33).

5. 'Memorandum SANU', *Duga*, Belgrade, June 1989; Vujačić refers to this document as 'the Serbian nationalist manifesto' (Vujačić 1995: [quoted from the Internet version of this article]. The SANU Memorandum presents the solutions for Yugoslavia almost as an ultimatum: either as a unitarian state under Serbian hegemony, or the creation of a Serbian ethnic state. See Magas 1993: 199–200.

6. See Magas 1999: 299.

7. After the failure of negotiations at the conference held in Rambouillet and Paris between February and March 1999, when the Serbian delegation refused to sign the agreement, the Western countries decided on NATO military intervention against Yugoslavia. The powers of the alliance started bombing military targets in Yugoslavia on 24 March. On 9 June, Yugoslavia signed its capitulation, at Kumenovo, and KFOR troops took over the control of Kosovo while, according to UN Security Council Resolution 1244, the governing of Kosovo was taken over by the UN Civil Mission in Kosovo (UNMIK) and the OSCE. See *The Kosovo Report*: 320–330.

8. Hundreds of thousands of Albanians participated in marching protests which came from all the towns to Priština, the capital of Kosovo. They were demanding a reversal of the decision to remove the Kosovar leadership, namely Azem Vlasi and Kaqusha Jashari, who had been forced to abandon their positions (Clark 2000: 47; Maliqi 1990: 179).

9. Later analysis would establish that: 'the defence of autonomy' was only a 'façade' or a 'mask' for more radical aims, namely the independence of Kosovo (Kraja: 150–153).

10. Only the Slovenian government organised a protest meeting, where it warned that Serbian claims were leading to the break-up of Yugoslavia (Kraja: 156; Magas 1993: 236–237).

11. They were, in fact, incarcerated in prisons where they were brutally beaten and mistreated, without any court procedure or criminal investigation, and without having been charged for having committed any criminal act or having the right of defence (Clark 2000: 53; Maliqi 1990: 273).

12. Because of the presence of armed units in and around the parliament building this act was soon dubbed 'The Constitution of Tanks'. Subsequent demonstrations which arose in Priština and elsewhere were brutally crushed by the Serbian police.

13. The KLMDNJ (Committee for the Protection of Human Rights and Freedoms), Yugoslavia's first opposition organisation, was founded on 9 December 1989. Then, on 23 December, this was followed by the foundation of the DLK (the Democratic League of Kosova) (Maliqi 1990: 273).

14. Special police forces (MUP – Ministarstvo Unutrašnjih Policija – [RH] had carried out massacres in Malisheva, Gllogovc and Zhur, shooting from armoured cars into accidental passersby or peaceful columns of demonstrators, obviously with the intention of provoking people's anger in a bid to win a *casus belli* (Maliqi 1990: 267–274).

15. LDK leaders claim that by the end of January 1989 this organisation had over 700,000 members. Although this figure is exaggerated, it is without doubt that signing up as a member of the LDK was taken as a 'kind of referendum'.

Also, within a week more than 400,000 citizens had signed the petition 'For Democracy – Against Violence', organised at the beginning of February 1990. The founders of the LDK claimed that their organisation 'was not a party in the traditional sense, but rather a movement'. One of its founders and ideologists, the writer Mehmet Kraja, called this period: 'The exit from political chaos', because: 'The people were convinced the LDK had replaced the structure of the governing establishment' (Kraja: 170).

16. If the free elections had been held under conditions in which Kosovo still formally enjoyed significant autonomy, Serbia would have risked losing control over Kosovo. Srdja Popović, a liberal and anti-regime intellectual, commented ironically on the Serbian regime as follows: 'I wonder about the Serbian intellectuals who are asking first to finish with Kosovo, then they would, as if, build democracy. Well how can you build democracy when you finish with them as you had planned to do so? With whom would you build that democracy? With those that you have already killed there?' (Popović).

17. This mistake would be paid for dearly, not only with the wars and the splitting up of Yugoslavia, but also by shackling Serbia itself to the chains of Milošević's chains of dictatorship (Perović 1993: 128).

18. The Assembly, government and public services.

19. Born in central Serbia in 1921, the author, politician and Serbian intellectual Dobrica Ćosić served in Tito's Partizans during the Second World War and became a strong supporter of the Tito regime until the 1960s. Fearing that Serbia's position within the SFRJ was under threat, Ćosić criticised the government for granting increasing autonomy to Vojvodina and Kosovo after 1968. This concern was perhaps best expressed in the populist slogan that a weaker Serbia meant a stronger Yugoslavia. Later he would become spokesman for Serbian and Montenegrin rights in Kosovo. It was also alleged that Ćosić had written the *Memorandum of the Serbian Academy of Sciences and Arts* (SANU) in 1986, though this has since been disproved. In 1989 he declared his support for Slobodan Milošević and two years later he helped Radovan Karadžić in his bid for the leadership of the Bosnian Serbs. In 1992 Ćosić became the first president of the Federal Republic of Yugoslavia, but in 1993 he would turn against Milošević and would subsequently be removed from office. Later in 2000, he would join OTPOR, the anti-Milošević resistence movement. Otherwise, his literary output included: *Daleko je sunce* (*Distant is the Sun*, 1951); *Koreni* (*Roots*, 1954); *Deobe* (*Divisions*, 1961) and *Bajka* (*Fable/Fairey Tale*, 1966). His best-known work is the three volume *Vreme smrti* (*The Time of Death*, 1972–1975) which recounts the fate of the Serbian people in the First World War. More recent works include the three volume *Vreme zla* (*Time of Evil*, 1985–1991) which describes Serbia's relationship with Stalinism. His non-fiction works include: *Stvari i moguće* (*The Real and the Possible*, 1983); *Promene* (*Changes*, 1991); and, *Prijatelji* (*Friends*, 2005) [RH].

20. Ostensibly because Serbian extremists had announced Dr Rugova's assassination. Later, it was claimed that Dioguardi himself had spread these rumours.

21. According to the Albanophone newspaper *Rilindja*: 'The Assembly interrupted its meeting after Ruzhdi Bakalli from Gjakova declared that: "The Kosovo Assembly made the decision, in 1945 that Kosovo should join Serbia as an autonomous province, this Assembly has the right to make a

decision on the separation of Kosovo from Serbia".' *Rilindja*, Priština, 26 June 1990: 1.

22. Nekibe Kelmendi, in his paper 'Kosovo under the Burden of the Serbian Discriminatory Laws: Facts and Evidence' provides a review of the legal acts which Serbia passed (Kelmendi 1993). I have quoted the Internet version of his study. See also *The Kosovo Report*: 301–318.

23. At the populist and nationalist meeting the main slogan was: 'Serbia from three parts – should be united'.

24. Serbs, who made up about 8 per cent of the total population of Kosovo, now took over complete control of the administration and the economy. Throughout that year, Albanians were expelled en masse from their jobs.

25. After the proclamation of the Republic, the members of parliament and members of government were sheltered for a certain time in Slovenia and Croatia, where they continued to work as a government and assembly in exile.

26. For example, the Albanian school system was not re-created, but continued to work in the scope and functions, that it had had previously, also, under the new conditions and outside of school buildings, which had been usurped by the Serbian authorities (Clarke 2000: 96). See also Kosotovićova 1997.

27. 'Albanian opposition in Kosovo... produced an independent and autonomous civil society under the very noses of the Yugoslav authorities – a counter-power unique in political history' (Schwartz 2000: 127–131).

28. A Serb anti-regime writer Mirko Ković concluded that: 'The Albanians are politically the most mature nation in Yugoslavia.' Slovenian philosopher Slavoj Žižek has a high esteem for the Albanian resistance, commenting that: '[They are] a European nation, which is characterized by patience, uses Ghandian methods in politics, which in the face of violence returns with non-violence' (*Borba*, 13 March 1992; Maliqi 1993: 20).

29. Clark 2000: 1. In his book, Howard Clark (2000), analyses in detail the weaknesses of the movement.

30. *Ibrahim Rugova: La Question du Kosovo – entretiens avec Marie-Françoise Allain et Xavier Galmiche* (1994). In this chapter the Albanian translation is used: *Çështja e Kosovës* [The Kosovo Issue] (together with Marie-Françoise Allain and Xavier Galmiche), Dukagjini, Pec, 1994, prefaced by Ismail Kadare, the renowned Albanian writer/novelist.

31. Also, H. Clark claimed that Rugovism doesn't have anything in common with Gandhism, nor, moreover, with pacifism in the true sense of the word. Clark comments that: '... it is a misrepresentation to call him [Rugova] a pacifist. Above all, he was pragmatic. He followed a peace policy broadly speaking, but at one stated seems to have favoured Kosovo having its own territorial defence system, and later he worked towards NATO intervention. Neither was he a Gandian. The Gandian strategy of non-violence is active, emphasizes self-reliance and a constructive programme as well as civil resistance, while Gandhi's personal philosophy was based on a dialogue for Truth' (Clark 2000: 6).

32. That kind of opinion, expressed in many papers, was openly supported by Henry Kissinger.

33. On 24 December 1992, American President George Bush sent a so-called 'Christmas warning' to the Belgrade regime, in which he stated that: 'in

the event of conflict in Kosovo caused by Serbian action, the US would be prepared to employ military force against the Serbs in Kosovo and Serbia proper' (Judah 2000: 73; *The Kosovo Report*: 56).

34. Serbian sociologist Duško Janjić in *Zeri*: 15.

35. Clark concludes that it has to do with both kinds of parallel institutions: first one arose through 'the transfer of the former autonomous organs to the self-declared Republic of Kosova', and the other from 'the construction of new systems'. He makes a detailed review of these parallel institutions in his book (Clark 2000: 95–117).

36. It had been a completely independent system, from the pre-school institutions through elementary and secondary schools to university, teaching training and publishing institutions (Clark 2000: 95–100; Kustovićova 1997; Maliqi 1998: 113–119).

37. A summary of the international reactions on Human Rights violations is given in *The Kosovo Report*: 301–318 (Annex 1, 'Documentation on Human Rights Violations').

38. In essence, Judah shares a similar opinion on this, but from the position of neutralism or with a little bit of a pro-Albanian connotation, when he says that Kosovo was not a case of 'violating human rights', as had been represented in many international forums, but rather a 'fundamental struggle between two peoples for the control of the same piece of land' (Judah 2000: 84).

39. The upshot is that the LDK was subsequently informed after decisions had been made (Kraja: 230).

40. As a member of the Presidium, Kraja serves as a credible source.

41. It should be noted that this struggle was not clearly articulated at the time, but had been developing behind the scenes and became more-or-less superfluous when the legalists achieved their main goals, namely the Declaration of Independence and the Proclamation of the Republic (Kelmendi 1998: 153–166).

42. Although it claimed to have the status of a government agency at the top of its daily bulletin, the KIC/QIK, which was also distributed in foreign language editions, also bore an LDK logo and was therefore a party organ.

43. In 1996, when the delegates' mandate had come to an end without them ever having held a meeting, Rugova, using his 'presidential decree', extended their mandate for two further years. Parliament remained a fiction, and Rugova by this gesture confirmed his position as the one and only authority.

44. Rugova barely said anything about his rivals. In the forward to his book of conversations he comments that 'I do not polemize with them', and he adds the ironic message: 'Please save us, if you have any other solution' (Rugova: 142).

45. Political excommunication was the job of the KIC and the only daily newspaper *Bujku*. The dirty jobs of blaming opponents and publishing insinuations and anathemas was left to the supplement of the *Kosovarja* magazine.

46. This formulation was referred to in the LPRK's publication *Pararoja* in 1990 (Kraja: 207).

47. In 1991, rather than create a 'National Council', the LDK and Rugova, after a period of several months of negotiations, agreed to create what would

be known as: 'The Co-ordination Council of Albanian Political Parties', in which Rugova would have the last word (Kraja: 223–229).

48. Demaçi became the head of the Kosovo Committee for the Protection of Human Rights and Freedoms.

49. '[Rugova] appeared to have gone into a form of political paralysis. He drove around Priština in his presidential Audi and simply did nothing' (Judah 2000: 138).

50. This was at the time that the Contact Group was created as an ad hoc international mechanism, which would play a great role in ending the war in Bosnia and bringing about the allied intervention in Kosovo.

51. It was military action against Yugoslavia over the Kosovo crisis, by a group of states without a mandate from the UN Security Council, in 1999, that was widely greeted as being the first international military intervention against a sovereign state for purely human rights purposes. While, on the one hand, this meant that many would object to both the legality and the justification for fighting this conflict, on the other hand, the Kosovo war has been the starting point for an ongoing debate on the 'Responsibility to Protect', which means that the moral obligation of the international community to intervene in situations in which crimes against humanity, war crimes and genocide are committed by states or non-state actors de facto rules (Hudson and Heintze 2008: 13–14).

4

The Paradox of the Solution: The Impact of the Kosovo Question on Macedonia

Maja Muhić

Introduction

This chapter provides a political analysis of the complex scenarios that could result from the final outcome regarding the status of Kosovo. It examines, in particular, the possible implications that the final decision on the Kosovo status will have on the Republic of Macedonia.[1] At the same time, it aims to show how an incredibly complex regional paradox would inevitably emerge, whereby, regardless of the outcome of the Kosovo question, the solution for Kosovo could inexorably integrate the majority populations in both Serbia and Kosovo, both in terms of their social realities as well as of their political agendas.

The paradox of the solution to the final status of Kosovo applies precisely to the case of Macedonia, if one takes into account the multi-ethnic setting of that country, where Albanians constitute the second largest ethnic group representing around 25 per cent of the total population in the country. Albanians also form a major constituent of the multiparty government, and their community is represented by twenty-nine members of parliament in the 120-seat parliament of Macedonia. The solution to the Kosovo status could bring not only both the Macedonian and the Albanian political parties and their opinions into confrontation with each other, but could also bring both ethnic communities into conflict, as was demonstrated in the spring of 2002.

This chapter will focus upon the events that have taken place in Kosovo over the past decade (1997–2007). It treats the current situation as the basis for an estimation of the most probable implications that might come about as a result of the final solution regarding the future status of Kosovo. It also analyses the plausibility of different trajectories in connection with political strategies, which the different possible solutions of the final status may produce. Concomitant with this analysis is a brief sketch of the social, economic, cultural and political impact on the region. This chapter will also address the changes of conditions for academic work on and in the region, including the author's own change in attitude over the past decade.

The background to the paradox

Although it was generally accepted that Macedonia was a unique former Yugoslav state due to its peaceful and bloodless secession from the Yugoslav Federation, in 2001 Macedonia was struck by an ethnic conflict, which brought about an eight-month period of unrest in the region. Even before the conflict, in January 2001, various research reports registered that:

> Relations between the ethnic Macedonian majority and the ethnic Albanian community were deteriorating, that the climate in the country was one of widespread pessimism, that dialogue and interaction between the two communities were virtually non-existent, that fears and a lack of trust dominated the attitudes of both sides. (Ethnobarometer 2002: 73)

The conflict started on 17 February 2001, when paramilitary Albanian groups (the NLA – National Liberation Army) entered the border village of Tanusevci (in the mountain range of Skopska Crna Gora).[2] In a short time span, the conflict between the Macedonian security forces and the NLA expanded to the Kumanovsko, Lipkovsko and Tetovsko region (all in the north-western part of the country) claiming the lives of 120 soldiers from the Macedonian army, and an unknown number of casualties from the NLA (although it is generally believed that the number of casualties on their part range up to about 1,200).

The Ohrid Framework Agreement, which was signed on 13 August 2001, finally put an end to the insurgencies and radically improved the conditions of the Albanian population in Macedonia. The former NLA members together with their leader, Ali Ahmeti, established the Democratic Union for Integration (DUI) and entered the coalition with the then ruling parties SDSM (Social Democratic Union of Macedonia) and LDP (Liberal Democratic Party of Macedonia). Since the 2006 parliamentary elections, these parties became the opposition, and a new coalition government has been established, with VMRO-DPMNE (the Internal Macedonian Revolutionary Organization) and DPA (Democratic Party of the Albanians) as its major constituents.

Now, seven years later, Macedonia is faced with yet another extremely dramatic challenge: to preserve its peace and stability in the whirlpool of already existing as well as newly arising complexities that arose from a turbulent decade that had witnessed: weakness in the economy; issues over the quality of political leadership; a deterioration in trust among the two major communities; and growing concerns with regard to the final status of Kosovo.

It goes without saying, then, that any version of the solution regarding the status of Kosovo, when taking into account the specificities of Macedonia, will inescapably lead to the deepening of mistrust along ethnic lines, and to a disintegration rather than an integration of Macedonian society. If the final outcome were to be a status of independence for Kosovo, this would almost certainly be seen as a highly destabilising factor for the Macedonians in Macedonia. The opposite scenario would bring about similar dissatisfaction among the Albanian population in Macedonia. It could be argued, then, that the political as well social conflict between the two parties is in a phase of incubation under the surface of Macedonian political reality, precisely because the status of Kosovo still has not been finally decided.

The likelihood of increased tensions, mistrust and conflicts in the reality of everyday Macedonian life increases as the solution to the status of Kosovo approaches. Similarly, the announcements of a possible postponement of the Kosovo final status[3] might also produce an avalanche of negative consequences and tensions that will inevitably affect Macedonian society. Given these circumstances, it is highly pertinent to analyse the paradoxical situation, whereby the solution to the Kosovo question will inevitably involve the populations of both Serbia and Kosovo. These two populations are directly involved in this problem and there is little doubt that they, in turn, could bring further instability to Macedonia, a country which is indirectly involved in this crucial issue, being marked by a number of related circumstances – the 25 per cent of the Albanian population being but one of them.

Future scenarios and trajectories of the solution to the Kosovo question

Any in-depth political and analytical treatment of the current situation in the region must inevitably include the two following aspects:

1. The local political, social, as well as 'inter' and 'intra' factors in the political agenda of Kosovo and the surrounding states; an analysis

that takes into account both the positive and negative factors that can affect the state of affairs in the region;
2. The politics and crucial role played by the International Community.

Without doubt, the future political situation in the region will be the outcome of the interplay of both these factors. A one-sided action that will not be the result of the interconnectedness of these factors is highly improbable. However, it may be expected that the final solution of the Kosovo question would almost certainly express the fundamental strategic interests of the International Community, whichever option prevails.

The following is an analysis of trajectories in accordance with the possible different solutions to the Kosovo question:

An independent status for Kosovo without partitioning and without the consent of Belgrade

Possibility A: *Macedonia recognising the independent status of Kosovo*

At the time of writing, this possible solution is dramatically close, as the date (10 December 2007) when the future of Kosovo is to be decided is fast approaching. Yet the outcome of the negotiation processes is still somewhat vague.

The first visit of the 'troika' – the international negotiating team of envoys from the United States, Russia and the European Union – to Belgrade and Priština in the first half of August, achieved little, as the two sides in the dispute simply reinforced their respective positions. Serbia offered everything but independence, while the Kosovo Albanians said they would have nothing other than that. 'The two international key players also remained entrenched in their conflicting positions – the Americans insist that *complete* independence is the only viable outcome, whilst the Russians say that any final decision must have the consent of Belgrade.'[4]

Since then little progress has been achieved in the negotiations of the 'troika'. Nevertheless, as 10 December is approaching, so the statements of the Kosovo people are intensifying in their sharp demand for independence. In 1999 a former general of the KLA (Kosovo Liberation Army), Rexhep Selimi, who was Kosovo's first Minister of the Interior, as well as serving as a member of the self-proclaimed provisional (shadow) government,[5] stated that: 'This is the first time since then, that I honestly believe we should declare independence unilaterally – after 10 December.'[6] It can therefore be assumed that the independent status for Kosovo is going to be a very feasible outcome of all the drawn-out and tiresome negotiations that have been taking place. This would imply that the combination of historical circumstances and events that have defined the past decade of Kosovo's existence could surely lead one to conclude that the aspiration of Kosovo for independence has now reached the point of no return.

Kosovo has a homogenous, ethnic composition, where the Albanians constitute 90 per cent of the population, the rest of the population being made up of Serbs, Turks, Montenegrins, Gorani, Bosniaks, Aškali, Roma and others. In a number of instances, the opening argument that the Albanians use as the basis for claiming greater rights in the region is their insistence upon the fact that they are the descendants of the Illyrians. The Illyrians had inhabited present-day Albania and most of the former Yugoslavia. However, the argument that the Albanians are the descendants of the Illyrians who settled in the Balkans around 2000 bc, and were therefore settled in the region long before the Slavs, who settled around the seventh century, has frequently been disputed by Serbian historians who claim that the Albanian presence in the Balkans goes back only to the eleventh century.[7] Regardless of all the historical disputes, the fact of the matter is such that in Macedonia, by contrast, there is no ethnic group or nation, irrespective of size, which cannot be considered autochthonous, thus creating the basis for a fragile ethnic balance in the country. As Muhić points out in his lucid analysis of the ethnic complexities in Macedonia, the three major ethnic groups in Macedonia (Macedonians, Albanians and Turks) can all lay various claims on the present-day territory of Macedonia (Muhić 1996: 236). While the Turks can lay claim to the longest tradition of statehood, but suffer the handicap of small numbers in Macedonia, the Albanians argue that they have the longest continuous habitation in the Balkans although they have never had a state on this particular territory. By contrast, the Macedonians are the most numerous on the territory of Macedonia and have had their own state (Muhić 1996: 236).

In addition, although the majority of Kosovars are Muslims, Albanians have never been characterised by a religious-based political movement. As Malcolm points out: 'If one looks further back into Kosova's past, one may find numerous examples of a mixed religious life' (Malcolm 1998: xxiii). Although there have been battles and wars in Kosovo over the centuries, there is a general belief among the Albanian elite that the starting point of their continuous calamity can be traced back to 1912, after the Balkan Wars.[8] As Kuci comments: 'the Albanian desire to break off from Serbia is not an aspiration born within the context of Yugoslavia's break down ... Since 1912, when Kosova was occupied by Serbia after the Balkan Wars the Albanians always wanted to escape Serbian rule ...' (Kuci 2005: 193).

However, it should be noted that, while Albanians feel that Serbia has been their occupier and that, ever since the Balkan Wars and the uneven division of the territories by the Great Powers, they have aspired to escape Serbian rule, during the period of the Kingdom of Yugoslavia (1918–1941) Macedonians found themselves in a similar relationship with Serbia. Cvijic (1987) even launched the term 'floating mass' to refer to the status of Macedonians. Within the Yugoslav Kingdom Macedonians found their ethnic identity and consciousness subjected 'to systematic pressure to assimilate to the Serbs. The concepts "Southern Serbs" and "Southern Serbia" were imposed within the framework of Vardar Banovina' (Muhić 1996: 237).

While one could go on to argue that sharing such similar historical circumstances of ethnic subjugation could bring the two groups closer together, the fact that Macedonians had legally and legitimately formed their own state (ASNOM 1944–1994)[9] and brought it into the federal community of former Yugoslavia, complicates the situation further and adds bitterness to the consciousness of the Albanians in both Kosovo and Macedonia, who did not receive equal treatment as the other federal units in former Yugoslavia. In a similar vein, Muhić has commented that: 'in different times, and in different parts of Macedonia, Greek, Serbian, and Bulgarian security forces have all tried to suppress Macedonian consciousness' (Muhić 1996: 238). He goes on to explain the vigour and pride with which the Macedonians now praise this state.

Although with the Constitution of 1974 Kosovo enjoyed almost equal rights and duties with the other federal units of the Yugoslav Federation, including having its own Constitution, as well as the right to veto, its autonomy was abolished in 1989, when Milošević came to power. In September 1991, however, Kosovo's parliament passed a decision to organise a national referendum on the Republic of Kosovo as an independent state. The referendum, which took place between 26 and 30 September 1991, expressed the Kosovars' desire for Kosovo as a sovereign and independent state. On 24 May 1992, Kosovo held multiparty, general and presidential elections, thus leading to the formation of Kosovo's shadow parliament and presidency. The Dayton Peace Agreement of 1995 did not consider the Kosovo question and was followed by a massive student movement in the autumn of 1997. In 1998, the situation in Kosovo became very volatile. From 1997 all international players became deeply concerned over Kosovo,[10] concerns which became more vibrant as the days of finalising Kosovo's status approached.

However, an independent status for Kosovo, for which most Kosovars aspired on the basis of the above-mentioned historical reasons as well as the complexities of the previous decade, will most likely produce deep changes in Macedonian–Serbian relations. Those changes would most probably develop in the following manner. The most probable outcome of this scenario, to name but a few cases, could be the retaliatory introduction of a visa regime and a drastic increase of the export/import taxes by Serbia on Macedonia. In addition, the deepening of the political distance and mistrust between these two countries can certainly be expected.

It is of the utmost importance to also point out that according to the current political situation in Macedonia and its intense endeavour for accession into the EU and NATO, it is highly improbable that Macedonia would oppose the recognition of Kosovo's independence even if it were to be achieved without Serbia's consent.

Developments of this kind would, on their part, produce intense dissatisfaction among the ethnic Macedonians and to some lesser extent among the Albanians. In this scenario, however, the Macedonians would put the blame on the Albanians; that is, they would identify Albanian nationalism as the major reason and source of their suffering, and would very likely see themselves as scapegoats for the fulfilment of the strictly narrow Albanian national interests that do not work for the benefit of the whole country.

Possibility B: *Macedonia delaying the recognition of Kosovo for strategic purposes*

In the case that Kosovo gains independence without partitioning, it might be expected that Macedonia would most likely follow precisely the above-mentioned pattern. Without hesitation, one can almost certainly annul the possibility of Macedonia taking a proactive role on the Kosovo question. Macedonia will under no circumstances be the first country to recognise the independence of Kosovo, which means that it will wait for at least two or three regional countries (Slovenia, Croatia, Bulgaria) to recognise the new status of Kosovo. Even in this case, strong measures towards Macedonia by Serbia might be expected, though perhaps not as drastic as in the first scenario.[11] However, the feelings of mistrust, both between the two countries as well as between the Macedonians and Albanians within Macedonia, will remain.

Independent status for Kosovo including partitioning and a most probable consent from Belgrade

This solution would be the most problematic one for Macedonia, since it would almost certainly generate a demand by the Albanians for the south-western parts of Serbia (Preševo, Bujanovac, Medvedja) and, along this line, it could trigger the nationalist feelings among the Albanians in Macedonia who could claim its north-western parts. This would create inevitable tensions in the region and would most likely be the least beneficial solution for Macedonia. It would encourage the extreme Albanian nationalists in Macedonia to revive the already suggested and formulated partition of the country[12] on the pretext of the already existing precedent.

The first talks announcing the possibility of the partitioning of Kosovo, in August 2008, resulted in Macedonia's President Branko Crvenkovski stating that 'the partition of Kosovo could harm Macedonia's interests'. In addition, a few days before this statement, President Crvenkovski summoned a meeting of the council, a body comprised of Macedonia's top officials, to discuss the possible partition of Kosovo, saying that redrawing the territory's borders could stimulate extremism in the region.[13]

This would create the same difficulties for Macedonia as in the first scenario, but in addition it would force Macedonia into considering the impact of the hypothetical partition of Kosovo on the demands for its own partition. Although political analysts do not see new conflicts arising in Macedonia in the light of the solution to the Kosovo question, there are a few analysts who also believe that the partitioning of Kosovo would bring about the partitioning of Macedonia and its disappearance from the map of Europe.

Respect for the principles of UN Resolution 1244 (1999) – Respecting the territorial sovereignty of Serbia, thus having Kosovo remain, at least formally, an integral part of Serbia

A solution to the Kosovo status that would unfold in this manner would again generate difficulties for Macedonia, only with the reversal of roles. In other words, the Macedonian population would be mainly satisfied, and the state of affairs would remain unchanged, while the official relationship with Serbia could be strengthened even further. However, the tensions between the Macedonians and Albanians, both in the political arena as well as at the social level, would increase tremendously especially now, when, according to many analysts, Kosovo's independence has reached a point of no return.

Moreover, it is worth mentioning that on 19 October 2007 the ruling Albanian political party in Macedonia, the DPA, organised a mass meeting in Tetovo (a city in the north-western part of Macedonia) bluntly calling for an independent Kosovo and thus taking a proactive role on the issue. Nonetheless, the slogan of this mass meeting was delivered under the pretext that they call upon an 'Independent Kosovo and Macedonia in NATO'. Hence the sole reason for the mass meeting, the insistence upon and the unreserved support for an independent Kosovo, has been hindered and balanced out by connecting it with Macedonia's aspirations for joining NATO. Nevertheless, this event showed that the Kosovo question is not only widening the mistrust among the population, but that confusion, disagreement and a lack of coordination dominate the Macedonian political scene as well. Combining the proactive support for an independent Kosovo with the call upon the acceptance of Macedonia in NATO probably served the role of bringing the Albanian bloc closer to the agenda of the Macedonian ruling parties. Instead, the Macedonian bloc remained rather reserved about this event, and a further distancing of the parties took place regarding the latest incidents related to the Macedonian Constitutional Court and the Law on the use of the flags of the national minorities in Macedonia, which came into force in 2002 after the signing of the Ohrid Framework Agreement.

In the last week of October 2007, the Constitutional Court of Macedonia annulled the right to display the Albanian flag on municipal buildings, local courts and state institutions where the ethnic community represents the majority. The decision was adopted one month before the Day of the Albanian flag (28 November), at a time when the Albanian community was more sensitive than ever regarding the issue of its identity in the light of the unresolved Kosovo status. As a result, two Albanian members of the Court resigned, including Mahmut Jusufi, the President of the Constitutional Court. The ruling VMRO-DPMNE and DPA accused the opposition of carefully planning this event in order to destabilise Macedonia and prepare a spring offensive. The ruling Albanian party, the DPA, accused the Constitutional Court of making 'provisional interpretations' while the opposition Albanian party, the DUI, went as far as saying that they would not respect the decisions adopted by the Constitutional Court. Such a statement would certainly be considered unprecedented since it is widely known that

Constitutional Court decisions are never commented upon, and must be accepted unquestionably.

The conflict within and between the two major Albanian parties on the one hand, and the two Macedonian parties on the other, as well as between the ruling Albanian and Macedonian parties has obviously weakened the coalition and supports even further the argument over Macedonia falling prey to further internal dissension. Even a problem like this proves that the level of social integration has been seriously damaged. In the final instance, one can argue that the problem is not really over the display of the flag, but rather the continuous attempt to express both parties' patriotic feelings, which are unavoidably furnished in relation to the Kosovo question.

In the light of these events and the above-mentioned scenario concerning the Kosovo question, it becomes obvious that the accumulation of the strong feelings of empathy towards and support for the Albanians in Kosovo among the Albanians in Macedonia, as well as among the Albanians in the political milieu of that country, would inevitably explode at some point. Macedonia would therefore most probably be faced with very strong pressure from both the Albanians in Macedonia and those from Kosovo. It might be expected that the Republic of Albania would also noticeably change its attitude and foreign policy towards Macedonia. The failure to realise their long-desired independence in Kosovo could lead to an even further strengthening of opinion with regard to claiming parts of Macedonia. The fact that all the symbolic fronts that give Macedonians a sense of unique being could be seen as a weakness and, at the same time, a major incentive for the awakening and strengthening of such aspirations. The state of mind of ethnic Macedonians was well expressed by Gareth Evans in his address, in 2001: 'Their language (Macedonian) is claimed by Bulgaria, their Church is contested by Serbia, and their chosen name is denied by the Greek diplomatic veto. Hence, there is a sense among the Macedonians that: "nothing in the country is really their own".'[14]

4. Freezing Kosovo's status until 2020

In their article regarding the possible freezing of the Kosovo status,[15] Krenar Gashi and Berat Buzhala announced the latest discussion by US diplomats. As they pointed out: 'a senior source within the State Department had described for *Balkan Insight* and Kosovo's *Daily Express*, parts of a draft proposal for Kosovo that is currently in preparation, whereby: "The US has two options: to recognize, together with a few other countries, Kosovo's independence and to cause thereby many global and regional problems; or to drop formal independence for some years, relaxing tension in the region and boosting Kosovo's economy".' 'A freeze on Kosovo's political status until 2020 means a period in which to boost Kosovo's economy ... as it is also foreseen that the EU and the US would inject up to €7 billions a year into Kosovo's budget, as a pay-off during this period.'

In February 2007, The UN envoy, former Finnish President Martti Ahtisaari recommended the internationally supervised independence for Kosovo, but did not receive the endorsement of the UN Security Council, due to objections from Russia. The additional 120 days allowed for further negotiations showed no signs of a breakthrough, which is why the announcements for the freezing of Kosovo's status could be a new solution in sight. However, even this scenario would not bring about any dramatic changes in the already proposed trajectories that Macedonia would take.

Implications for academic work on and in the region

The aforementioned analysis of the past decade's developments in the region and the possible trajectories of Macedonia in the light of the Kosovo question bring us to the indisputable conclusion that, whatever the final status of Kosovo will be, it will offer an extremely exciting terrain for academic work of any kind. Regardless of the outcome of the Kosovo dispute, it will unavoidably lead to deep controversies and stimulate further research on the region. Just by way of illustration, if no independence were to be granted, the triumphalist consciousness of the Serbs could offer a rich basis for a raft of deeper analyses in the disciplines of sociology, history, politics and psychology, among others, just as Kosovo gaining the status of an independent republic would open up new vistas for research into the triumphalism of the Albanians.

In addition, it is my deepest conviction that the past decade has brought about major changes that should provide a sufficient incentive for certain alterations in the academic approach. Taking the anthropological stance, I believe that, looking at the events in former Yugoslavia and the region from 1992 onwards, it could be argued that an extremely sceptical approach towards the capacity of grand theories in the social sciences should be developed. By this, I mean a development of scepticism towards the pure objectivist interpretation of history, which naturally marginalises the human factor. I argue that a social interpretation of history as an objective series of events and a scientifically explainable process is unattainable. Instead of talking about social science that deals with the analysis of objective events, the furthest one can go is to talk about the existence of social description and social psychology only.

I derive those arguments from the fact that events from 1992 onwards (and not only these) have proved that one can hardly talk of social *causes*, but rather, only of social *motives/programmes/plans* and accordingly of actors who rush into the realisation of these plans, ignoring the objective factors and often even going against them. This by no means announces my revocation of the existence of objective factors. On the contrary, while fully affirming their existence, I would also like to point out that the scientific theory as a sum of objective circumstances is simply unattainable in the sphere of social events.

While the objective circumstances have never been even close to announcing the break-up of Yugoslavia, it did however take place. Just as the objective circumstances of the 1920s did not suggest the development of the USSR as a world power, so the objective circumstances in the late 1980s did not suggest the break-up of a major socialist system. Although the majority of analysts claim that the USSR dissolved because it was, among other things, economically unsustainable, I would argue again that it was the *people's motivation* to keep it alive, just as the loss of that *motivation* announced its death. Indeed, many other factors play a crucial role in shaping people's motivation, propaganda being but one of them. Macedonia has been called the People's Republic of Macedonia, the Socialist Republic of Macedonia and, in the past decade, the Former Yugoslav Republic of Macedonia (FYROM). All objective factors prove that a flexible approach whereby Macedonia would finally accept some other formula to its constitutional name due to the neverending dispute with Greece would almost certainly bring about benefits to the country. Yet the *motive* of the Macedonians, especially when taking into account that there is a sense among them that 'nothing in the country is really their own' as every other aspect of their identity is being disputed, brings them to the point of claiming that under no circumstances will they agree to a name other than the constitutional one. This understandable yet stubborn approach does not take into account the objective factors, that Macedonia will have to face the consequences for not agreeing to another name, which can go as far as Greece preventing Macedonia from joining NATO.

Hence the objective factors in the social sphere are neither crucial nor do they decide the outcome of events. The chances for an individual, populist, political or any other response of that kind to that which we refer to as objective factors, always remains present in the social reality. To further clarify this, I argue that social reality offers a vast space for scepticism towards the general, traditional model of historicism, that is, the *causal* model of interpreting changes in a society. This could lead the historian, anthropologist, sociologist or philosopher to pay greater attention to the social, psychological and mental characteristics of the given region, its people, political parties and the country's leading figures. In their analysis, the social scientists will have to focus more on the cultural and other idiosyncratic factors of the given circumstances, as well as the motivational structure and psychological factors of the specific situation, political parties, or the country's leading politicians. This could gain even more clarity if a further in-depth analysis is made to show that frequently the leaders epitomise what is, incarnate, the will of the majority of the population and not vice versa.

Conclusion

This chapter has explored, politically and analytically, the complex set of scenarios that could result from the final outcome regarding the status of Kosovo. It examined the possible implications that the final decision regarding the status of Kosovo will have on the Republic of Macedonia. It argued that the specific ethnic composition of Macedonia, whereby Albanians represent 25 per cent of the population, in combination with its historical complexities, led to the unavoidable conclusion that whatever the outcome of the Kosovo question will be, it will inevitably have a disintegrating effect on Macedonia. At the same time it will have an integrating effect on the Serbs in Serbia and the Albanians in Kosovo. Even the Special UN Envoy for Kosovo Martti Ahtisaari's recommendation for an internationally supervised independence for Kosovo has increased the integration of the social as well as political reality in both Serbia and in Kosovo, while leading to a decline in political confrontations over integration in Macedonia. While the Macedonian political parties and the government remained more restrained with regard to this plan, the Albanian factor in Macedonia (both within the opposition and the ruling Albanian party) radically and openly supported it. Disintegration and a further deepening of mistrust, fear and the distancing of the two major groups in Macedonia has become inevitable.

However, the first scenario of Kosovo gaining independence would most probably be the one that would offer the best opportunity as a source for stability in Macedonia and for a regional balance unlike all the other scenarios, which are more threatening especially with regard to Macedonia. While the disintegration of society would still most likely occur, it would almost certainly be a more *benign* process.

Notes

1. The territory of what is today Macedonia was until 1913 the last part of the Balkans to be ruled by the Ottoman Empire. After 1919, Macedonia entered the Kingdom of Yugoslavia under Serbian jurisdiction and without any administrative autonomy. This kingdom was defined as the Kingdom of Serbs, Croats and Slovenians, without any reference to the Macedonians. After 1945, Macedonia was constituted as the People's Republic of Macedonia within the framework of Yugoslavia. After the break-up of Yugoslavia, Macedonia was admitted to the UN on 8 April 1993 as the Former Yugoslav Republic of Macedonia (FYROM) until an agreement could be reached with Greece which had claimed that some of the articles of the new Macedonian Constitution, following the declaration of independence, on 8 September 1991, made territorial claims on the Greek province of Macedonia. The issue regarding Macedonia's name has still not been resolved, with Turkey being the first state to recognise the country under its own constitutional name, that is, the Republic of Macedonia. For the sake of clarity and ease of expression in the text, I shall be using the term Macedonia, although the debate with Greece is now reaching a boiling point, especially after the latest United Nations Special Envoy, Matthew Nimitz's proposal for adding two names for the country in its Constitution. Macedonia is a landlocked country covering 26,000 square kilometres with a population of approximately 2 million and the capital is Skopje.
2. Although Macedonia had been spared the inter-ethnic violence that had broken out in Croatia and Bosnia and Herzegovina following the break-up of Yugoslavia in the early 1990s, the country came close to civil war ten years later, in February 2001. Rebels led by the Albanian NLA (National Liberation Front), which had been largely officered and equipped by the KLA, staged an uprising in the name of greater rights for ethnic Albanians. Months of skirmishes followed in an insurgency which witnessed a wave of refugees, before the president of Macedonia, Boris Trajkovski, was able to strike a peace deal with the ethnic-Albanian leadership. Under the Ohrid agreement, the NLA insurgents laid down their weapons in return for greater ethnic-Albanian recognition within a unitary state [RH].
3. Read more in 'US Ponders Freezing Kosovo's Status Until 2020' by Krenar Gashi in *Balkan Investigative Reporting Network* 29.10.2007. www.birn.eu.com/en/110/10/5411/ (accessed 21 December 2007).
4. Balkan Investigative Reporting Network, 16.08.2007, *Serbs Mull Over Partitioning of Kosovo*, by Aleksandar Vasovic, Belgrade, http://birn.eu.com/en/99/10/3863/ (accessed 21 December 2007).
5. It should be noted that he had not been recognised by the international authorities [RH].
6. Balkan Investigative Reporting Network, 26.10.2007, *Kosovo Albanians Look beyond December Deadline*, by Krenar Gashi, Pristina, http://birn.eu.com/en/109/10/5399/.
7. Dimitrije Bogdanovic: *The Kosovo Question Past and Present* (Belgrade: Serbian Academy of Sciences and Arts) Monographs, VOl. DLXVI, Presidium No.2.
8. The London Conference and its final decisions brought on 29 July 1913, divided the Albanian lands by giving Kosovo to Serbia, Peja and Gjakova to

Montenegro, and Janina and Epirus to Greece. Although Austro-Hungary argued that all Albanian inhabited lands should be included in the newly established Albanian state, Serbia's protector power, Russia, as well as France opposed this idea. (See more on this in Malcolm 1998: 256.)

9. ASNOM – The Anti-Fascist Assembly for the People's Liberation of Macedonia (Antifašističko sobranie na Narodnoto Osloboducanje na Makedonija) [RH].

10. See a more in-depth analysis of the 1992–1998 circumstances in Kosovo in the European Centre for Minority Issues (ECMI) Working Paper No.1, 1998, by Stefan Troebst, *Conflict in Kosovo: Failure or Prevention? An Analytical Documentation, 1992–1998.*

11. Both Macedonia and Montenegro recognised the Independence of Kosovo on 9 October 2008, establishing full diplomatic relations between Skopje and Pristina on 17 October 2009. This stimulated an outburst from Serbia, but in the case of Macedonia, the lure of the Europe, as a candidate for EU membership, proved far stronger [RH].

12. The partitioning of Macedonia along ethnic lines has been vigorously supported and suggested by Arben Dzaferi, the leader of the Democratic Party of Albanians (DPA), currently in coalition with the ruling VMRO-DPMNE (Internal Macedonian Revolutionary Organization), The Macedonian Academy of Arts and Sciences (MANU), as well as former Prime Minister (1998–2002) Ljubco Georgievski from VMRO-DPMNE, which later divided into two parties – VMRO Narodna (with Georgievski) and VMRO-DPMNE, presently the ruling Macedonian party with Prime Minister Nikola Gruevski.

13. Balkan Investigative Reporting Network, 24.08.2007, *Macedonian Security Council against Partitioning of Kosovo,* by http://birn.eu.com/en/100/15/3934/ (accessed 21 December 2007).

14. Gareth Evans, the Trilateral Commission, in his address: 'Advancing Balkan Stability', delivered on 11 November 2001. Mkakademija, 15 November 2001. One could also add that in Serbia the Macedonian language is treated, on a populist level as a variant of Serbian [RH].

15. Read more in 'US Ponders Freezing Kosovo's Status Until 2020' by Krenar Gashi in *Balkan Investigative Reporting Network* 29.10.2007 www.birn.eu.com/en/110/10/5411/ (accessed 21 December 2007).

5
Pride and Perplexities: Identity Politics in Macedonia and Its Theatrical Refractions

Ivan Dodovski

Film and television are largely considered to be the dominant media of social constructivism today. In earlier times, and notably since German Romanticism, it was believed that nation-building depended on an established national literary canon. Modern nations as imagined political communities were consolidated through the considerable influence of both the press and literature (Anderson 1991). However, in the age of the new media, literary (including dramatic) representations are said to count only as expressions of the individual from the global village. In the contemporary world, one finds compelling the argument that theatre has lost its mobilising power and can no longer sustain a social synthesis. Still, it remains relevant to see how the theatrical medium refracts social convulsions, particularly in societies which undergo an immense political and economic change. This paper considers the intricacies of the Macedonian case. After a few contextual details at the very beginning, I will analyse four performances which communicate the crucial national perplexities of the past decade.

Following political change in the early 1990s, the Republic of Macedonia entered a process of social transition common to all former socialist countries in Eastern and Central Europe. What appears unique in that context, however, is the fact that Macedonia as a newly independent state, unlike the others, faced a denial of its identity from without as well as amended identity definitions from within. The referendum on independence in September 1991, supported by a vast majority of Macedonian citizens, brought a peaceful end to the era of 'brotherhood and unity' (*bratstvo i jedinstvo*, in 'Serbo-Croat') shared with the other Yugoslav nations and peoples.[1] Ethnic Macedonians, being the constituent nation of the state which had been established in August 1944 and thereafter integrated as one of the six republics of federal Yugoslavia, were now living out the dream of many generations: namely, that of a free, independent Macedonia. The country gradually came to be known as, or rather perceived itself as being, an 'oasis of peace' amid the Balkan horrors. However, this 'dream come true' would soon have to confront serious challenges. Neighbouring Greece imposed an embargo, claiming an exclusive right to the name Macedonia and thus denying any attribute of a distinct Macedonian national identity. Pressurised by the threat of economic devastation, Macedonia made concessions. It agreed to change its flag, the Star of Vergina, associated with ancient Macedonia, to amend its constitution, thereby giving assurances to Greece that it held no territorial aspirations, and to discuss the differences over the name issue under the auspices of the United Nations. The embargo was lifted in 1995 but the dispute remains. Moreover, it gave rise to a new narrative of Macedonian national identity. Some Macedonians embarked upon a new definition of their ethno-genesis, claiming an amalgamation of ancient Macedonian and Slavonic roots, although now placing emphasis upon the former, rather than the latter – as it was defined until the 1990s. Needless to say, this perfectly suited national imaginings, according to the principle 'the older, the better'. At the same time, Bulgaria, as throughout the twentieth century, continued to deny the distinctiveness of the Macedonian language and the existence of Macedonian national identity as such.[2] Officially renouncing any territorial aspiration, Bulgaria nonetheless claims that the Macedonians were 'Bulgarians by blood', seduced by a Macedonianist propaganda that has allegedly been fabricated by the Serbs. Conversely, the Macedonian Orthodox Church, perceived by most Macedonians as being an eminently national institution, remains unrecognised in the Christian Orthodox world. This is due to the refusal of the Serbian Orthodox Church to acknowledge it as a canonical church within present-day Macedonia, a territory over which the Serbian Orthodox Church gained jurisdiction only in 1918; a century and a half after the illegitimate abolition of the autocephalous Archbishopric of Ohrid, in 1767, of which the Macedonian Orthodox Church claims to be the rightful heir and re-institutor.

Along with its efforts to counter the denials of its neighbours, Macedonia also experienced an internal crisis. In 2001 the National Liberation Army (NLA), an ethnic Albanian extremist organisation, took over parts of the territory of western Macedonia and threatened to instigate a civil war. The inter-ethnic armed conflict was brought to a halt with the signing of the Ohrid Framework Agreement. The amended Constitution gave a new definition of statehood, stipulating mechanisms for the protection and enhancement of the rights of ethnic communities. Thus, new multicultural values were introduced in Macedonian society. In the so-called post-Ohrid era, ethnic Macedonians faced the necessity of sharing the state with other constituent members, which implied abandoning the idea of a mono-ethnic nation-state. The citizens of Macedonia – the Macedonian nation, and parts of the Albanian, Turkish, Serb, Roma and Bosniak nations living in the Republic of Macedonia – were acknowledged as constituent communities by the Constitution. In practical terms, this meant that substantial power was delegated to ethnic Albanians. They comprise slightly more than 25 per cent of the population and refuse to be called a 'minority', opting for the politically correct euphemism 'non-majority community' in politically correct public discourse.

These contextual facts can help us to understand two opposing trends in Macedonian society today: the first trend, which calls for a new type of nation-building, based on multicultural values and civil loyalty (in other words, a political nation where Macedonian signifies citizenship rather than ethnic background); and a second trend, which advocates cultural pluralism but, in fact, introduces biculturalism (Macedonians and Albanians) and a communitarian definition of identity in ethnic terms. Although multiculturalism seems appealing, public space is dominated by the cultural nationalism of the two dominant ethnic communities. There are hindering factors to the multicultural prospect, too. As the Macedonian philosopher Branislav Sarkanjac puts it, 'multiculturalism without acknowledged identities is just a farce'; in other words, Macedonians, being persistently denied outside, become a 'frustrated majority' inside[3] (2005: 22). The common perception is that ethnic Macedonians are giving up their national identity defined in modernist terms in order to embrace a liberal concept of multiculturalism before their modern national narrative was generally confirmed in the first place. That is why, concludes Sarkanjac, the postmodern discourse on national identity in the context of the Balkans cannot be a prerequisite but a consequence of mutual recognition and respect: 'The Macedonian situation clearly illustrates this. Given the modern historic discourses of the countries surrounding Macedonia, a postmodern one (in Macedonia) can stand no chance' (2004: 74). We need to keep this in mind, particularly when discussing deconstructionist attempts to represent identity on the stage.

With regard to the theatre, most of the state companies still featured the syntagma 'national theatre' (*naroden teatar*) in their name. When they were established in the late 1940s and 1950s, this adjective had a strong ideological meaning: it was related to the socialist concept of 'the nation'. The intention to exploit theatre in the promotion of national identity was not excluded, although national drama never dominated the repertoires. What seemed emancipating was that plays were performed in the Macedonian language, something which had rarely happened in the past due to oppressive regimes. For example, a few folklore melodramas (so called *bitovi drami*) performed in a local dialect in the 1930s were being restaged after the Second World War as de facto 'classics'. Given the ideological constraints of Yugoslavism, major national identity issues did not appear on the stage until the late 1970s and early 1980s, with the exception of the famous play *Darkness* (*Crnila*, 1961) by Kole Čašule, which I discuss below. In the 1990s, social transition seriously affected the concept of the national theatre. First of all, productions were expected to employ a different ideological paradigm. Like society as a whole, theatre encountered two alternatives: to give voice to the emerging nationalist discourse or to resist it in a deconstructionist manner. In fact, both responses took place as an odd resonance of shifting national values. A prominent metaphor of this change is, perhaps, the dissolution of the traditional nineteenth-century model of the Macedonian National Theatre (MNT), which comprised drama, opera and ballet. This supreme national institution was eventually split into two separate entities, though still defined as national. However, neither the transformed MNT nor any of the other theatres across the country remained strategically focused on a clear national agenda. Instead, the repertoires reflected transitional complexity, every so often turning the stage into an arena of national perplexities.

The spectacle *Macedoine – Odyssey 2001*, a joint production of several companies, opened the international Ohrid Summer Festival in July 2001. This was only weeks away from the signing of the Ohrid Framework Agreement, while the fighting was still going on. The premiere took place in the ancient Ohrid amphitheatre, which at the same time was inaugurated as a newly reconstructed archaeological monument and theatre venue. For almost 2,000 years the site had remained underground and only now was it spectacularly opened to serve the purpose of identity politics. Prior to the performance, both the Macedonian Minister of Culture and the European Union Special Envoy to Macedonia gave long speeches. It was a moment of pride: Macedonia was rediscovering its ancient heritage, interpreting it as a generous contribution to a united Europe. The performance itself followed the same interpretative pattern. It was envisaged as a journey through Macedonian history to the present, depicting a long and dramatic struggle from denial to glory. It was also an optimistic message which coincided with the official political aspirations towards entry into the EU and the euphoria of the millennium. The script was a patchwork of texts, legends, historic figures and events which marked the collective consciousness of the people living in Macedonia. Let us mention but a few: Alexander the Great; the fall of the Ohrid Archbishopric; the romantic poet of Macedonian nostalgia Konstantin Miladinov; and the Kruševo Manifesto, which called upon all ethnic communities to support the 1903 Ilinden uprising against Ottoman rule and the attempt to establish Macedonia as the first republic in the Balkans. Other events and the historical characters of note are: the unfulfilled love of Kemal Ataturk, a Muslim, for the beautiful Eleni, a young lady from a rich Christian family, at a time when the future 'father of modern Turkey' was just a cadet at the Military Academy in Bitola, and the gory destruction of Tito's Yugoslavia.

Ivan Popovski, a Macedonian director with a career in Russia and Europe, played with the amplitudes of national pathos, adding here-and-there carnivalesque ritual, folk humour, and parodied Bogomil dualistic cosmology. The performance, however, demonstrated a high level of political correctness in its representation of ethnic communities other than the Macedonians. Also, there were several scenes in which the actors spoke in both Albanian and Turkish. The very opening scene, representing the symbolic expelling of the plague, seemed to connote the current political effort to exorcise the evil blood of history. In contrast, the ending, evidently triumphant, suggested a happy multicultural prospect. Skating on the thin ice of spiritual and historic as well as present political circumstances, the performance sparked manifestations which appeared to be noteworthy from a sociological point of view. The audience in Ohrid, numbering more than 3,000, almost all coming from different parts of the country and perhaps comprising predominately middle-class men and women, reacted to the stage representations in an ambiguous, if not contradictory way. For instance, there was an audible shout of appreciation when the old flag – the Star of Vergina – was displayed over the entire stage. By the end of the performance, however, this very same audience, mesmerised by its national identification with ancient symbols, demonstrated a nostalgia for the Yugoslav identity pattern. It started with the Yugoslav anthem in mumbled tones, but went on with a collective recital of musical refrains from the 'former' Yugoslav pop scene. Thus, somewhat ironically, the title befitted the effect: given that *Macedoine* refers to a type of salad with various fruits; so too the performance was a mixture of national pathos, bits of history, humour and – naturally – a politically correct appeal. Then again, what did 'Odyssey 2001' stand for in the title? Perhaps that, in spite of everything, Macedonia has embarked upon a jolly millennial future?

National discourse, however, relies on perceptions of the past. It is not an exaggeration to say that much of the Macedonian perception of history was synthesised in the title of the famous play *Darkness* (*Crnila* 1961) by Kole Čašule, which marked the beginning of Macedonian modernism on the stage. The play dramatises the political assassination of Ǵorče Petrov in 1921. As a prominent figure in the Macedonian liberation movement, he opposed the pro-Bulgarian faction within the Macedonian revolutionary organisation VMRO and opted for an independent Macedonian state. In this context, he is also considered a symbol of the struggle for the expression and recognition of ethnic Macedonian identity. *Darkness* relates to an act of national betrayal by those members of the VMRO who plotted to kill the legendary hero of the Macedonian struggle for freedom. Although the characters are fictitious, the play has the cathartic power of mobilising the Macedonian national consciousness – a quality which seems to have remained ever since its premiere at the MNT in 1961. Over the years, the play has been staged more than fifteen times, both at home and abroad, making it one of the most striking myths of Macedonian theatre. Still, in 2005, Slobodan Unkovski, a teacher of directing at the Faculty of Dramatic Arts in Skopje, who was celebrated across former Yugoslavia, decided to direct a completely deconstructed version of *Darkness*. Symbolically enough, it was staged in the transformed MNT.

In *Darkness 005* Unkovski subverted both ideological content and theatrical form. On the one hand, the play was a comment on the re-emergence of nationalism. It questioned the integrity of the national party (the modern replica of the former Macedonian revolutionary organisation) whose leaders, in reality, became rich by means of organised crime. In this adaptation, the political assassins were just a miserable bunch of criminals, terrorists, drug addicts and drunkards caught amid the social transition of the 1990s. Hence, nationalism was brought as a master narrative to serve the purpose of camouflaging crime and moral degradation. On the other hand, Unkovski undermined the pathos of the original script, inserting citations from current news headlines as well as his own voice which attempted to explain how theatre could resist the whole-embracing discourse of corruption in politics. Consequently, *Darkness* was converted from a modernist play about betrayed national ideals into an abrasive comment on national-ist manipulation with identity. Two aspects of the play deserve further elaboration: national betrayal and gender relations.

For contemporary Macedonians, the assassination of Ǧorče Petrov instantly prompts an evocation of the Bulgarian attempts to eradi-cate any trace of Macedonian national identity. However, in the play *Darkness* it is a group of Macedonians with questioned national identity and weak personal morality who take it upon themselves to carry out the assassination ordered by their superiors from within the upper ech-elons of Bulgarian political circles. Indeed, the entire dramatic tension in the play relies on the fact that the assassin is a young Macedonian whose life was once saved by Ǧorče Petrov himself. As a little boy, he witnesses the killing of his family by the Turks and becomes a protégé of the revolutionary hero whom he would never see again. As a sign of his indebtedness, as well as a way to revenge, the young man joins the organisation. Years later, in a mission in Sofia, he does not know whom he is going to kill, but he unconditionally trusts the directives given by the organisation. At the end, finding out that he has actually killed his saviour, the young man commits suicide. Thus, the play dramatises the myth of 'the self-exterminating national gene' of the Macedonians, which often augmented the positions of Bulgarian nationalism, but also served as an alibi for political mistakes in Macedonia. And while the mimetic story on the stage implied that history was repeating itself, an intervention by Unkovski maintained that it was time to dismiss the notion of darkness. In the closing scene, when all the assassins kill each other and finally lie dead in shallow water and mud, amid the darkish setting of history, an actor approaches the audience and, with sophisticated cynicism, declares, 'The end'. Read in a simplified interpretative fashion, this finale holds a heuristic illumination: today Bulgarian nationalist policy towards Macedonia makes no sense; the time of Macedonian national betrayal is over; the nation now has other priorities, such as fighting corruption and organised crime. (Oddly enough, these very words reflect the current political discourse of the international community towards Macedonia.) In a similar emancipat-ing manner, the young assassin in *Darkness 005* was converted into a female. In all dark episodes of history, Macedonian women were usu-ally treated as objects, lacking any agency in the national liberation struggle. Nation-building was considered a machismo business. In this performance a woman became the subject of political assassinations, pushed in the very same historic arena along with the macho-men to exterminate her own national ideal. Gender balance here received a sardonic overtone: women assumed a macho-nationalist agenda rather than men becoming gender sensitive. Conceiving these identity representations, Unkovski seemed to suggest that theatre had no other option than to subvert nationalist manipulation, albeit being powerless to impose a new national synthesis. But he was neither a herald nor alone in the deconstructionist drive. Several plays considered to be at the apex of the national canon (including the 1930s melodramas) were restaged during the period of social transition. Still, the most successful ones, such as *Darkness 005*, served seditious ends and, on the whole, detracted the pathos of earlier productions. A further piece can exemplify this tendency in some detail.

In December 2000, Aleksandar Popovski, a disciple of Unkovski, staged anew the Macedonian cult play *Wild Flesh* (*Divo meso* 1979) by Goran Stefanovski. Its first version, directed by Unkovski and restricted within the ideological precincts of former Yugoslavia, referred to the Macedonians of the late 1930s who lived under the double hegemony of global German ascendancy and a Serbian oppressive regime as its regional derivation. Premiered at the Dramski Theatre in Skopje just a few months before the 2001 inter-ethnic armed conflict started, the new production became a dark prophecy. The opening line of the play reads: 'There's going to be a war.' It is augmented by an immediate reply: 'We've had enough of this so-called peace, anyway'[4] (Stefanovski 2002: 83). Thus, the restaging, as Stefanovski himself claimed in a note to the performance, was situated amid the contemporary Balkan wars and the exercise of muscle by the new world order. The performance had less to do with Macedonians being denied and threatened by war; ultimately, it was about the prevalent state of a crisis of identity at the beginning of the new millennium.

The differences in relation to the original script deserve attention. Stefanovski's dramatic story evolves around the ambition of Stefan Andreyevitch, a young individualist with a promising career in a foreign automobile agency, to fulfil his dream of success. His father Dimitri is an invalid, former house builder, who adheres to his traditional belief in honest work, and has ample experience to mistrust foreign values. The conflict between modern and patriarchal values culminates when the German visitor Hermann Klaus, entrusted by the power of the Third Reich, arrives to replace the manager of the agency, Herzog, who is a Jew. Klaus also offers to buy out the house of the Andreyevitch family so that the agency can extend its offices onto the main street. Stefan sees no problem, but this is out of the question for Dimitri. While Stefan fantasises about Western European progress, his ecstatic mother Maria, like Dimitri, illustrates a negative attitude through the metaphor of 'wild flesh': the foreigner, the other, that is Western values; is this wild hair intruding into the throat which suffocates the local self.[5] But the conflict is redirected: Stefan gradually comes to understand that the mistrust towards Klaus displayed by his family members stems from their experience of repression by various regimes; in short, they seem to believe that alternating one master with another does not fulfil their need for recognition and freedom. Hence, Stefan aborts his individual ambition and seems to restore dignity by joining the collective resistance. In the crucial tenth scene, Klaus invites Stefan to a hotel room and exploits his inferiority complex by describing the South Slavs as the masochistic other of Europe. Further, he speaks of Balkan suspicion towards foreigners, stubbornness and unwillingness to learn, particularly from experience. He gives a diagnosis of the local people as ones who feed on pettiness and provincial ideals. Yet, he persuades Stefan to become a possible exception: 'I'm offering you the chance of severing the umbilical cord tying you to this tribe of yours and of rising to achieve an identity of your own.' With a typical colonial arrogance, Klaus invites Stefan to join him in Germany so as to perfect the German language, refine his taste, get his body into shape, and improve his mind with selected readings. The intention is to transform Stefan into a 'mature and sophisticated' person, whose previous 'simplicity and rusticity' have been 'filtered and purified through education and culture'. This cultural project aimed at providing Stefan with European identity is further explained in sexual terms: 'You're still at the stage of *naive* innocence. You haven't yet lost your hymen... You need to be raped... You need somebody to grab you by the hair, break your bones, open up your eyes and ears and nose, stir you up, mince you, pound you and remould you into a new human being' (Stefanovski 2002: 128). Eventually, Stefan, in a state of shock, rejects Klaus's openly homoerotic approach. The shot that he fires from the illegal gun of his brother Andrei, a communist, symbolically suggests that the arrogant West was no longer admired or feared, but to be resisted.

Although the main storyline depicts a struggle of the Macedonian subject vis-à-vis German neo-colonialism in the Balkans before the Second World War, some details also expose an image of a Serbian nationalist hegemony moulded on the German model. Namely, in the perception of Klaus, all that is not European (or in radical terms – German) is equally despised as barbarous, be it Slavonic or Jewish. Local differences do not make sense to Klaus; he sees what is already a fashioned image of barbarous Slavs in a city which is 'all dirty and smells of the farmyard'

(Stefanovski 2002: 100). However, the members of the Andreyevitch family do make a difference between themselves and the Serbs, who impose a system of dominance locally. In the eighth scene, for instance, Klaus observes that the language spoken in the house of the Andreyevitch family is not purely Serbian, and he receives an ironic explanation: 'You see, we live in the Vardar Province, so we speak Vardar Provincial' (Stefanovski 2002: 119). The terms are, in fact, those used by the official Serbian regime to replace and proscribe any sign of Macedonian national identity. Even the Serbian form of the surname Andreyevitch (in Macedonian it is usually Andreevski or Andreev) reveals the practice of renaming which was usual at the time. Furthermore, Sivitch, a Serb, who works as a consultant in the automobile agency and whose brother appears to have a high rank in the police, offers his underhand services to the new manager Klaus, organising, as well as profiting from the eventual eviction of the Andreyevitch family from their home.

Still, Popovski's new production seemed to sidestep this twofold struggle and makes it ambiguous. There was a suggestive set design made up of the collapsing pillars of a family house which was separated by a simulated glass facade from the world of the rich. The chronology of the dramatic story was inverted and some scenes were redone. The intercultural and gender relations in the play were transposed: Klaus was transgendered, transpiring as a woman rather than a dominant man; the whole issue of transculturation in his monologue was represented though a martial arts exercise. Other male characters like Herzog and Sivitch were also played by actresses, which gave a psychoanalytical touch to the issue of dominance and subordination. The old mother Maria was played by a very young actress adding metaphorical connotations to mystified national fragility. Thus, the performance brought forward an image of a patriarchal world in demise rather than a promising national gestalt. Unlike the politically consecrated spectacle *Macedoine – Odyssey 2001*, it disclosed a twilight vision of Macedonia amid economic, ideological and geopolitical changes. Moreover, rather than depicting some local resistance to global capitalist expansion or a foreign (Serbian, Bulgarian, Greek or Albanian) nationalist foray, it addressed a state of the general volatility of identity positions which an individual experiences at the end of all post-isms. History, nation, culture, language, family and gender – all concepts, Popovski seemed to suggest, were unstable or fell apart yielding a world of irrational violence and barrenness of meaning.

Another production may also help us to unravel the present complexity of Albanian national representations on Macedonian stages. In 1998 the Macedonian director Vladimir Milčin directed the play *Late Coming Bones* (*Koskite docna doağaat*) in the Theatre of Nationalities – Albanian Drama, Skopje. The script by Teki Dervishi is based on motifs from the novel *The Palace of Dreams* (*Nënpunësi i pallatit të ëndrrave* 1981) by the famous Albanian writer Ismail Kadare. Mark-Alem, the main character of this novel, is a young man from a prominent Albanian family that has long-established ties with the Ottoman rulers. Thanks to his powerful uncle, Vizier to the Sultan, Mark-Alem rapidly ascends the ranks of imperial bureaucracy in Istanbul. He becomes the chief interpreter in what appears to be a macabre Kafkaian archive. The dreams of all imperial subjects are stored in this Palace of Dreams, then sorted and interpreted, in order to prevent any possibility of overthrowing the ruler. In the performance *Late Coming Bones*, Mark-Alem discovers dreams that speak of his origin. The key question turns out to be: What is his true identity? In the Sultan's realm, he is known as Abdullah, a Muslim name which also associates him with the dominant Turkish culture. However, he discovers that he was originally called Gjerg, an Albanian Roman Catholic name. The latter triggers an allusion to one of the leading figures of Albanian history, Gjerg Kastrioti, also called Skenderbeg, who was forced to convert to Islam and won many victories for the Sultan, but eventually turned against the Ottoman ruler, reverting back to Christianity and even receiving the title *Athleta Christi* from the Pope. The inner antagonism of Mark-Alem between two opposing identity positions, Islam versus Christianity, becomes an ethno-cultural struggle to preserve his Albanian roots from coercive Turkishness. In the end, he accepts the name Mark-Alem, which indicates an Albanian crypto-Catholic identity. In a recent study, Ger Duijzings argues that: 'because in Albania and Kosovo Islam was imposed in a much more violent manner, most converts were only nominally Muslims' (2000: 15). He specifically elaborates the experience of conversion and mimicry of the *laramans* or crypto-Catholics in the village of Stublla in Kosovo who used to feign being Muslims in public, but preserved their Roman Catholic beliefs privately. He also notes that in the church registers the priests frequently recorded two names for a baptised child of *laraman* background: 'Apart from the Catholic name, they also wrote down the Muslim name given by the parents, which would be the one used in public' (Duijzings 2000: 101). Mark-Alem would seem to be a representation of this practice. This leads us to the conclusion that the performance reflected the current superimposition of national over religious identity, which was encapsulated in the avowal of Albanian nationalists that their true religion was Albanianism. In this context, it is worth mentioning the observation by Shkëlzen Maliqi, an intellectual from Kosovo, who wrote that in 1989 many Albanians thought of a collective return to Roman Catholicism in order to obtain Western backing for Kosovo (Duijzings 2000: 104). So the issue of Albanian identity was considered alongside the global concerns of West–East, Christian–Muslim relations. However, this should not make us believe in a simplified or unequivocal definition of present Albanian identity as crypto-Catholic, particularly when discussing ethnic Albanians living in Macedonia, where Islam and Albanian ethno-cultural specifics usually go together. The significance of the performance *Late Coming Bones* seemed to be augmented by targeting ethnic Albanian Muslims for whom even a mention of the retrieval of their former Christian identity remains controversial. Following the premiere, for instance, it was not a surprise to see the play informally denounced as anti-Albanian and anti-Muslim. In contrast, the ethnic Macedonian (predominantly Christian) audience which had a chance to see this production (though it was – by all accounts – limited in number) seemed to have a positive response; such were the reviews too. The performance won foremost awards at the Macedonian theatre festival Vojdan Černodrinski in Prilep. However, this can also be related to another aspect of the production. Namely, in what seemed to be a crucial scene, Mark-Alem was put in a tub so that the collective nightmares of identity might be washed out from his memory and eventually replaced by a politically correct vision approved by the Sultan. Thus, the performance opened the issue of collectivist demands versus individual freedom in an attempt to criticise the ethnic communitarian, if not tribal, delineation of identity that leaves no space for cross-cultural exchange or personal choice. As the title of the performance suggests, the bones of the ancestors need to be taken back to their imagined homeland. But it is never too late to do so because their true homeland is within the person.

The productions analysed in this chapter illustrate the controversies of identity representation in Macedonia in the 1990s and early 2000s. Some performances, like *Darkness 005* and *Wild Flesh*, though being adaptations of national classics, demonstrated a genuine disbelief in a mythologised construction of the nation, warning of political manipulation and common conceptual impasses in our time. Others, like *Macedoine – Odyssey 2001*, aimed at provoking strong national pride, inaugurating, inter alia, a new perception of the ancient Macedonian heritage. Then again, some directors and playwrights dared to question collectivist obsessions, opening historical taboos, such as the appraisal of former Christian identity of ethnic Albanians in the play *Late Coming*

Bones. In this light, I hold the view that the Macedonian theatre has captured significant aspects of the politics of national identity in a period of social transition. Many of these aspects were highlighted on purpose: to comply with or resist official discourse. No matter what the purpose was, though, the representations on the Macedonian stage, as some cultural synecdoche, refracted a tension between past national imaginings and current challenges: a paradoxical crisis, as it were, of a nation that arrives at its long-awaited recognition.

Notes

1. In former Yugoslavia, the terms *narod, narodnost* and *manjina* (in Serbo-Croatian) were used to make a distinction between *nation, people* and *minority*, respectively; sometimes *nation* and *people* were used as synonyms meaning 'constitutive nation/people' in contrast to 'local minorities', while occasionally and debatable expression *narodnost* is translated with *nationality*. For the sake of clarity, I follow the first way of distinction.
2. The period of Georgi Dimitrov's rule in Bulgaria (1946–1949) makes the only exception to this approach. A census held in 1946 recognised Macedonians as a separate ethnic group mainly populating the south-western part of Bulgaria known as Blagoevgrad Province (or Pirin Macedonia); teachers as well as theatre and other professionals were brought in from Yugoslav Macedonia to organise schools and cultural production in the Macedonian language. This policy was reverted, in 1948, when Yugoslavia left the Cominform due to the *Informburo* discord between Tito and Stalin.
3. Author's translation (as are all quotations from Sarkanjac).
4. Pagination refers to the original, though I have used the English translation by Patricia Marsh-Stefanovska from a manuscript which was made available by the courtesy of the author.
5. The metaphor of 'a hair' used by Stefanovski derives from local folk beliefs that if someone's hair somehow gets into the body of an other person, it will grow into a deadly tumour ('wild flesh').

6
A Re-examination of the Position of the Student Movement in Serbia

Vladimir Marković

The idea of the 'end of history', which was launched at the beginning of the last decade of the twentieth century, more or less proclaimed the beginning of a conflict-free epoch that would be concomitant with the introduction of undisputed economic and political liberalism.[1] The experience of the collapse of the East European system of real-socialism meant that it would no longer be possible to imagine a world that was radically better than the present one, nor a future which would not be a capitalist one. Due to the escalation of armed conflicts, motivated by nationalism in the former Yugoslavia, this area became the European exception to those predictions of entering a period of eternal peace created by the free market system. However, when the conflicts were over and the regimes which had once led and inspired them had been overthrown, representatives of the economic and political interests of the leading Western governments optimistically concluded that the 'end of history' had finally arrived in the region. In other words, the situation had matured enough to speed up the process of the realisation of those transitional obligations which had been delayed due to the unregulated business conditions that had arisen from the wars alongside the politically unstable systems that had been put in place.

After the collapse of the Milošević regime in 2000, it was thought that the students and universities in Serbia who had often been heavily involved in the political turbulence of the gloomy decade of the 1990s would now be able to play a more important role, in a period that would witness the accelerated integration of the Serbian state into the West European political and economic system.

Indeed, between 1996 and 2000, there had been a period of dynamic political activity within the Serbian academic community, when confrontation with Milošević's regime was broadly articulated through the flourishing of independent students' organisations which found themselves in a dynamic relationship with the opposition parties and non-governmental organisations within Serbia. So, while there were expectations that in a way treated students and universities as a vital reservoir of qualified and competitive layers of society who would support the project of a social transformation based on the principles of political and economic liberalism, in reality, this community had become marginalised, depoliticised and stripped of any attributes of being a leading force in the public criticism of socio-political life, during the decisive moments of the struggle against Milošević's regime. This development coincided with a period that witnessed a decline in the role played by students in the criticism of social, political and public affairs. In reality, all that the academic community had gained was greater autonomy in dealing with specifically academic and operational problems, such as the reorganisation and reform of the universities. All this meant that the 'end of history' in the Serbian universities had resulted in their total pacification. Yet, ultimately, this pattern of events would be broken in the autumn of 2006, which witnessed the student protest in Belgrade.

The protest in question was inspired by the need for social change. The main demands formulated during the 2006 student protest concentrated on the question of students' fees in the state-run universities.[2] The protest started in October and lasted until the end of December, starting up again between March and April 2007. The protest involved students from many of the faculties of Belgrade University as well as from the Belgrade Faculty of Art, the University of Novi Sad and some Higher Technical Colleges. In contrast to the occasional sporadic demonstrations of student discontent in the previous five years in Belgrade, which had been isolated examples within some faculties or faculty groups, this protest was articulated on a much broader level of unrest that went way beyond the general situation in which higher education in Serbia found itself.

The university between privatisation and reform

The situation that the students revolted against came about as a result of the reorganisation of the education system, especially in the area of higher education, which had been becoming increasingly more market-oriented and less able to live up to its universal social and educational values. Over the previous decade, the higher education sector had been showing signs of being one of the most profitable areas in the economy, which was reflected in the number of privately established faculties and universities throughout Serbia. There are justifiable reasons for assuming that in most cases the main motive behind establishing new higher education institutions had been that of making a profit.

At the same time, one should note that, in the absence of a strict quality control system for higher education, private initiatives in the sector served to undermine the credibility of the higher education system.[3] The second characteristic of this process was the continuous cutting back of state funding from higher education which, in turn, has benefited the move towards the deregulation of the universities, in a process whereby many university lecturers and officials, with greater or less enthusiasm, are beginning to behave like private entrepreneurs. Problems of corruption and the usurpation of one's position in the area of higher education are to be found, not only in cases of students bribing lecturers in order to pass a module or to get a university diploma, but also in attempts by some lecturers to achieve financial gain at the expense of university students. The fact is that many universities now enrol an excessive number of self-financing students although many of them are fully aware that they do not have the capacity to organise sufficient teaching for all of them.[4]

The emergence of so-called 'external university sites' as well as the introduction of 'distance learning' programmes, which often do not satisfy even the minimum of standards required for this type of teaching, tells us enough about the intentions of replacing good quality education by the short-term demand for profit. An even more drastic demonstration of the desire for profit-making as the ultimate goal of higher education can be found in the practice of charging students additional fees, for activities such as registering on modules, changes of lecturers, the issuing of various certificates, and so forth, which should have been included in the fees as they already exist. Problems with which students and universities are being confronted are given an extra dimension in the process of the reform of higher education. On the one hand, reform is treated as an obligation resulting from the accession of Serbia, in September 2003, to the Bologna Process, which is a project for the organisation of a unified European space for higher education. On the other hand the reform was understood as being a set of measures made to get out of the long-term trend of reducing the effectiveness of studying (reflected in the high average duration of studying as well as in a small percentage of those students who managed to complete their studies within the normal university-regulated time period.) In the recent past, many discrepancies emerged between some of the aims of reform and the resources that were made available for their realisation. Trying to increase the proportion of the population in higher education presented an almost unachievable task when the additional educational funds required for the realisation of such reforms were not readily available. Furthermore, the greatest responsibility for paying tuition fees and expenses was passed on to the students and particularly to that part of the student population that was not budget-subsidised but self-financing. At some universities, in the past three years, student fees have been increased by 90 per cent and in some cases even by 170 per cent, which does not accord with annual inflation rates.[5] In practice, this means that accessibility to higher education is being significantly reduced for the broader section of the community, at the same time that students' rights and entitlements were under threat.

The student protest in 2006 directly demonstrated the complex nature of the conflict between a public interest in education and the existing situation in higher education. In the formulation of their demands, students who actively participated in the protest strove to take into account all the existing financial problems incurred in the higher education system and to point out unacceptable attitudes of the different ruling instances towards the public importance of education. The most important student demand, for the reduction of student fees and the establishing of clear criteria for their regulation in the future where their social situation would be taken into account, shows us a well-measured approach in the formulation of their aims and the form the challenge would take towards the opposing side. An explanation of this demand expresses the need for the condemnation of the 'robbery of students at some universities, by justifying such actions by given autonomy to the universities to set up their own student fees in a bid to secure the salaries of university lecturers in the region of up to 200,000 dinars'. At the same time people are demanding that the state 'starts fulfilling its financial obligations towards the universities', due to the fact that the state 'finances only 25 per cent of the universities' running costs, which is only half the amount the state is responsible for in the finance of the higher education system'. The conclusion of the explanation of the main demand of the student protest explicitly defined the main motive of the protest and its main direction of 'exerting pressure in order to avoid a further deterioration of student living standards whereby students will be forced to pressurize the government to respect its decisions by which the university's part in the financing of higher education will be reduced'.[6]

The articulation of the social protest

In line with the general thrust of student activities during the student protest of 2006, the main participants directly confronted a raft of relevant and important officials from the Serbian government and the world of higher education, on several occasions. These officials included Vojislav Koštunica (then prime minister of Serbia) and Jan Figel, (European Commissioner for Education and Culture), Slobodan Vuksanović, (Serbian Minister of Education and Sport), Dejan Popović (Rector of the Belgrade University) and a number of university deans from different faculties. The student representatives were able to present their demands to these officials in a convincing way, and this gesture of directly confronting the main political and higher education officials would enrich the usual forms of public protest as expressed by young people (which are normally characterised by cheerfulness, an attractive atmosphere, loud music and colourful posters) by providing them with an important dimension that was seriously and courageously articulated from both a political and social perspective.

This standoff reached its heights during the occupation of the Belgrade Faculty of Philosophy building which the protesters occupied continuously between 22 and 28 November. Students gathering when the sit-in of the faculty building was announced adopted the proclamation in which the reasons for the sit-in were justified by the cynical shifting of responsibility between the government, the Ministry of Education, the University of Belgrade and the university administrations. For the first time, they came out with their demands, and demonstrated just how serious they were about these issues. The proclamation condemned the tendency of prolonging the actual problems of students, universities and society in order to create a space for political manipulation as well as to enable some universities to make a profit by taking extra money from students, thus treating knowledge as a mere consumer product. This document states that Serbia, during the 1990s, was destroyed, impoverished and morally devastated, but the protesters were not prepared to lower the level of civilisation any further. Their key points were presented in the following proclamation:

> We do not accept being persuaded that education is a consumer commodity, rather than being for the public good. We do not accept living in a society in which inequality will be reproduced with a good quality education only being accessible to the rich and the privileged minority. Our generation is being given the opportunity to resist the

logic of those who argue that knowledge is a consumer product and that it costs as much as someone is ready to pay for it. We are here to prove that there are still some people whose integrity is not for sale and who believe that their knowledge is considered to be something that can help the advancement of the whole of society.[7]

The radicalised social motivation of this protest is highlighted in the key points of this proclamation, which go beyond the problems of higher education and connect with the consequences of a society that is suffering as a result of the dominance of a neo-liberal approach to the economy and social politics. This is not a demonstration of some rudimentary egalitarianism, that is very often linked with a traditionalist value orientation characteristic of the Serbian rural heritage from the period of its political formation in the nineteenth century, but rather a clearly articulated sign of an authentic leftist position which corresponding with modern tendencies and the imperatives of a democratic struggle that is directed, in a variety of forms and on the global level, against the hegemony of capitalism.[8] In this way the student protest in Serbia joined other protests that had been taking place in France, Chile, Greece and other countries throughout 2006, in a struggle for the protection of social rights.

The organisation of the 2006 Student Protest is reflected in the high degree of devotion to an idea of equality and democratic practice. The protest was started up on the basis of a self-organised student initiative. The horizontal structure of the organisation held a dominant role in the coordination of student activities, so that all decisions about students' actions were made at student gatherings where all the participants had equal rights in decision-making. The operational bodies of the student protest, such as the Protest Committee, negotiating teams, the PR team and the team for technical support were elected at the gatherings. They had an important mandate and they were re-elected by the protesters. This model of a students' organisation was something that the participants in the protest readily emphasised in their proclamation: 'Occupy the universities because knowledge is not a commercial product.'

Led by this idea, we organised ourselves independently at our universities, participating in open and democratic discussions at students' meetings and gatherings during which the main demands of the protest were formulated. Insisting on the democratic principles and on authentic social demands we found ourselves in opposition to the regime supported by student organisations and young politicians who through these student organisations were gaining some political credit. This protest will neither become a tool of the political parties nor of someone's election campaign nor the platform for the creation of some of the new, young political leaders.[9]

There were signs of confrontation with the 'official' student organisations (The Students' Association of Belgrade and The Students' Union of Serbia) which were mainly absent during the student protest, and at some moments of crisis this rivalry turned into an open conflict, having at its origins the strategic differences in the prioritisation of student demands.

The traditional student organisations joined the protest out of the motive of undermining the importance of demands for a critique of student fees and the social position of students and that all student activities be exclusively concentrated on the position of students over the issue of the status and equality between the Bachelor's degree and the Master's in accordance with the new legislation introduced by Bologna, while the main reason for putting this issue on the agenda of the self-organised protest was due to the direct interest of some faculties in non-equality so that graduates would have to pay extra in fees for an additional year of study. The fact that the protest was coincidentally taking place at the same time as the campaigns for the parliamentary elections in Serbia helped it to become an issue for daily political exploitation so that the student protesters had to make an extra effort in confirming their organisational independence.[10]

This was fully expressed on 22 November 2006, when, led by the established Belgrade student organisations, a musical concert was organised in front of the Belgrade Faculty of Philosophy which commemorated the tenth anniversary of the beginning of the Student Protest of 1996/97. The plan was to hold a gathering with some of the former leaders of that protest. At the same time a large group of students invaded the Faculty of Philosophy building and at their gathering made the decision to blockade the building while two of the former leaders of the Students Protest of 1996/97, Čedomir Antić and Čedomir Jovanović, now members of the political establishment in Serbia, were shown their way out of the building followed by angry shouts from the students in an attempt to avoid any possibility of questioning the protest's academic autonomy and its political independence.[11]

It is interesting to note that on 22 November 2006 the demonstration to commemorate the Student Protest of 1996/97 was launched at the same time that the six-day picket of the Faculty of Philosophy building began, which was one of the most important actions of the Student Protest of 2006. An important characteristic of this event was that the activities of the new protest movement overshadowed the remembrance of the old protest. This might well indicate that the importance of the Protest of 1996/97, as a symbol of civic struggle against the authoritarian Milošević regime, had gradually declined in its significance with the distancing of time. The regime had been overthrown and there was now a need for a new mobilisation potential, and this required resisting the current forms of oppression in Serbia, all of which were to be found in the ideas and models of the new protest.[12]

In order to have a rational and well-balanced approach towards the experiences of the previous demonstrations of the student protest which could help these fresh political ideas break through into the protest culture of contemporary students, it is necessary to revisit the ideological positions of the Student Protest of 1996/97.

The student protest of 1996/97 and OTPOR (Resistance)

The student and civic protests that were held in 1996 and 1997 were a reaction to the attempted election fraud carried out by the Milošević regime after the local elections in Serbia, in November 1996. Many accounts of this process refer to the dominant picture of their imagination, irony and the presence of 'a carnival atmosphere' that captivated the charm of this 'postmodern spectacle'. An important contribution to these protests was their rejection of any parochial political culture for the sake of building modern, democratic and participatory politics.[13]

Recent literary interpretations of the Student Protest of 1996/97, as expressed in the novel *Kandže* (Claws) by Marko Vidojković, are closer to the facts because they strove to describe the atmosphere of the protest in order to add a more realistic dimension to the political and ideological confusion at the time. Based on his personal experience, this Serbian writer from the younger generation described the organisation of the Student Protest of 1996/97 as a relatively inflexible structure of political consensus between the daily, political interests of the opposition parties and the conservative-oriented students who were essentially closed to any demonstration of irony or humour. The writer's attempt at being realistic demonstrates the dominant orientation of the 'Great Protest' that would be more successful if he had not engaged himself into additionally constructing the possibility of radical disagreement with the dominant Serbian ideology shared by the protesters. The main character in the novel, the writer's alter ego, during the protest argued against clericalism while implicitly criticising the crimes committed in Srebrenica.[14] In contrast to the fiction, in the reality of the Student Protest of 1996/97, critical gestures of that kind were successfully blocked because the leadership of the protest saw clericalism as a catalyst for its anti-communist orientation, while creating their perception of the wars in Croatia and Bosnia and Herzegovina from the romantic position of the ideology of a Greater Serbia. Traditionalism and nationalism were important characteristics of the Protest of 1996/97, where the protest organisers did not operate against the system because they wanted to confirm their belonging to the 'moral majority' while asking for support from the nationalistic intellectuals, the Serbian Orthodox Church, the Serbian Academy of Sciences and Arts as well as from other 'national institutions'. It is important to note that before each gathering, in front of the Belgrade Faculty of Philosophy building, during three months of protest, students were listening to the clerical-nationalistic 'Hymn to St Sava' while one of the leaders of the protest (Čedomir Jovanović) whose responsibility was to announce the programme of protest for each day greeted the crowd with the three-fingered salute and the expression 'God help us'.[15] The discourse of 'democratic nationalism' and of a 'returning to Europe' that was promoted during the Student Protest of 1996/97 as an authentic revolt of the middle class, was necessarily defined with the aspiration of excluding some class groups from participating in the political community and a rigid understanding of the desirable cultural model.[16] This can be best seen in the programme of the *Narodni Pokret Otpor* (People's Resistance Movement). Otpor is an organisation which was formed by part of the leadership of the Student Protest of 1996/97 and gradually became a movement which managed to mobilise a large number of young people who made a decisive contribution to the political activities engaged in the overthrow of the Milošević regime in the autumn of 2000. Unselfishly financed by governmental and non-governmental organisations from the USA and Western Europe, Otpor successfully developed the necessary and effective marketing strategies for reaching the widest possible audience. There is no doubt that Otpor politics were deeply influenced by neoliberalism. In *Deklaracija* (Declaration), a document in which we find the main aims of Otpor, this organisation supports: 'the transformation of the economy, the creation of conditions for a free market and unavoidable privatisation as well as the opening up of a space for foreign capital with legislative guarantees for secure investment'.[17]

However, it is very interesting, from the point of view of understanding modern democracy, that the proclaimed metaphysical aspect of

Otpor's aim is presented in the document entitled 'A Memorandum' which was adopted at the first congress of Otpor, in February 2000. This is a document where the essence of the conflict between the two cultural models which crucially affected the collective identity of Serbia and the Serbian people is explained. European, civic Serbia with attributes of being urban and individualistic and according to the Otpor ideologists, with its authentic liberal and democratic characteristics inherited from the traditions of St Sava's Serbian orthodoxy, is opposed to the picture of a primitive, oriental and unauthentic Serbia, a product of the centuries-old Ottoman rule, to say nothing of five decades of the socialist regime.

In this Memorandum it is stated that:

> Still the dominant Asian model is trying to destroy the European roots in Serbia but in the long term the chances of achieving this are non existent. There are futile attempts to turn Serbia into an *Ostrvo Gubavica* (leper colony)[18] isolated from the rest of the world by barbed wire, because of its regime, dangerous ideas, and trends. Attempts at preserving this model still succeed, but only in forgotten societies such as Cuba, but this is impossible at the crossroads of Europe, in a state such as Serbia.[19]

Based on this discourse, it can be noticed that neither Otpor nor the Student Protest of 1996/97 with their achievements, as impressive as they were, managed to reach over the horizon of the ideological matrix so dominant in Serbia in the 1990s, and in the current decade. Therefore it is as much as it might be expected as being essential to having a critical analysis of that protest even after the distance of ten years.[20] The historical distance and 'experience of transition' in Serbia have created a space for the new generation to get out of this political dead end.

The potential of a progressive movement

Precisely by distancing itself from the superficial, non-critical and politically opportunistic commemorations of the previous student protest which left its traces on the last decade of the twentieth century, the Student Protest of 2006 opened up a space for the development of an authentic student and youth movement that could initiate questions relevant to solving the acute social problems that burden the everyday existence of Serbian citizens. Although the protest activities at some universities between the end of 2006 and the beginning of 2007 were on a relatively modest level, it was already possible to notice signs of the strategic importance of the achievements of the protest. From a formal perspective, the greatest achievement of the protest was the joint proclamation of the *Naučno nastavnog veća* (Faculty Board) of the Faculty of Philosophy and the protesters, which as a platform for the entire Belgrade academic community was accepted at the meeting of the Senate of the University of Belgrade, held on 28 November 2006. This document demanded that all the relevant Ministries of the Serbian government engage in the creation of a long-term strategy for the development of higher education, including the formulation of a clear statement from the government towards the state universities and their financing, as well as aiming to reduce student fees for university students.[21] On the other hand, a long-term achievement of the Student Protest of 2006 was that of mobilising a large number of students to imitate on behalf of genuine social questions.

Observed from this perspective, the Student Protest of 2006 can be seen as a manifestation of the historical continuity of a socially engaged and politically progressive student movement in Serbia and Yugoslavia in the past two centuries. It was the *Velika škola*,[22] which preceded the University of Belgrade, where the organisation of the cultural activities of the first Serbian socialists started, who, led by Svetozar Marković, in a wretched, backward and semi-colonial Serbia, supported the concept of peoples' education and democratisation.[23] Students of the University of Belgrade were among the first to resist the dictatorship and they organised anti-fascist activities in Yugoslavia in the period between the two World Wars. In order to sanction these activities, the regime of the Kingdom of Yugoslavia, at the beginning of 1935, established a concentration camp for communist- oriented Belgrade students in Višegrad. Well-organised students participated in Belgrade's anti-fascist demonstrations in 1937, while, during the Spanish Civil War (1936–1939), a significant number of students from the University of Belgrade took part in a bid to defend democracy. In 1940, the university became a centre of conflict between progressive students and members of Ljotić's youth movement[24] and the following year, when Yugoslavia was occupied, a large number of students took an active part in organising the anti-fascist uprising.[25]

Finally, in the summer of 1968, when student protests were spreading across the world, the students of the University of Belgrade occupied the Faculty of Philosophy building, turning it into the epicentre of the critique of an increasingly class-divided Yugoslav society, which was the direct result of the economic reforms in 1965. This protest was based on open criticism of the bureaucratic usurpation of social power and the demands for authentic socialist solutions for the existing problems while at the same time it pointed to the limitations of access to higher education for young people from a working-class or peasant background as well as the ever-increasing privation of students and universities due to decreasing budget subsidies caused by the market driven – economical transformation of society.[26] Systematic comparative analysis of the characteristics of the student movement in its historical continuity could provide a framework for explaining the conditions in which the current protests took place and predicting possible directions of their further development.

For the time being, it is only possible to give a preliminary judgement on the achievements of the Student Protest of 2006. It is true that the demands of this movement had not been met by the end of 2006, while during 2007 some new problems occurred in relation to the possibility of sorting out longstanding problems within Serbian higher education. However, the organisation of a large number of students who had very clear aims spread an awareness of their justification and the possibility of their realisation more widely; concomitant with the wish to strengthen solidarity among students from different universities who were studying under different conditions but experiencing identical social problems already indicates the creation of a potentially respectable student movement.

From a wider perspective, the Student Protest of 2006 succeeded, at least in the area of higher education, in articulating the legitimate resistance of the majority of the population against the neo-liberal transformation of Serbian society. Students in the protest, identifying with the oppressed, highlighted the important aspect of social engagement that had been systematically neglected in the calculations of everyday party politics. In refusing to accept that politics should be reduced to a choice between the conservative, nationalistic, 'patriotic bloc' on the one hand, and a Westernised 'reformist bloc' on the other, within the Serbian political scene, but instead insisting without any ambiguity on solving the economic side of problems in society, this protest was demonstrating that the dominant political concept in Serbia since 1990 had gradually become outdated, while social forces which were going along with the world trends of democratic struggle against inequality and dominance are strengthening their positions.

Notes

Translated by Adem Repeša and Robert Hudson – Both members of the Identity, Conflict and Representation Research Centre at the University of Derby.

1. Francis Fukuyama, *The End of History and the Last Man* (New York: Avon, 1993): 46.
2. Ivana Milanović, 'Studenski protest: Spontanost, organizacija i pare' (Student protest: spontaneity, organisation and money), *Vreme*, 830 (30 November 2006): 32–33.
3. See: Ladislav Novak, *'Ključne zablude koje ometaju reformu visokog školstva u Srbiji'* (The basic mistakes which are hindering the university reform in Serbia) in Aljoša Mimica and Zoran Grac Grac(eds), *Visoko obrazovanje u Srbiji na putu ka Evropi četiri godine kasnije: Zbornik radova* (Higher education in Serbia on the road to Europe four years later: Collected works) (Belgrade: AAOM, 2005, pp. 298–299).
4. See: Srbijanka Turajlić, *'Visoko obrazovanje u Srbiji između tradicije i realnosti'* (Higher Education in Serbia between tradition and reality) (Belgrade: AAOM, 2005): 292. Along with these examples of abuse of the financial autonomy of faculties, one should also add the practice of some lecturers of purchasing their textbooks directly, without the opportunity of their being borrowed from the library, thus placing considerable conditions on the outcome of the exams.
5. For example, tuition fees for the Philosophy Faculty of the University of Belgrade amounted to 45,000 dinars in the academic year 2003/04; these increased to 51,000 dinars in 2004/05; 69,000 dinars in 2005/06; and 86,000 dinars in 2006/07. In the Architecture Faculty of the University of Belgrade, fees increased from 90,000 dinars in 2003/04 to 100,000 dinars in 2004/05; then from 160,000 dinars in 2005/06 to 240,000 dinars in 2006/07. By comparison in the whole period from academic year 2003/04 to 2006/07, tuition fees in the Mining and Geology Faculty in Belgrade did not change and were set at 30,000 dinars. Information supplied on enrolments and admissions was published in the *Prosvetni pregled*.
6. Reasons for the spread of the 2006 student protest, published on their official Internet website: http//protest.zbrka.net (accessed 22 December 2008).
7. *'Blokada fakulteta, jer znanje nije roba: Proglas studenskog zbora koji je odlučio da se blokira rad Filisofskog fakulteta'* (Blockade of the faculty, because knowledge is not a commercial product: Proclamation of the student assembly which decided to blockade work in the Philosophy Faculty on 22 November 2006), attainable from http:// protest.zbrka.net (accessed 22 December 2008).
8. Vincent Navarro, 'The Worldwide Class Struggle', *Monthly Review*, LVIII, 4 (September 2006): www.monthlyreview.org/0906navarro.htm (accessed 22 December 2008).
9. *'Blokada fakulteta, jer znanje nije roba: ...'* (Faculty blockade because knowledge is not a commercial product ...) www.monthlyreview.org/0906navarro.htm (accessed 22 December 2008).
10. *'Ni studenti nisu neka bili'* (Even students aren't what they used to be), *Glas javnosti*, 17 November 2006; also, Milanović, 'Studenski protest: Sponatanost, organizacija i pare', *Vreme*, 830, 30 November 2006: 33.
11. Milanović, ibid.
12. Todor Kuljić,, *Kulturna sećanja: teorijska objašnjenja upotrebne prošlosti* (Cultural memory: a theoretical explanation of the use of the past) (Belgrade: Čigoja štampana, 2000): 273–335.

13. See: *Sociologija*, Vol. XXXIX, No.1, January–March 1997 (Special number dedicated to civil and student protests in Serbia); Čedomir Čuprić (ed.), *Duh vedrine, Kultura protesta – proteste kultura: građanski i studentski protest 96–97* (A Clear Mind – Culture of protest – protest of culture: Civil and student protest 96–97) (Belgrade: Faculty of Political Science, 1998); Anđelka Milić and Ljiljana Čičkarić, *Generacija u protestu: Sociološki portret učenska studenskog protesta 96/97 na Beogradskom univerzitetu* (A Generation in Protest: A social portrait of the participants in the student protest of 96/97 at the University of Belgrade) (Belgrade: The Institute for Sociological Research (*Institut za sociološka instraživanja*), Faculty of Philosophy, 1998).

14. Marko Vidojković, *Kandže* (Claws), 5th edn (Belgrade: Samizdat B92, 2005): 29, 48.

15. See: Vladimir Rubić, '*Studenski protest 1996/97, između političke heterogenosti i strateškog konsenzusca*' (The student protest of 1996/97, between political heterogeneity and strategic consensus), in Gordana Gormović and Ildiko Erdei (eds), *O studentima I drugim demonima: etnografija studentskog protesta 1996/97* (On students and other demons: Ethnography of the Student Protest of 1996/97) (Belgrade: Filozofski fakultet, 1997, pp. 6–7). Also, note that in Serbian the expression 'God help us' is rendered as *Bože pomoze nas*, to which may be ascribed both religious and nationalist connotations, along with the Serbian three-fingered salute [RH].

16. James Robertson, *Discourses of Democracy and Exclusion in the Streets of Belgrade 1968–1997* (Sydney: University of Sydney Press, 2006): 76–77.

17. *Deklaracija OTPORA za budućnosti Srbij'* (The OTPOR declaration on the future of Serbia) (Belgrade: Srpski Otporaš (pamphlet), 1999).

18. Literally a 'leper colony', symbolically emphasising Serbia's political and social isolation [RH].

19. Memorandum, 'OTPOR!' www.otpor.com (accessed 25 July 2000).

20. An interesting account of this position can be found in Ljubiša Rajić, '*Ostrvo usred stvarnosti*' (Island in the middle of Reality), in Čedomir Antić (ed.), *Decenija: spomenica studenskog protest 1996–2006* (A decade: commemorative volume of the student protest 1996–2006) (Belgrade: Evoluta, 2006, p. 85).

21. '*Zajedničko saopštenje povodim materijalnog polažaja studenata*' (Joint Report regarding the material situation of students), 21 November 2006, Internet presentation of the Faculty of Philosophy, University of Belgrade, www.f.bg. ac.yu. (accessed 22 December 2008).

22. *Velika Škola* is an archaic term that literally means a 'high school'; this was the institution that preceded the University of Belgrade. There was a tradition of Serbian students going abroad to complete their higher education in European universities, particularly in France and Germany, at the end of the nineteenth century and before the First World War [RH].

23. Vaso Milinčević, '*Omladinska levica na Velikoj Školi (1863–1875)*' (Left-wing youth in the *Velika Škola* (1863–1875)), *Ideje i pokreti na Beogradskom univerzitetu od osnivanja do danas* (Ideas and movements in the University of Belgrade from its foundation to the present-day), Book 1 (Belgrade: Centar za Marksizam, University of Belgrade, Belgrade, 1989): 59–71.

24. This is a reference to Dimitrije Ljotić, 1891–1945, a right-wing Serbian politician who collaborated with the Germans in the Second World War. Having graduated from the Faculty of Law of the University of Belgrade, he served

in the Serbian Army in the Balkan Wars and the First World War, and later became a politician in the Serbian Radical Party. In 1935, he was elected president of the newly formed ZBOR party (*Jugoslovenski narodni pokret Zbor*, or Rally/Assembly), which militated against the communists and has been compared with other fascist movements prevalent in 1930s Europe. After the German Occupation of Yugoslavia, in 1941, Ljotić was seen as the ideological leader of the Serbian Volunteer Command (*Srpski dobrovoljački korpus*), made up of 3,600 men, which was the key fighting unit of Milan Nedić's military collaboration with the Germans in combating Tito's partisans [RH].

25. Đorđe Stanković, *'Revolucionarni studentski pokret i fašizam'* (Revolutionary students' movement and fascism), *Beogradski univerzitet u predratnom periodu, narodnooslobidilačkom ratu i revoluciji* (Belgrade University in the pre-war period and the peoples' war of liberation and revolution) (Belgrade: Centar za Marksizam, University of Belgrade, 1983): 73–83.

26. Mirko Arsić and Dragan Marković, *Šezdesetosma: studenski bunt i društvo* (68: Student rebellion and society), 3rd edn (Belgrade: Istraživačko – Izdavački Centar SSO Serbia (Research and Publications Centre of Serbia), 1988): 216–223.

7
Bosnia and Herzegovina: Citizenship versus Nationality

Neven Andjelić

In order to gain a better understanding of the nature of citizenship and identity in Bosnia and Herzegovina, it is necessary to understand how tightly interconnected the religious and ethnic identities of the ethnicities in Bosnia and Herzegovina are.[1] Ethnic identities in 'Bosnia and Herzegovina have been cast from a primarily religio-cultural mould', as has been discovered by Mitja Velikonja.[2] If one takes into account other possible influences in the development of national consciousness throughout Europe, one will find that they are all lacking in this particular country. The language factor, for example, which was actually decisive in the creation of nations and nation states throughout the greater part of Europe in the nineteenth and twentieth centuries, must be discarded in the case of Bosnia and Herzegovina because ethnic groups in this country speak very similar languages, if not indeed the same language, while naming the language after their own ethnic groups. Neither political unity nor territorial cohesion was ever a factor in nation-building and the formation of Bosnian and Herzegovinian national identity.

Many analysts, including Coady, found that the: 'Bosnian Muslims and Bosnian Serbs thought they shared the same history and culture until only very recently, but this is precisely what the zealots on both sides now deny'.[3] If that analysis had also included the Bosnian Croats, the result would have been just the same. Since differentiation could not be based on a territorial principle either, as can be seen in the example of the two parts contained in the very name of the state and the pre-war ethnic heterogeneity of the territory, the basis for collective identification in Bosnia and Herzegovina became based upon religion. It was on this foundation that the process of ethnic building was to be based.

All the nationalist movements in Bosnia and Herzegovina have been successful at politicising the above differences by way of precise ethnic arguments to which the population, undergoing economic deprivation, is particularly susceptible. In this sense, one can talk about the complete dominance of ethnic nationalism in the political space of Bosnia and Herzegovina, with only the barest traces of nationalism present.

If one were to compare the various ethno-nationalist movements, even within the same ethnicity, it would be impossible to find significant ideological differences. The arguments during their pre-electoral campaign, as well as their policies upon coming to power are virtually identical. In this context, a vote for the Alliance of Independent Social Democrats (SNSD)[4] or the Serbian Democratic Party (SDS)[5] is not as different as it may have been some ten years ago, because the former party has in the meantime significantly altered its attitude towards nationalism and from having once opposed the Serb nationalist movement it has now become a contestant in the scuffle for votes based on nationalism.

The political struggle between the two Croat Democratic Unions (HDZ and HDZ 1990)[6] is rooted in almost exclusively personal dislikes, as there are no ideological differences between these two parties. There is no difference in political aims or even in the ways of how to achieve them, as their policies are identical. The ideological differences between the two Bosniak parties may be similarly described. The original pseudo-multiethnic party for Bosnia and Herzegovina has always been a Bosniak party with very few non-Muslims among its top ranks that can be presented to the international community to give the impression that this is a non-nationalist, or even a non-ethnic party. Their policies, by contrast, are exclusively Bosniak-oriented and nationalistic; while their party membership is almost entirely made up of Bosniaks. These tactics have been followed by the Party for Democratic Action that also included some non-Muslims in its top ranks but hardly any within the lower party ranks.

In the case of each of the three ethnic groups in Bosnia and Herzegovina, there is no universal political mobilisation on the level of the entire state; instead mobilisation is carried out in opposition to the other two ethnic groups and, in the Bosniak case, in opposition to the neighbouring countries of Serbia and Croatia. Additionally, every national mobilisation in the region is, without fail, reflected in Bosnia and Herzegovina and results in mobilisations within ethnic groups and a further dismantling of society and the state.

The present situation in Bosnia and Herzegovina, whereby Serbs carefully guard their own entity, and Croats repeatedly demand the creation of their own, while Bosniaks actually request the recreation of a unified state where their ethnic group and ethnic policies will be dominant, is a result of these well-known and basic nationalist principles. The problem is that three different ethnic nationalisms co-exist on the same territory, they are all constitutionally non-minority groups and, regardless of numerical differences, equal to each other in terms of their rights.

It is common for minority groups to base their political demands on several arguments, and Bosnia and Herzegovina is no exception to this as these arguments can easily be applied to the country. Cultural specificity is the latest argument used in public debates, although historically there are no significant differences and cultural specificities within Bosnian and Herzegovinian society. They are only over the past two decades being developed as part of the ethno-nationalist projects.

The historical argument is very popular in nationalist rhetoric, but it lacks any territorial concentration in the past of a single ethnic group to strengthen these kinds of arguments for ethnic separation. The ethnic territorial distribution of the population arose as a consequence of the recent war, or more precisely the war crimes committed during the first half of the 1990s. Invoking the injustices of the past is a very effective argument because individuals are prone to finding justification for their own failures in claims that it is all a consequence of injustices wrought against the collective. Thus collective cohesion is gaining strength as nationalist policies become ever more attractive to larger masses of the population. It clearly worked and still works for the majority of South Slavs and it is arguably at its strongest in Bosnia and Herzegovina.

Another approach is more liberal in character and is reflected in the call for the universal equality of all groups in society. Nationalists are quick to accept this and then stretch its application to the point of being absurd. This argument is also a problematic for the general understanding of liberal democracy because if certain groups within society demand and achieve some special status and special rights, then the equality of individuals, as a supreme principle of liberal democracy, is not only endangered but abandoned or rather sacrificed for the purposes of ethnic peace.

Finally, the argument currently used to support all demands for the political autonomy of ethnic collectives is a purely nationalist one, because it holds that national groups, and in this case ethno-national groups, are so specific that they require a separate state or separate state-like administrative bodies to protect a 'distinct cultural and political life'.[7] This argument lies at the heart of all the policies of the nationalist leaders in Bosnia and Herzegovina. While Bosniak leaders do not argue for a set of separate institutions, their argument actually favours a unified state, the way they practise their policies in state institutions is hegemonic and the result might easily be the creation of the minorities out of the Serbs and Croats in Bosnia and Herzegovina.

An additional burden for the common state community is the identification of two of the three constituent ethnic groups, the Serbs and the Croats, with the country's neighbouring states. This inevitably leads to identification with the state on the part of the most numerous group without a nation state in the neighbourhood, namely, the Bosniaks. Paradoxically, this pronounced identification of Bosniaks with the state of Bosnia and Herzegovina repels the Serbs and Croats from the idea of a Bosnian and Herzegovinian state as their own and directs them even more towards the nation states of the Serbs and Croats, respectively. Neighbouring nation states thus become transmogrified into matrix states in the nationalist psyche.

The problem has been complicated further by the Bosniak identification with other Slavs of Islamic denomination in the wider region; although in reality they share very little in common. Yet this only serves as yet another testimony to the religious roots of ethnic identities in Bosnia and Herzegovina. Furthermore, it is very difficult to interpret in any other way the representation of Macedonian Muslims as Bosniaks in the Sarajevo media. Indeed, this pan-Bosniak perception of some neighbouring ethnic groups only serves to exacerbate existing problematic relations within the region.

In that sense, as absurd as it may seem, it might be necessary to weaken this sort of identification of Bosniaks with the state of Bosnia and Herzegovina, because this would be the only way for the same state to seem to be potentially attractive to Serbs and Croats so as to inspire their more intense identification with it as their homeland without the now already established fears of majority rule and Bosniak hegemony. In relation to the outside world, these two ethnic groups must also find a modus vivendi for their identification with Serbs and Croats in their nation states without jeopardising the statehood of Bosnia and Herzegovina. However, a simple solution is not so readily applicable in a state that is claimed by three ethnic groups.

There is a clear problem when it comes to the citizenship of Bosnia and Herzegovina. Michael Kenny in his theoretical consideration of the problem of citizenship realised that: 'the commonality and unity of purpose that citizenship requires may be imperilled if citizens are overly aware of group differences'.[8] The problem in Bosnia and Herzegovina seems to be the existence of the ethnicities of three nations or ethno-nations, within only one state. That is why ethno-nationalist movements never fail to attack the legitimacy of the state order as part of their political strategies. The nationalists insist that, by definition, the only legitimate form of state government is national, which in their terminology actually means ethno-national.[9]

Consequently, if one were to attempt to get to the core of the majority of political conflicts in post-war Bosnia and Herzegovina, the most crucial problems would be those of determination; in other words, the level and scope of the autonomy of territories, where certain ethnic elites have come to power. The recognition of this situation, however, only serves to indicate the continuation of policies from the time of the Dayton Peace Agreement of 1995. The differences in the articulation of demands stem from a number of reasons, some of which can be explained by the existence of certain differences between the nationalist parties, as well as the varying degrees of policies of tolerance towards others, but the general characteristics are common to all ethnically based political parties in Bosnia and Herzegovina.

The ultimate consequence of these demands by nationalist parties could be the territorial division of the country, be this official or just in practice. The first step is the division of government; it boils down to a mutual agreement over which nationalist party would take control over which ministry. This part is usually the easiest; because it comes down to appointing the state's civil servants who then go on to undermine that very state because they act exclusively in the interests of their own nationalist elites. When such policies become absolutely unacceptable to partner nationalists, they then move on to dividing the territory into areas that can be governed completely by single nationalist groups.

However, since the same parts of the territory are often claimed by more than one group, political conflicts have arisen in the aftermath of lethal armed conflict and are overcome by the suspension of legitimate government, so that the state is effectively governed by externally imposed institutions under the common umbrella of the Office of the High Representative. External supervision was necessary throughout the post-conflict period, as has been readily demonstrated by the numerous examples of all decisions pertaining to the construction of politico-national identification and the creation of national symbols. They were all devised by a foreign governor (the Office of the High Representative) because the local political leaders could not find a common denominator for Bosnia and Herzegovina that would satisfy the requirements of ethnic identification, as had been witnessed in the cases of: the currency; the flag; the coat of arms; the national anthem; and car registration plates.[10]

All other national symbols still in use in Bosnia and Herzegovina stem from the former para-state formations of the ethnically organised entities. The popular acceptance and identification of citizens with these former para-national symbols is actually a reflection of the general state of society in Bosnia and Herzegovina and the paradigm of its division. Citizenship and nationality are two separate and often confrontational issues in present-day Bosnia and Herzegovina. One should bear in mind, however, that it was not uncommon for many other European states to be faced with similar problems in the past.

Guy Hermet refers to the French example of striking the right relationship between citizenship and nationality as a form of 'secular republicanism', while the German case was different and based on 'constitutional patriotism'.[11] Jacob Levy noted that: 'given the prevalence in the world of the nationalist idea and of national minorities to seek their own states, states have a strong reason to nationalize their populations'.[12] This is exactly the process that has proven impossible to achieve so far in Bosnia and Herzegovina or, at least, governing structures were not competent enough to initiate it.

The two examples that have often been referred to by both Bosnian politicians and foreign mediators are Switzerland and Belgium, as it is in Switzerland that the relationship between nationality and citizenship 'was reconciled, not without difficulty, with people's cantonal and federal identities', while in Belgium, although specific linguistic, ideological, and religious identities were never really reconciled to the concept of Belgian-ness, a raft of competing political and economic actors centred on regional institutions has nevertheless created a model that can work.[13] Normally, however, provincial institutions in Bosnia and Herzegovina resist the nationalising of the policies of the state, as was the case of both Serbian entity and that of the Croat-dominated cantonal institutions in the Bosniak–Croat federation. It is often the case that a state-level institution would actually defend the particularities of the provincial entity, that is, an ethnically based institution, as the state-level portfolios were divided up between the three sets of nationalists while state officials continued to promote the policies of their ethnic groups and not those of some imaginary state ideology.

The problem with the Bosnian case was that nationalist elites kept proving in the past that they were not really interested or were not capable of creating a workable solution. The only new political players that have managed to impose themselves onto the political scene have to come through the nationalist structures because otherwise they lack credibility and legitimacy. It seems that collective identification has passed the point of no return when it comes to the introduction of the possibility of redirecting historical processes towards the strengthening of a political and national Bosnian and Herzegovinian identity. In the absence of any revolutionary change of this carved-out historical course, one may expect the complete disintegration of society. This is not an unknown feature, as secessionism is a rather common political idea that creates a fear that: 'groups which develop too much of an independent identity and set of allegiances might withdraw their support from a state's central institutions', as Daniel Weinstock has already demonstrated.[14]

Therefore society in Bosnia and Herzegovina could be developed in one of two directions. The first, and currently more apparent, option is the continuation of the empowerment of ethnic identities and an insistence on their dominance. The final consequence of this development is the complete disintegration of society and probably that of the state itself. The artificiality of the political entities only serves to empower the role of ethnicity. Not a single cantonal identity has been developed since their creation that could rival any sense of ethnic belonging. Moreover, some cantonal governments were paralysed in their work because of ethnic rivalries. *Republika Srpska*, in this sense, reminds one of the creation of Padania in northern Italy, as both have been created artificially and neither *Republika Srpska* nor Padania have been based upon any historical grounds, unlike Catalonia, Scotland or Wales, which had all been independent at one time or another. While Padanian identity remains largely underdeveloped, the *Republika Srpska* has grown into a sacred polity for the Bosnian Serbs with which the majority have identified. Ethnic identification, in this case, coincides with territorial identity and it works well for the politics of political identity. The moral basis of this type of identity (ethnic cleansing) is entirely lacking but this did not prevent any sustained growth in the sense of belonging among Bosnian Serbs.

National civicism in Bosnia and Herzegovina was attempted during the period of communist rule in this country but the events of the 1990s proved that it has not been successfully rooted. Educational tools were used for this purpose over several generations but it seems that family ties and ethnic traditions, largely based on religious customs, were of greater importance for the citizens. Another tool in the development of national civicism, as Hermet describes it, has been the military.[15] It was through conflict that nations were developed or strengthened in the past. In Bosnia and Herzegovina, unfortunately for the process of building national identity, conflicts were experienced that were to a large extent based upon ethnicity. Thus the armies were mainly, though not exclusively, ethnically organised and the camaraderie among the conscripted young men brought about a stronger sense of belonging to the ethnic group and a common religion than anything else, ever before in their lives, including the failed educational projects for building up the national civicism of the communist state.

National culture in the Bosnian case is ethnic, and should be measured, as Debeljak suggests: 'according to the handshake of collective solidarity which draws its sustenance from the communal ligatures'.[16] It was during the war that the ethnic dominance of developing group cultures and communal solidarities took over society in Bosnia and Herzegovina, creating the conditions of three distinctive ethno-cultural and politico-territorial spaces. The last fragment, namely that of territory, has not as yet been created for separate identities but everything else seems to be coming into place.

There is little doubt that it was violence during the military struggle that developed *Republika Srpska* as an ethno-territorial identity. Hermet, while concentrating on a different period and region, actually laid the ground for understanding this case. It was 'conscription and the growth of chauvinistic nationalism' in the context of the wars in former Yugoslavia that was the determinant factor 'in the decisive allegiance that citizens swore to this polity'.[17]

The very same factor played an important role in strengthening Croatian ethnic identity but since the Croats had failed to achieve any territorial recognition, it remained largely personally based. However, political efforts to achieve the territorial determination of Croat identity in Bosnia and Herzegovina keep coming back onto the public and political agenda. One could argue that Serbs and Croats in Bosnia and Herzegovina are actually ideal examples of how differently autonomy could be organised for the ethnic groups with supposedly equal rights. The Serbs' autonomy is territorially based and recognised by the Dayton Peace Accord, while the Croats' autonomy is personally based as a consequence of the Washington Agreement. Any analysis of contemporary society in this state clearly recognises greater satisfaction with the state order (as the economy has been ignored for the purposes of this study) among the Serbs than the Croats, which provides further proof of the dominance of the territorial principle for the development of autonomy and identity.

This is an irony as the Washington Agreement has created a federation of Croats and Bosniaks, but the entities of this federation are not officially organised on ethnic lines and, as a consequence, autonomy has been personalised, therefore it is cultural rather than territorial. Political practice based on the actual numerical dominance of either the Croats or Bosniaks in several cantons created a practical territorial autonomy but this situation only causes further inter-ethnic grievances as the newly created minorities call upon the Constitution in order to protect their own rights. Thus a further power-vacuum appears even at some local levels and it only serves to make the whole system even more unworkable.

The Bosniaks swore their allegiance to the state during the war and this fact, alongside the struggle they went through, made this connection significantly stronger than before the violence started. Those who had a stronger sense of national belonging to the state than to their ethnic group usually sided with Bosniaks because of this kind of allegiance. Some of them even ended up in Bosniak nationalist political parties.

Although members of all three ethnic groups in Bosnia and Herzegovina suffered from horrible war-crimes committed by the 'others', there is little doubt that the crime of genocide against the Bosniaks was the most heinous of all. Schopflin found that: 'groups subjected to ethnic cleansing or genocide do not forget such a traumatic experience...which becomes a constitutive part of their identities, thereby encoding antagonism and enmity against ethnic cleansers for generations'.[18] Therefore, it would be very optimistic to expect the creation, or rather re-creation, of a unified identity in Bosnia and Herzegovina because neither of the two groups wants it, and the third, while claiming commitment to it, is actually working against it.

The other possibility, less likely as it seems, is the partial repression of the ethnic identification of each group, a more cautious attitude towards the past because what is a celebration for one group is a memorialisation for the other. The consequence of such events is that particularism is strengthened on both sides and social mobilisation remains ethnic. The development of the mutual understanding of certain differences present among others, without insisting on concurrent reciprocity as a necessity at this stage of social development. In the long term and under such circumstances it should be possible to construct a more powerful national identity for Bosnia and Herzegovina where citizenship would mean more than the mere need for a passport.

The problem is that: 'nation-building, the deliberate creation and imposition of a central national identity, naturally invites a backlash',[19] which might be overcome with mutual trust between the ethnic groups. Such trust is non-existent because society in Bosnia and Herzegovina has one permanent feature in that, ever since the creation of nation-alist movements, this has resulted in conflict, whether by violent or by peaceful means. The state of conflict prevents any development, no matter how slow, of mutual trust, and this could result in a failure in the nation-building process. This correlation has been missed so far by local political leaders and by the imposed foreign representatives whose supposed role has been to assist the process of nation-building.

Whichever way the nationalist leaders decide to lead their followers, which is an overwhelming majority of the citizens of this state, the whole of Bosnian and Herzegovinian society, or the three separate societies, would probably see greater economic and social development, because even the formation of national territories with which the groups could easily identify would facilitate the strengthening of the institutions of the system and the structuring of societies as economically rational and sustainable units. The reason is that for now at least two groups, namely the Serbs and Croats, find themselves situated involuntarily in the state of Bosnia and Herzegovina, while the third, the Bosniaks, could hardly be described as being happy with the present constitutional order and intra-state relations between the ethnic groups.

It is only if the status quo in Bosnia and Herzegovina is maintained that all three societies within the state and the state itself would con-tinue along a path of development that would run counter to all mod-ern European trends based on social prosperity. Nationalism is not unknown to European societies and it is even possible to talk of its ren-aissance, but identification with the ethnic group sometimes yields to other processes for the purpose of progress and general prosperity. This is not the case in Bosnia and Herzegovina, and ethnic identification, along with politicised ethno-nationalism, are primary forms of express-ing belonging in almost all spheres of life.

Whether Bosnia and Herzegovina is possible without a Bosnian and Herzegovinian identity is a question that will not remain unanswered for long in historical terms. The present prospects are bleak, to say the least, because the citizens of this state, when they depend on their state to provide security and civility for them, often find it absent and a fur-ther disappointment in the state develops without realising that it was actually the very same citizens' insistence on ethnic identity, which they imagine as national identity, that prevented the state acting in a protective way unlike the role played by nearly every other European state.

The ethnic groups in Bosnia and Herzegovina in their own search for such a neutral space have created exclusively ethnic spaces that possess some legitimacy, albeit within only one ethnic group. Thus ethnic elites are further undermining the common state in the interest of their respective ethnic followers and with the full support of those followers.

One could argue that it was violence that put nationalist elites in the position to act in this way in the first place. On the positive side of the argument is a fact, noticed by Gagnon when analysing one particular area of conflict that: 'violence was not coming from below, but rather was being imposed on these communities from above'.[20] This was certainly the case throughout the violent years in Bosnia and Herzegovina. Whatever is chosen in the future, it certainly cannot be worse than the present situation. If the external supervisory powers wait much longer, the local nationalist elites might be prepared yet again for a violent solution. In order to prevent this, it might be advisable: 'to force responsibility onto local elites', as Ignatieff advised in his argument on nation-building.[21] It is possible that either a real new nation of Bosnia and Herzegovina will be born out of this process or that three practically new national para-states will be created in the Balkans.

Notes

1. M. Velikonja, *Religious Separation and Political Intolerance in Bosnia-Herzegovina*, (College Station: Texas A&M University Press, 2003): 91.
2. Ibid.: 288.
3. C. A. J Coady, 'Nationalism and Identity', in I. Primoratz and A. Pavković (eds), *Identity, Self-Determination and Secession* (Burlington: Ashgate, 2006, p. 62).
4. SNSD Alliance of Independent Social Democrats (*Savez Nezavisnih Socijaldemokrata*), the Serbian party in Republika Srpska, led by Milorad Dodik.
5. SDS Serbian Democratic Party (*Srpska Demokratska Stranka*), originally led by Radovan Karadžić and now by Mladen Bosić.
6. HDZ (*Hrvatska Demokratska Zajednica*) originally led by Franjo Tuđman and now led by Jadranka Kosor, while the HDZ 1990 was a breakaway Bosnian Croat party, founded in 2006 and led by Boz Ljubić.
7. A. Pavković, 'Self-Determination, National Minorities and the Liberal Principle of Equality', in I. Primoratz and A. Pavković (eds), *Identity, Self-Determination and Secession* (Burlington: Ashgate, 2006, p. 124).
8. M. Kenny, *The Politics of Identity* (Cambridge: Polity Press, 2004): 43.
9. M. Suzman, *Ethnic Nationalism and State Power* (London: MacMillan Press, 1999): 13.
10. This process had not eluded Bosnian intellectuals. In seeking an alternative to what he described as an impasse in his article published in *Forum Bosnae*, on the civic elements of compromise in the crippling implementation of the Dayton Agreement, Dražen Pehar acknowledged that one option might

be to transform Bosnia into a protectorate in which the OHR (Office of the High Representative) would probably be the one to take the role of a 'BiH emperor' who would 'rule over Bosnia in a fashion not unlike that of the period of Austro-Hungarian rule in the late nineteenth and early twentieth centuries (D. Pehar, 'Civic Elements of Compromise and the Crippling of Dayton', *Forum Bosnae* 'Reconstruction and Deconstruction', 15/02, 2002). See also R. Hudson, 'The Return of the Colonial Protectorate: Colonisation with Good Intent in the Western Balkans', in M. Aguirre, F. Ferrándiz. and J.-M. Pureza (eds), *Before Emergency: Conflict Prevention and the Media* (Bilbao: University of Deusto Press, 2003, pp. 103–124).

11. G. Hermet, 'States and National Cultures', in A. Dieckhoff (ed.), *The Politics of Belonging: Nationalism, Liberalism, and Pluralism* (Maryland: Lexington Books, 2004, p. 74). See also M. Rady, 'Minorities and Minority Protection in Eastern Europe', in R. Hudson and F. Réno (eds), *Politics of Identity: Migrants and Minorities in Multicultural States* (Basingstoke: Palgrave Macmillan, 2000).

12. J. T. Levy, 'Constitutionalism and Nationalizing States', in A. Dieckhoff (ed.), *The Politics of Belonging: Nationalism, Liberalism, and Pluralism* (Maryland: Lexington Books, 2004, pp. 162–163).

13. G. Hermet, 'States and National Cultures', in A. Dieckhoff (ed.), *The Politics of Belonging: Nationalism, Liberalism, and Pluralism* (Maryland: Lexington Books, 2004, pp. 74–75).

14. D. Weinstock, 'The Problem of Civic Education in Multicultural Societies', in A. Dieckhoff (ed.), *The Politics of Belonging: Nationalism, Liberalism, and Pluralism* (Maryland: Lexington Books, 2004, p. 107).

15. G. Hermet, 'States and National Cultures', in A. Dieckhoff (ed.), *The Politics of Belonging: Nationalism, Liberalism, and Pluralism* (Maryland: Lexington Books, 2004, p. 75).

16. A. Debeljak, *The Hidden Handshake: National Identity and Europe in the Post-Communist World* (Oxford: Rowman and Littlefield Publishers, Inc., 2004): 23.

17. G. Hermet, 'States and National Cultures', in A. Dieckhoff (ed.), *The Politics of Belonging: Nationalism, Liberalism, and Pluralism* (Maryland: Lexington Books, 2004, p. 76).

18. G. Schopflin, *Nations, Identity, Power: The New Politics of Europe* (London: Hurst & Co Ltd, 2000): 62.

19. D. Weinstock, 'The Problem of Civic Education in Multicultural Societies', in A. Dieckhoff (ed.), *The Politics of Belonging: Nationalism, Liberalism, and Pluralism* (Maryland: Lexington Books, 2004, p. 112).

20. V. P. Jr Gagnon, *The Myth of Ethnic War: Serbia and Croatia in the 1990s* (Ithaca, NY and London: Cornell University Press, 2004): p. 163.

21. M. Ignatieff, *Empire Lite: Nation-Building in Bosnia, Kosovo and Afghanistan* (London: Vintage, 2003): 126.

8
Singing the Politics of the Croatian Transition

Ines Prica

In their frozen and perplexed shape, many of the items that had been 'formerly understood' as being crucial to national-oriented politics in Croatia, are now casually left to the field of pop-cultural representation. This means that in practice, the trivialisation of political discourse makes contemporary Croatia an awkward example for revisiting *the state of nationalism and antagonism* as a symptom of its post-Yugoslav condition. This chapter will refer to two intriguing examples of Croatian pop-ideology by which we will demonstrate the paradoxes of the cultural critique in coping with the *mimicrycal* nature of its traditional object.

The lighter contemporary Croatian identity becomes, with the gradual loosening of its historically rooted affiliations, the harder it is to conduct an investigation of the 'former' Yugoslavia through the concept of nationalism(s). The fading of national-centred discourses from the Croatian public scene partly indicates that such discourses are no longer required. The main goal of independence has been achieved, and the international processes of post-conflict political normalisation have been initiated and developed, despite all the controversies over events that took place during the Homeland War, along with the perceived 'anachronous' claim of the national state. Now we are, gladly or reluctantly, turning to the implementation of democratic procedures and minority-talks, along the 'one-and-only path towards Euro-Atlantic integration' (as the phrase goes).

As a result of all the regulatory programmes introduced by international politics, the valid conclusion, for the majority of the population, is that independence has been 'earned' exactly on the basis of *the historical continuity of Croatian national identity*, with all the pronounced 'irrational' support of the notion.[1] Possibly, such a consensus of the internal and external participants, allowed a different understanding of the meanings of the current process of political justification, is the crucial point of further debate on the confined *status of nationalism and antagonism*. Mutual agreement on the basically procedural nature of *the execution of democracy* opened an arbitrary space between pragmatic deeds and *ideological minds*. Metaphorically, what was once considered to be a national-oriented politics, 'with a democracy in one's heart', has now become democracy-oriented politics, 'with the nation in one's heart'. Thus, a possibly superficial move towards *the tolerance of politics* functioned as a sufficient move towards *the politics of tolerance*.

The aim here is to disclose the ambiguous object of the conversion of *national into transitional narration*, the process which lay at the core of identity politics in 1990s Croatia. It was pushed by the ambition to spectacularly envision the new, capitalist and democratic nature of state politics, but also to diminish the opaque routes of capital that marked the period of the 'first Croatian transition'.[2]

For that purpose, the elastic, radiating and frivolous scene of pop-cultural values and representations has functioned as the most appropriate ground, at least the one for the latest discovery of its interest in courting with the scratchy items of national politics. While, from the beginning of the 1990s, the mass media arbitration of the Croatian state-building discourse switched popular culture to an acute political instrumentalisation such as that of *singing patriotism*,[3] the victory of oppositional coalition parties in 2000, and, above all, the public withdrawal from the nationalist discourse after the 2003 elections, and the comeback of a thoroughly reformed HDZ,[4] triggered the cocooning of the suppressed political content in this domain. It composed a quasi-political climate where one could more credibly 'vote' for 'politically conscious' entertainers than for a recognisable party programme. But it also revealed an acute rupture in the legitimate matrix of political diversification. The blurring of the principles 'formerly known' as being representative of the left and right political option, including those related to the issue of national-identity politics, has opened up a stretched space of the hypothetical 'liberal esteems' – a flamboyant platform able to provide all the persuasive rationalisations or 'whatevers' of the Croatian transition, while dismissing the findings of common reasoning and the 'old-fashioned' social critique.[5]

Beyond the critical pertinence of numerous insights into the mentality of the South-East European transition, led by the anticipation of social 'normality' to which they need to be striving, the aim here is to show something of the opposite routine. How the anomalous facets of global, neo-liberal capitalism find their ways to settle down in the 'laissez-faire' transitional environments, disclosing the upsetting flow of common analytical tools and critical practices.

A pair of Croatian 'pop-political personalities', known worldwide for their exhibitions on the Internet,[6] has caused a lot of serious trouble for their critics, both figures are ephemeral in their creative sphere, yet remain the absolute for their faithful consumers and supporters.

'I just sing'

> Thin red line? No! Long red carpet
>
> Cvijetić 2000[7]

The transformation of Severina Vučković from an 'innocent' and approachable *village girl* (as the title of her popular song suggests) at the end of the 1980s, to today's untouchable icon of Croatian glamour-culture, represents one of the most highly extolled, but also most strongly disputed examples of a non-criminal success story of the Croatian transition.

Through the scenario of her own biography, encapsulated within the words of her famous song 'I just sing, and have no reason to get upset', she has achieved the prototypical *transitional dream*. The winning-path has led her from professional incompetence (amateurism) and the working-class milieu, with the aid of a strong desire for change and the abandoning of old communal values, to her becoming a figure of huge public influence and private possessions. However, while the process of the legalisation of the 'original sins' of Croatian *tycoons* has worked out fine, with any objections too wretched to 'get them upset', Severina, as a metaphoric personality of an inappropriate *female transition*, seems to be constantly obliged to explain her 'primary accumulation of capital'.

Nevertheless, despite the brief setback caused by the recent sexual scandal that arose from the Internet broadcasting of her stolen home video, she was soon back again, with a changed image referring to the 'new person' she can always be, in the wholeness of her arbitrary pop-culture personality. The porno-scandal (with the involvement of an identifiable married man) exposed the pop star to both mockery, due to conservative values that she otherwise promotes (holy marriage, Holy Mother and the football team Hajduk from her hometown Split) and pity for her as a victim of the abuse of privacy, here included the Croatian Helsinki Watch Committee rejoinder. But this was only an unplanned reference to another controversial representation by Severina.

Her wholehearted commitment to the political iconography and participation in the political campaigns of the HDZ (with Franjo Tuđman's name proudly displayed on the protruding parts of her T-shirts), proved her total political indifference to her sudden and scandalous 'crossing-over to the Left'. The 'nationally aware' pop figure, to the astonishment of the narrow circle of intellectuals with their worn-out feeling towards political engagement, appeared at the dawn of the 2003 election campaign as the trump card of the HDZ's harsh opponent, the Social Democratic Party (led by the recently deceased Ivica Račan).[8] The pop heroine, until then naively linked to the politics of her former employers, was now raising the rating of the new ones, performing a concert in Zagreb's central square (newspaper gossip that was never refuted buzzed about a fee of some €200,000). As is known, the SDP, together with the coalition, lost the 2003 elections. Obviously, Severina was 'just singing', and the potential voters knew it very well. So, how come the intellectual critics, cultural analysts and writers of enlightened newspaper columns found 'reasons to get upset', trying to decipher whether Račan had finally announced his pragmatic pandering to the Right, or his incurable inclination for 'communist-luxury', or was he simply the victim of a 'just-singing' American marketing?

The head of the SDP announced such a possibility long before the campaign began: he explained in an interview that it would be quite convenient if he lost the election. He would rest, catch up on his sleep, and live the comfortable life he had been used to. For some time now, he has been behaving in public like a loser, going around with a sullen look, without a smile, as though he wanted to intimidate and drive away potential supporters. Someone has already observed that his main electoral acquisitions – 'Cro Cop' [Mirko Filipović, a popular figure in the Ultimate Fight sports, and a member of parliament during the coalition government] and Severina – are an expression of his subconscious desire to lose the elections. This selection is fully in the spirit of his recent behaviour. He had been kowtowing to the Right throughout his mandate, even though this had never produced any benefits, nor had it attracted anyone from that side – while it had repelled his own people. That's the way it will be this time, too. The American advisers who had proposed such a road-show treatment of the election campaign had made a bad mistake. In that respect, 'Croatia is not yet America, thank God, nor is Račan a Schwarzenegger' (Lovrić 2003: n. p.). Or is it so that, by announcing that he could bring to his political court *the most beautiful belly-dancer*, he only confirmed the social insensitivity of Croatian Social Democracy (!), that draws its historical link from 'communist

Tsarism', as is suggested by a dramatically intoned social variant of the commentary on the event.

   Are the parties facing up to Croatian reality, given that living conditions for the elite are so very different from those of the majority of the population. How much do they know about the deprived, the invalids, those who are trying to find their dead ones, and how much do they respect the fresh graves upon which some of them have built up wealthy empires? For the unfortunate fate of this country must never again be repeated. As in wartime, Croatia needs strong people and strong programmes, lots of work and the return of hope, of which Pope John Paul II had spoken so eloquently during his visits, and as Cardinal Bozanić has repeatedly pointed out. Can hope include a pre-election entertainment event, which, if the newspapers are to be believed, will cost the SDP €200,000 (from our budget) for Severina Vučković's pre-election concert? With her status as a freelance artist, thanks to the Ministry of Culture, she could, 'generous' as she is, share the money with all the other freelance artists, from writers to musicians, who often go hungry. Is Croatia transforming into the worst possible *Cabaret* or into some kind of Ancient Rome that falls under the burden of its own humiliation? Severina is the last to blame for that. Why shouldn't she take what is so generously given to her? It is money snatched from those without homes, from workers who do not receive their wages, and from those missing arms and legs – so that the circus can continue, so that the party can last, even though the lights have been dimmed. Where on earth are the intellectuals, unless impoverishment has made them humble slaves at some of the ministries? It is as though the intellectuals have ceased to exist. The communist mentality is entrenched at the universities and in the schools (apart from some honourable exceptions) and the tentacles of this mentality also encompass the thirst for Severina and Brioni [Tito's Island]. The Dictator loved them and why shouldn't the little dictators enjoy them as much as he did. Their intellectual work includes running the relay races [for Tito's birthdays, celebrated on Youth Day] and attending the Kumrovec School [the Party's ideological school], 'with the psychological component of brain-formation, with its ideology creating slavish souls' (Ivanišević 2003: n. p.).

   Anyhow, the most stinging slap in the face to a serious 'over-analysis' of that quasi-political event can be found in the interpretation of Severina in the role of 'Cosmo Girl intervention', an appearance still insufficiently understandable within the unadventurous Croatian social scene. From that indifferent and light-hearted premise, we are invited to penetrate into 'the deeper' layers of the affair, and that would be the way she was dressed, her sex appeal, and the eternal envy which is spun around this successful 'manager of her own body', in the atrophied environment of the average Croatian voter – the cursed 'who will never have a chance to meet Severina'.

There have always been controversies about her songs, and particularly about her star status. So far, Severina is still on the credit side. A considerable majority continues to have a positive opinion about her, or at least only adds that mythic 'but', which maintains her position at the top of today's show business. Anyone *who has had an opportunity to meet Severina* will agree with Miljenko Jergović's conclusion that she is much cleverer than the songs she sings, while she herself is not inclined to an excessive mystification of her own job. Because of all this, it would be interesting to see the consequences of Severina's political adventure in which she has placed her star status, her charisma, and – let's be frank – her sex appeal at the service of the SDP's election campaign. It would have been most interesting to compare the reactions if Severina had agreed to perform for some ultra-Right option, and for a symbolic fee. In that case, 'the female Thompson' would not appear to be acting so strangely. Severina herself claims that she only agreed to sing for those who offered the best conditions. And while the public is shocked at her hefty fee under the circumstances, politicians too, even those from the party for which she is 'doing battle', are objecting, along with the rockers who carried the entertainment load on their backs in the last SDP election campaign, and for much less money. The cynics could comment that Račan once appeared at the rock stage arm-in-arm with Budiša,[9] but that this time he has chosen a well-thought-out media option for himself and the party that he leads. And if elections were to be won on the basis of such criteria, there is not a man who would not vote for a comrade who replaced Budiša with Severina. However, *a return to the more serious part of this story* brings us back to Severina who is, once again, doing her job in a professional manner. She doesn't talk about politics, but obviously knows her way around politics. Anyone who doubts this should take a look at the clothes she wears at her pre-election concerts. None of the tight bodices and hotpants of the type she usually wore at her concerts, but instead there was a more restrained choice of a woman who knows that any contribution on her part to a possible SDP victory would never be acknowledged, but that she could easily be singled out and blamed for any 'crushing defeat' (Radović 2003: n. p.).

So it seems that only intellectually and politically 'uptight' commentators are in need of mistakenly focusing on 'the Singer and the

Politician' as symbolically crucial figures of the political status of culture, rather than misrepresented actors in a flow of transient transitional incidents. People listened to the free concert by the well-loved singer under the 'social democratic organisation' and then went off tranquilly to vote for the opponents. There is nothing scandalous in that. Quite the contrary, what could better represent the average voter's reasoning than the absurdity of this political event, 'irrationality' of which does not lie within the sharp differentiation of trivial and purely political values, but in what that imbroglio has been condensed to: the accumulated experience of political concessions which turns the democratic elections into a farce of *just voting*.

Over-analyse this!

> They proclaim patriotism to be fascism, that's how they shield
> their communism.
>
> Thompson, *Once upon a time in Croatia*

By contrast, does Marko Perković Thompson 'just sing'? The contentious entertainer claims that he clearly does not, when it goes for the clean patriotic and Christian values he promotes in his lyrics. But he obdurately refuses to stay behind the obnoxious connotations he evokes in his concerts and otherwise.

The village boy who has never abandoned his devotion towards the 'stone genes' that have made him as proud and tough as he is, stepped clumsily into the popular culture of the war, with a rural voice hoarsely running from a toothless mouth. Nowadays he is an internationally renowned, although controversial character,[10] but also a heavily refashioned musician, with a huge stage support behind him. He owes his publicity, contrary to Severina, to a deadly serious, though charismatic performance, designed around outlandish 'gothic emblems', with a sword as a central character of his 'medieval' narration about the lost roots and other dissoluteness of modern civilisation. The captivating lyrics of the Croatian shepherd-rocker have been mostly devoted to a historical lament over the Croatian people and national heroes, who had been the victims of the previous, and apparently ever-present 'communist' regimes. The Croatian war for independence has been criminalised, and its heroes are squatting in The Hague while the fruits are enjoyed by hypocritical politicians ingratiating themselves with the new world masters – this is, in short, *the manifesto* of Marko Perković, called Thompson in favour of his beloved gun from the good old days of national defence. Some features of the manifesto are not very far removed from the suppressed Euro-sceptical and legitimate anti-globalist claim, but they are far too close to the murky legacy of the Croatian historical stigma. The problems for him, but simultaneously also for the incredible publicity, both at home and in the Croatian diaspora, which resulted in thousands of visits to both his concerts and websites, started at the moment when public attention began to turn more to the 'ephemeral', contextual signs of his performances.

The place where the phenomenon of Thompson, by now a shabby stumbling block of various *pro et contra* arguments, almost hit its 'limits of interpretations', was quite indicative. The obscure performance of criminalised songs extolling the concentration camps of the fascist NDH,[11] has in the end emerged on exactly the same independent site where Severina's joyful video was revealed to public eyes. Indicative for the *gender essence* that the two most politicised pop scandals of the Croatian transition have been abridged to, it was also a moment for Thompson to face a painful question addressed to his heroic maleness.

When her porno was released on the Internet, she owned up to it, admitting that it was indeed her, and asking them to give her back her tape. 'When the scandal concerning your performing of "Jasenovac i Gradiška Stara" had burst, why didn't you show up publicly to say what you had to say?' (Vodopivec 2004: n. p.).

As Thompson kept defending himself in a *just-singing* manner,[12] the scandal was pushed to the cul-de-sac of its procedural arbitration. In a desperate search for the grain of political credence within the miraculous travesties of Croatian pop-ideology,[13] it turned to a general question of who, at what point, and with which outcomes, stays for the haphazard consequences of such an 'elaboration' of its most painful items.

The singer made it obvious that it was not him, but the officials not being able, or willing, to react properly. Not only that some of them enjoy Thompson's music, so they are *just listening and having no reason to get upset* with its wasted connotations. It is neither just a matter of the blurred constitutional law on national-racial hate speech, formulated primarily in a way to avoid any resemblance with the notorious, over-policed and totalitarian one of the previous regime. It is also because Thompson's music, by means of its harshly achieved un-ideological criteria, ought to be recognised separately, from its evident content and not for its hidden intention. As we have seen in the previous case, everybody can choose from the random marginalia of the context, mixing up fallacy with the substance or vice versa. Aren't many of Thompson's messages only a matter of the carnivalesque epic genre, like the maxim 'Lady Mary, could you maybe do that, take Stipe and get Franjo back'?[14] So, up to what point are we going to go, exaggeratedly and dimly, in the end, with our literal interpretations of the pseudo-historical signs and plots which are actually symptoms of 'something else'?

Thanks to such a 'hermeneutic' hesitation, Thompson's case is turned into the hard-boiled dispute on national identity with uncertain rationales.

> He has been turned into a kind of Croatian God Janus? For his admirers he is a symbol of 'the days of pride and glory', and for those that despise him, a primitive nationalist, who 'does not sing but bray'. Grown from the traditional patriarchal and epic culture, from the folklore of heroic songs and 'stone genes', by his songs he obviously woke up the long hushed-up and forbidden national ethos. While many, also among his listeners, can not understand and forgive him the scandalous blasphemy known as Jasenovac i Gradiška Stara, to his critics it comes as crucial evidence of his Ustashi-inclination. For the mentioned part of Thompson's public, it is unacceptable that someone who claims to live Christian values can be connected with something so monstrous. But, essentially, Thompson is a singer of a disappointed and frustrated *Croatianship*, those who did not expect that the creation of Croatia could be a bare legislative and political act, but a national revival, Thompson is the singer of their warrior's pride and post-war disappointments. (Jajčinović 2007: n. p.)

For now, his only prohibited concert was one which should have taken place in Sarajevo in April 2007.[15] More recently, Thompson's concert in Canada has almost been forbidden due to the Simon Wiesenthal Center's veto. Instead, 'the Croatian neo-Nazi star on 2 November 2007, performed in the town of Velvet Underground, the Ramones and Patty Smith',[16] thanks to permission of the New York's Archdiocese, and after having presented the English translation of the lyrics. They were clean.[17]

Towards a conclusion

The awkward mixture of Croatian pop ideology has led to the fall of an engaged critical thought, defeated at the same point where it was anchored. Whereas the disclosure of the transitional 'monstrosity' of undesirable works in favour of launching, the primarily denounced, cultural 'authenticity', they are gradually giving up 'the country in which mountain clans collide with global-consumerist hype and the post-modern with feudalism' (Pavičić 2004: 18).

Possibly, the cultural analysis generally misses the point when it obsessively picks up the political meanings of the pop-cultural phenomena.[18] But couldn't it be also the contrary, in the 'cunning' circumstances of transitional reason, where the cultural trivialisation generally works as mimicry, excluding the suppressed political content both from the reach of social critique and legislative procedures.[19]

Transitional cultures seem no longer to be graspable in terms of some credible relation between social knowledge and social phenomena. Copying with signs that *may not mean anything*, but a kind of phenomenological 'flirting' constantly seeking for deeper layers of analysis, put the social understanding on the borders of suspicious over-interpretation: an 'excess of wonder' which leads to: 'overestimating the importance of coincidences which are explainable in other ways' (Eco 1990: 167).[20]

Still, how are we supposed to know what is at work here: professional deformation of inventing subversion within banality, or a bigger cognitive deceit which pushes the 'leftist imagination' to be lulled into curing its analytical paranoia and social decline?[21]

Croatia has surely entered its post-political era, as putting the former practices of nation-centred identification aside, and turning to the processes of democratic political 'normalisation' ahead. In relation to the position in 1993, one may speak about some radical cultural change that has occurred here. But, with too many instances, there are also changes pushing it to the edge of social and cultural normality, or, at least, the common reasoning about it. As Zoran Roško, a Croatian representative of the new, post-theoretical thought would put it: 'something simultaneously frightening, exciting and boring is happening here. Things are changing so rapidly that they are becoming imperceptible, so that they no longer evoke shock but rather indifference: a *horror-porno-ennui*' (2002: 120).

Notes

1. For the rationality versus irrationality in the case of Yugoslavian disintegration, see Bates and De Figueiredo 1998.
2. Srećko Pulig instructively points out that the notion of 'second transition' in Croatia is based on a crafty liberal invention. 'As they understand the war only as an obstacle for political transition, they needed the alibi for joining the political life, despite the consequences of the criminal war-transition'

(Pulig 2007: n. p.). About the devastating economic consequences of the 'first transition', see Vojnić 1999.

3. See Ramet (2001), but also Crnković (2001), for the 'underground Anti-Nationalism in the Nationalist Era', and Velikonja (2002), Port (1998) and Gordy (1999) for the Balkan pop culture.

4. HDZ (*Hrvatska Demokratska Zajednica*), the Croatian Democratic Union, is the nationalist party formerly led by President Franjo Tuđman. By the insistence on the reforms and procedures of joining EU after 2003, they painstakingly changed their political language and attitude, forcing their extreme right wing into forming their resentful opposition.

5. According to Daskalovski: 'Intellectuals in the Balkans, an infamous region that has produced such great thinkers as Mircea Eliade, Julia Kristeva, and Slavoj Žižek, have had difficult times coping with the democratization process. Ten years after the changes of the political regime five categories of intellectuals are now discernible in the Balkans: émigrés, businessmen, politicians, technocrats, and *influentials*' (Daskalovski 2000: n. p.). As for Boris Buden's interpretation, it is: 'the understanding or misunderstanding of the West that is still a key element in the interpretation of the "authenticity" or "non-authenticity" of things occurring within' (Buden 1996: n. p.).

6. Official pages, for Marko Perković: www.thompson.hr, and for Severina: www.severina.hr.

7. 'Although nearly four months have passed since their landslide victory in the parliamentary elections, the new Croatian ruling elite (the coalition lead by the SDP – Social Democratic Party) still seems to be in a state of shock. Accustomed, over the past ten years, to the state of mind in which the execution of power is something that is, to paraphrase Milan Kundera, 'somewhere else', or, in other words, a matter of a nice but distant dream, it had been fairly unprepared for a sudden and harsh awakening. And in this dizzy state, it tends to engage in activities that would make for an excellent fable filled with subtle irony, were they not politically disruptive and potentially very dangerous' (Cvijetić 2000: n. p.).

8. The SDP (*Socijaldemokratska partija Hrvatske*) previously led by Ivica Račan, is now led by Zoran Milanović.

9. The former leader of the Croatian liberals, who owes his charisma to his leading role in the Croatian national movement from 1971. Known, otherwise, as the Croatian Spring.

10. About the Internet aspect of Thompson's popularity see Senjković and Dukić.

11. NDH (*Nezavisna Država Hrvatske*) – the Independent State of Croatia, founded in April 1941 and existed until May 1945. Led by Ante Pavelić (1941–1943) and then by Nikola Mandić (1943–1945).

12. 'I do not know who those people with Ustashi signs are. I don't bother with that' (Vodopivec 2004: n. p.).

13. On the misuse of ideology in pop culture, see Đurković 2003.

14. A saying inspired by the results of last Croatian presidential elections, which Thompson also uses in his concerts. It alludes to the contemporary and liberal Stipe Mesić, and the late ex-president of Croatia, desiring to change their places in earth–heaven terms, and by the intercession of the Holy Mother of God.

15. Thanks to the joint veto of Jewish and Islamic Community, as well as Union of Anti-fascists BiH.
16. 'Marko Perković Thompson on the world tour'. Halter, electronic newsletter of Croatian alternative. 25.10.2007. www.h-alter.org/tekst/simon-wiesenthal-centar-protiv-thompsonova-koncerta-u-new-yorku/6945#hotHalter, H-rvacke ALTER-native
17. 'Mr. Weitzman urged Cardinal Edward M. Egan, the Roman Catholic archbishop of New York, to cancel the concerts at a cultural centre operated by the Croatian Church of St. Cyril & Methodius, at the 10th Avenue and 41st Street. Joseph Zwilling, a spokesman for the archdiocese, said church officials had been investigating but had found nothing to substantiate the accusations. Mr. Perkovic's tour is to take him to Toronto; Cleveland; Chicago; Los Angeles; Vancouver, British Columbia; and San Jose, Calif.' (*Croatian Rocker Draws Anti-Nazi Protests*, By *The New York Times*, 1 November 2007).
18. As Meaghan Morris suggests (1990).
19. 'All the classical political ideologies in the era of mass media and pop culture get transformed meanings, which can lead their immanent dialectics towards utterly dangerous political consequences' (Đurković 2003: 1).
20. Eco's distinction between interpretation and over-interpretation, as a usage of text 'entirely for our own purposes'. For wider debate, see Fetveit 2001: 180.
21. According to Serbian Philosopher Mile Savić, in the renovation of the idea of 'engaged intellectual', 'the paradoxical mixture of political *decisionism* and social escapism' we are witnessing a general nostalgia for 'the heroic role of Marxist's intellectual avant-garde' (Savić 2002: 1).

9
The Gender Dimension of Conflict and Reconciliation: Ten Years After: Women Reconstructing Memory

Vesna Kesić

In the former Yugoslavia, political transition exploded into ethnic conflicts and widespread ethnic violence that heavily affected women. Gendered nationalism silenced and de-politicised women, but women's groups mobilised and resisted war and nationalism. Women's groups cooperated across ethnic and national lines in an attempt to prevent conflicts and promote peace. Nowadays, there is a tendency to forget about these efforts. Wars, peace-building, reconciliation and social renovation are gendered processes. If we want a just and democratic society and a sustainable peace, women's memory needs to be reconstructed and included in the collective memory.

The Center for Women War Victims (CWWV) was founded in 1992, in the midst of a bloody war raging in Bosnia and a frail peace imposed by international forces in Croatia. Its mission was to help and support women refugees 'regardless of their ethnic backgrounds and other differences', as was stated in our founding document, 'The Letter of Intentions'[1] and to advance and empower women in general by enhancing women's human rights. Throughout its existence, CWWV worked with thousands of refugee and displaced women by organising self-help groups in refugee camps, distributing humanitarian aid, organising psychological and legal counselling and other forms of what we referred to as *feminist* social work. At the same time, the activists from the Center fought numerous social and political battles opposing warmongering, hate speech, nationalism and – in particular – denouncing the militarised war violence against women and the further misuse of women victims of sexual war abuses for the purposes of Tudjman's nationalistic regime. During the war, besides being victims of sexual

144

war crimes, women in Croatia and the other newly established nation states of former Yugoslavia were exposed to increased domestic violence, economic, social and political discrimination and were increasingly marginalised.

The Center initiated, co-organised or participated at some of the first regional women's meetings and peace conferences: in 1993, in Zagreb and in Geneva, and in 1995, in Istria. We also helped launch the first all-Bosnian women's conference in Sarajevo, in 1996. The women from the Center regularly participated at the Women in Black meetings in Novi Sad and other regional meetings, as well as at the most important world meetings on women: the UN conference on human rights in Vienna, 1993 and the Beijing conference, in 1995. The Center was a resource and a supporter of international initiatives for the establishment of the Hague Tribunal, and the recognition of wartime rapes as war crimes. CWWV participated in local and national actions: from organising the petition for keeping abortion in Croatia safe and legal in 1995 (which was successful), to the election campaigns from 1995 to 2000, as well as in writing the shadow report for the UN CEDAW committee in 1998 on the status of women in Croatia. The Center is one of the initiators and the founding member of the Women's Network of Croatia that today includes some 50 women's groups from the whole of Croatia and became one of the strongest initiatives in developing Croatian civil society.

During that time, the Center and its members were targets of sometimes severe and threatening public attacks, and denigrating and political confrontations: from the famous case of the 'Witches from Rio' to attacks in the Croatian parliament and media.

It is a well-recognised fact that women's groups have been since the late 1970s the first initiatives, in the reconstruction of civil society in the former Yugoslavia that was blurred within the state-established and state-controlled mass organisations, including women's organisations in which everybody was enlisted, but none really participated. Women's feminist initiatives from the late 1970s and women's groups and projects from the early 1980s were among the rare collective of social actors who pronounced their independence from the state-controlled public sphere. During the war, it was mostly the women's groups that had developed from these earlier initiatives that built organisations and networks that cut across national and ethnic lines; women led peace and trust-building initiatives.

Nevertheless, women's efforts in resisting war and nationalism are today largely marginalised and forgotten. Women's human rights are nowadays acknowledged at the level of state legislation, but because of the marginalising of women's groups, these achievements seem to be more the result of imposed pressures from the outside, the international community, for example, than as a result of the continuous activities of women's groups within the former Yugoslavia. Women's suffering, and wartime experiences, as well as women's resistance to wars and nationalism became repressed in collective memory. But at the same time, in a Foucaudian manner, the same repression started to provoke the numerous projects throughout the region that attempt to recollect and reconstruct women's memory from the period of war, as well, as from the socialist period. Once again women, as a marginal group, are on the cutting edge of social research initiatives, as well as initiating many important social changes in the region.

The CWWV is presently working on the conference: Women Recollecting Memory: the Gender Dimension of War and Nationalism.

Women's memory projects start from the premise that the extent of the preoccupation with the past and its remembrance is essential for reconciliation, sustainable peace and democratic development, particularly in transitional and post-war societies. Central research issues of that project are:

1. The construction mechanisms of nation and ethnicity from a gender perspective and the connection between nation, nationalisms and war from a gender perspective. Political transformation processes are gendered processes. When transition occurs under the weight of nationalistic movements, it can incite ethnic conflicts and, as was the case in former Yugoslavia, explode into warfare in which ethnic and sexual violence intertwine and become the widespread form of war violence.
2. If a large part of the past is repressed and detached from the collective memory, this can result in restoring the 'old balance of power' in which the gender dimension plays a major role. The question of reconciliation, sustainable peace and the development of democratic processes includes the question of the involvement of men *and* women in these processes.

Transition research in Eastern Europe

In recent years, a number of different scholarly disciplines have been devoting increasing attention to the question of violence in connection with political transformation processes,[2] whereby the political discourse surrounding the question of human rights has become a central point in this debate.[3] Two German scholars point out an important conceptual aspect of the debate. 'The struggle for human rights begins with the dispute surrounding the concept. It is an essential instrument of rulers to expropriate the means of expression – the political language which constitutes a condensation of the memories of wrongs experienced, collective memory, as well as claims to, and promises of a better life – for human beings who have become cognisant of their oppression and seek to emancipate themselves.'[4] Concrete instances of this connection between collective memory and its expropriation are provided by the changes and upheavals in former socialist countries, which were often associated with the restoration of symbols from the past. During the years after 1989 in these countries, the symbols of their former power – statues of Marx or Lenin, the red five-pointed star, and so forth – were dismantled or replaced, and thereby removed from the 'public memory' and shifted into the collective unconscious. Nowadays, we can see that the confrontation with the past takes on a tremendous significance for the formation of the collective memory and the identity of a society. On the political level, the question that arises is what consequences the ban on reality (the prohibition on mentioning realities) has on political, social and cultural concepts and symbols. Women's projects on memory go into greater detail about the possible effects of such prohibitions and ways of coming to terms with them, both with respect to the individual as well as the collective and gender dimension. The perspective assumes central significance to the extent that symbols express a significant substance of historical relationships, and a 'cleansing' of symbols – as this has been demonstrated in connection with the dismantling of socialist symbols – can ultimately lead to a state of desperate speechlessness and further social traumatisation.

During the early 1990s, the former Yugoslavia (SFRY), underwent a twofold transformation/transition. The political and socio-economic order changed to a 'rule of market and democracy' and the multi-ethnic federation disintegrated into the new, ethnically centred nation states. Both transitions were mediated and enforced by strong ethnic and gender identity politics. Women became the markers of differentiation on both levels – ethnic and political. In the non-democratic socialist state, patriarchal gender relations became an integral part of political regime and social structures. Therefore, women enthusiastically supported the democratic changes. In some fields and professions, such as journalism or the organisation of civil society initiatives, women were the leading initiators of these changes. However, when nationalist political parties came to power, with the first multiparty elections in 1990, they started to re-patriarchalise political and social life and their institutions, with ethnicity and gender becoming the central focus. For instance: one of the main squares in Zagreb, '*The Square of the Victims of Fascism*', which after the Second World War had served as a reminder of the dark period of Croatian history, and the collaboration between the so-called Independent State of Croatia (NDH) and Nazi Germany was, almost immediately after the elections in 1990, renamed '*The Square of Croatian Great Men*' by President Tudjman. What was at work here was what Katherine Verdery describes as a nationalist discourse: 'presenting history as an endless sequence of male heroes, sprung out one after the other, almost like a series of biblical "begets," producing the impression of the nation as temporally a deep patrilineage.'[5] After ten years of organised protest against the erasure of the memory on the fascist episode of national history, as well as the anti-fascist resistance – the protests in which most of the Croatian women's groups participated eagerly, and added to them the gender specific actions, such as the memorialising of 8 March and, anyway rare, memorials on women members of the anti-fascist resistance that were also dismantled – with the political changes that occurred with the 2000 elections, the old name was returned to the square. But to accommodate the nationalistic, patriotic layers of the population, which did not disappear with these elections, another nearby square which was traditionally named *Trg Burze* (Exchange Market Square) was now renamed the 'Square of Croatian Great Men', while none of women's monuments or street names were renamed. Besides the continuation of the erasure of memory on women's history, with the renaming of *Trg Burze* into 'Croatian Great Men', one of the capitalist society's anxieties, or schizophrenia as Renata Salecl calls it, was also created.

With the beginning of war in Croatia in 1991, the image of warring and attractive young women in military uniform appeared in the mass media as a part of promulgating national homogenisation. Women, victims of sexual war violence became embodied symbols and turned into national metaphors ('*A raped Croat woman stands for the raped Croatia*'). Women were established as victims on whose bodies nationalism(s) inscribed their state-building projects and embodied their dreams. Feminist women's groups that did not conform to state-sponsored nationalism were pronounced as traitors and 'un-womanly'. Immediately after the war ended in Croatia, the suffering of women and their sexual abuse ceased to be an issue and benefits and the honour of the male war veterans became highly exaggerated. Although peace is now celebrated, the role of the women's groups that opposed war and nationalism[6] is not acknowledged. Repressed or silenced memories have in general become one of the major obstacles in social reconciliation and reconstruction throughout the region.

Gender, age groups, social classes, occupational groups, subcultures and regional affiliations likewise, provide the potential criteria of differentiation. Depending upon their specific social definition, they also open up specific alternatives for action. On the one hand, gender-specific differences in the construction and representation of (national) identities need to be examined, but there is also a need to show how women participated in national political processes. Women were the victims of ethnic conflicts and nationalism, but women also played an active role in opposing wars and ethnic conflicts. Political and social stability are (not only in the case of women) being created at the cost of forgetting and repressing, instead of upholding an actively pursued 'policy of remembrance'. Women were never included in the official peace negotiation initiatives and missions, although this had been requested by several UN documents, such as the *Beijing platform for action* and Security Council Resolution 1325 that, among other things, recommends:

- An International Truth and Reconciliation Commission on violence against women in armed conflicts;
- Gender experts and expertise to be included at all levels and in all aspects of peace operations and peace-building;
- A review of training programmes from a gender perspective for conflict resolution and peace-building;
- Gender issues to be incorporated in peace-building and post-conflict reconstruction;
- The assessments of gaps in international and national laws and standards pertaining the protection of women in conflict and post-conflict situations;
- An increase in the women's approach to media and communication technology, so that gender the perspective and woman's expertise can influence public discourse and decision-making on peace and security;
- The systematic collection and analysis of information and data by all actors, using gender specific indicators to guide policy, programmes and services for women in conflicts and post-conflict situations.

The ceasefire, democratisation and reconciliation processes in the countries of former Yugoslavia were, more often than not, the result of international pressure and economic interests, rather than of the thought-fully led processes of understanding and reconciliation. The Hague tri-bunal is, by now, the only instance where testimonies and memory on sexual war crimes against women are recalled. The local courts, as far as we are informed, have not yet brought to trial the perpetrators of sexual violence against women and accused them for war crimes.

On the one hand, gender-specific differences in the construction and representation of (national) identities are to be investigated within memory projects; on the other hand, we will also look into the extent to which women are made into a central component in the construc-tion of nationality/identity and ethnicity. In this connection, we define 'nation' as a historical project located at the nexus of the past, self-representation and a future in which: 'Women are represented as the atavistic and authentic body of national tradition, embodying nation-alism's conservative principle of continuity.'[7] Aside from the historical component in the construction of nation, it needs to be shown how women participate in national political processes. According to Anthias and Yuval-Davis, women are brought into the national/ethnicised polit-ical discourse along the lines of the following points: 'a) as biological reproducers of members of ethnic collectivities; b) as reproducers of the boundaries of ethnic/national groups; c) as participating centrally in the ideological reproduction of the collectivity and as transmitters of its culture; d) as signifiers of ethnic/national differences, that is, as a focus and symbol in ideological discourses used in the construction, repro-duction and transformation of ethnic/national categories; e) as partici-pants in national, economic, political and military struggles'.[8]

In this context, sexual violence against women (such as rape during wartime) can be described as an example of 'genderising nations'/'genderising ethnicity': The sexualised violence was not treated as an act of violence committed by men upon women, but rather as a 'nationalist offence'.[9] Thus the nation was raised to the status of vic-tim, and – as a last resort – its masculinity had to be restored to it. Accordingly, such a rape metaphor constituted an important form of preparation for the ensuing national wars. But this also enables us to see – at least partially – that 'the female (constitutes) the specific center for the overall organization of nationalist and racist thought' in the violently waged confrontation surrounding the reconstruction of mas-culinity/the patriarchy.[10] Putting the image of the raped woman on the level of the highest form of violence – namely, positioning it on a national basis – was always a precursor to, or a means of justifying excesses in society.

It has been, first and foremost, scholars in the fields of cultural studies and gender studies who have investigated the representation of the nation by means of women, and social scientific analyses have attempted to explain the differing participation of women and men in the construction of nations. 'The understanding of nationalism as a gendered phenomenon indicates gender-specific involvements in nation building and in the construction of national identities, even as it demonstrates how "woman" symbolized the "nation" – in this case nations struggling to find themselves and become independent.'[11]

Two things can be brought to light with this approach: first, the fact that one element that belongs to national defence – as this is formulated by scholars such as Geoff Eley – is the will and the wish to die for the nation. 'This became the extreme heroic form for melting the individual and the nation together.'[12] Second, it can be made evident that the militarisation of the men led to a familialisation and privatisation of the women. 'The emerging nation may have been militarized and masculinized, but it was also "familialized," construed as a "patriarchally and hierarchically organized folk family." Within that family, women, embodying the canon of female virtues, found their properly subordinate and dichotomous place as defined by the new bourgeois gender order.'[13]

Out of this short illustration of how the intersection between the categories such as nation, state, ethnicity, men and women worked in the transformation processes in former Yugoslavia, particularly in the incitements of the sexual and ethnic violence committed in time of war, I want to point out once again that there is a critical need to recreate the gender dimension of public memory and women's role in peace-building, because if women are excluded from recent memory, they are also excluded from contemporary social and political processes. Sustainable peace and reconciliation in former Yugoslavia cannot be achieved without the participation of women, among all the other reasons, because women 'bear' the memory of the continuous peace and reconciliation efforts.

Notes

Considerable parts of this paper are being used from the 'Project Proposal Political Transformation Processes in Former Yugoslavia under the Gender Perspective' that my colleague Dr. Doris Goedl from Salzburg and I submitted to the Fonds zur Förderung der wissenschaftlichen Forschung (FWF) in Vienna. I also want to thank my friend Doris Goedl for allowing me to use our common work here, and to thank the FWF for giving us the two-year grant to work on our project.

1. See: M. Belić et al. (eds), 'Centar za žene zrtve rata: Zbornik' (Zagreb: Ženski informativno-dokumentacijski centar i Centar za žene žrtve rata, 1994): 119.
2. In Europe, for example, the collapse of the Socialist regimes in 1989 and the break-up of Yugoslavia in 1991; in Latin America, for example, Chile in 1990, and in Africa, the political changes in South Africa and Algeria.
3. On this subject, see: G. Smith and A. Margalit (eds), *Amnestie oder Die Politik der Erinnerung* (Frankfurt, 1997). This collection of essays includes papers by numerous authors connected with the Einstein Forum Potsdam, an international conference that took place in 1996 in Berlin. The articles printed in this volume constitute expanded and revised versions of the papers presented there.
4. O. Negt and A. Kluge, *Maßverhältnisse des Politischen* (Frankfurt, 1992).
5. K. Verdery, 'From Parent-State to Family Patriarchs: Gender and Nation in Contemporary Eastern Europe', *East European Politics and Societies*, 8, 2 (Spring 1994): 238.
6. Not all the women's groups opposed warmongering nationalism, though. This will also be demonstrated thorough the projects research.
7. S. Wenke, 'Gendered Representation of the Nation's Past and Future', in I. Blom, K. Hagemann and C. Hall (eds), *Gendered Nations: Nationalism and Gender Order in the Long Nineteenth Century* (New York and Oxford: Berg, 1999).
8. See F. Antias and N. Yuval-Davis, *Women-Nation-State* (London: Macmillan, 1989): 6–11.
9. See V. Jalusić, *Die Funktionalisierung von Vergewaltigungen im Vorkriegs-Jugoslawien* (1994).
10. Ibid.: 125.
11. Ida Blom: 6.
12. G. Eley, 'Culture, Nation and Gender', in I. Blom, K. Hagemann and C. Hall (eds), *Gendered Nations: Nationalism and Gender Order in the Long Nineteenth Century.* (Oxford, New York: Berg, 1999): 27–40, 29.
13. Ibid.: 46.

10
Unable to Heal: Debate on the National Self in Post-Socialist Slovenia

Irena Šumi

The independent state, eighteen years on

On 23 December 1990, voters in Slovenia were invited to answer a historic question: 'Should the Republic of Slovenia become an independent state?' No less than 88.5 per cent of the total voters responded in the affirmative and, together with the remaining 12.5 per cent, made up of the disinterested or the sceptical, they escaped the old federation with barely a scratch, unlike the majority of other ex-Yugoslavs. Eighteen years later, Slovenia is about to emerge from the first four years of a rightist coalition that had succeeded the leftist Liberal Democracy of Slovenia (LDS) which had had three mandates and had remained in power for twelve barely interrupted years.[1] This chapter will address the following three questions: Apart from gaining independence, what kind of state has Slovenia become? Is Slovenia's period of transition over? Has Slovenia become a truly Western democracy, or not? To obtain these answers, one must ask oneself, what is the debate on the national self that has spanned roughly two decades of statehood all about?

Following the brief rule of the DEMOS coalition in 1990,[2] the political arena soon split into two more-or-less balanced halves, that may be perfunctorily labelled the right and the left, that have since managed to keep the body of voters divided proportionally. This nearly symmetrical split clearly situates Slovenia among those countries where people essentially vote against a political leadership that is deemed to be depleted of ideas, devoid of efficient policies, or has become totally corrupt, rather than vote in favour of the best programme on offer. This is certainly true of the last parliamentary elections, in 2004, when the

153

voters turned against the LDS en masse. Similarly, the last presidential elections in 2007 were won by a relatively unknown candidate, Danilo Türk, basically due to visceral opposition to Lojze Peterle, the perceived favourite who had mounted the longest and most aggressive campaign.[3] Although essentially bipolar, if not at the same time bipartite, given that political parties dissolve and unite constantly, generally by way of left–right regrouping in the face of elections and subject to negative voting, the Slovenian political space now seems to be stable.

Slovenia attained its place in the international community, and among its achievements, the most frequently quoted are: Slovenia's membership of the UN, NATO and the EU; the adoption of the Schengen Agreement; and, of course, Slovenia's presidency over the EU, in the first half of 2008. The corresponding internal structural changes bear witness to the formal success of Slovenia's systemic transition. Slovenia had obviously managed to adopt all key legislation transposing the *acquis communautaire*; the reintroduction of capitalism and the massive collapse of socialist industrialism without causing any serious social unrest; while the constitutionally guaranteed social welfare state, although drastically reduced, had nevertheless nominally survived.

A closer inspection would reveal that the political discourse, while completely innocent of any political correctness, at least takes place in an atmosphere of transparent opposition and dialogue. Basic democracy would seem to function despite the frequent evidence that the judicial system is practically dead,[4] that capital and power are still generated in both illegitimate and illegal ways and that vital social systems such as health care are irreparably crippled, while the notion of political opposition uniformly translates into that of political enmity, which would all seem to indicate that while a lot goes wrong, little goes unexposed. As is normal in a democracy, there are the constant occurances of scandals, excesses and irregularities that shake up the political arena and capture the attention of the public.

These scandals are cyclical, repetitive, incessant and reported on in most alarmist tones. However, equally persistent is the public impression that none of the transgressions are ever rectified and brought to a close. It is a matter of widespread public consensus that the most outrageous cases of daring large-scale theft, blatant injustices and the misuse or neglect of office inevitably go unpunished. This results in a kind of collective fatalism that is rooted in Slovenian history and goes as far back as anyone can remember, so far that it has been affirmed in folk wisdom. For example, the most cherished proverbs insist that: the Slovenians are serfs by nature; the Slovenian 'national character' is lacking in pride, courage and self-esteem; power corrupts, especially in the circumstances most frequently detected in Slovenia which proverbially involve an ignoramus risen to a position of power and wealth; Slovenes never had a state, and do not even know how to go about creating one; and, finally and irrefutably, nothing can be done about any of these things. The state and local powers, the newfangled capitalists and autocratic directors of state-owned monopolies who harvest a mythical income in defiance of state norms on the salaries of public servants, political parties in power and, as of late, academic monopolists are all seen as essentially unstoppable in their frivolousness.

All these social arenas teem with people who have, or are on their way to having, unbelievable post-socialist careers. Infallibly, they will give the impression of being the worst possible choice: positions of authority seem to be reserved for the demonstrably incapable. It would seem that there is no limit to how ignorant, rude or sometimes silly these people can be; as long as they ignore every criticism, proof and challenge, they will enjoy their position of authority. The circumstances in which blatant narcissism is the only quality needed for success produce barely articulate politicians, alongside economic tycoons who seem to turn up overnight from the most humble artisan backgrounds, and top academics whose careers may hitherto have been in the more conservative industries in the Third World, or in the obscure bastions of the nineteenth-century-style social sciences. Their narcissism is structural rather than personal: once they are recruited into the winning team, no amount of public criticism, no proof of incompetence, no exposure of any kind can make them engage the critics, explain or justify themselves, or stand their ground on the basis of honour preserved, much less step down when proven to be at fault.

For the onlookers, this creates the schizophrenic impression that these public actors are not really all that they seem, and that these public figures are partaking in another game that is being played out behind the scenes. Paranoid impressions abound among the general public, complemented by a fatalism, whereby 'they' would seem to be opposing each other, while, in fact, their true game is being fought out in secret; 'they' never seem to be concerned with the public good, or ideals and professionalism; and, 'they' have their own self-serving, hidden agendas. This peculiar marriage of unbounded mistrust and categorical fatalism equally pervades the media and the general public who make use of the media reports. The cycle goes something like this: a newspaper launches a dramatic corruption story. Since any medium is either decidedly pro-government or zealously against it, the reaction of the incriminated, and the opposing public, exposes the fact that the seeming 'objectivity' of the initial report has gaps in it of a yellow press nature, duly casting doubts on its very veracity: things are not what they seem; there is a hidden agenda. While the protagonists will most likely keep their silence, or limit themselves to court appearances and enigmatic statements, the readers of the print media have to come to terms with a small confessional war being fought out between the opposition fans, and the government fans. Ultimately, both come together in the opinion that nothing will be done about the issue, and that nothing can be done about anything in the first place. A few idealistic, or else militant, readers may add that with the next parliamentary elections, things are sure to change. Upon which, they will invariably be told to 'dream on'.

Public actors are not the only ones constructed in the public view as being essentially feudal in their imperviousness to responsibility; so too are the state institutions. A case in point is the ongoing debate on the state taxation system and its concomitant amendments, given that Slovenia has one of the highest tax rates in the EU. While there are many arguments over the fairness of the system and still more its feasibility from the perspective of the taxpayer, never once can one detect any kind of debate over the very reasons why taxes are collected in the first place. Indeed, the notion that the taxpayer should get their investment returned in the form of an improved infrastructure and better public services would seem to be totally alien to the Slovenian general public. Collecting taxes is understood as a means of approximating a kind of social equilibrium, not as a public investment towards a set of goals. The tax authorities are seen in medieval terms, as the indisputable power that confiscates surplus wealth which, once collected, disappears from the public eye and ultimately, and inevitably, enriches the wealthy and the powerful, if not directly, at least by means of covering up their mistakes in ruling the country. Put simply, the collection of taxes has become the 'cost of having a state'.

A thousand-year dream, give or take

But as to dreaming, the reality of the independent Slovenian state is uniformly seen as being a historical inevitability, a self-fulfilling prophecy. It may not work well, but it was written in the stars. In a sense, this state had always existed as a future reality, and all the life paths of all Slovenes that ever existed inevitably led to its formation. Between libertarian laypeople, professionals and politicians alike, and the right-wingers across the same span, there exists only a nuance of difference: the latter shamelessly celebrate independent Slovenia as 'a thousand-year-old dream come true'. The former will have heard that this may be somehow objectionable as being not 'scientifically' concise enough, and somewhat dubious in the sense of being not quite chic and cosmopolitan, while – for one unfathomable reason or another – it is potentially racist, so they choose to confine, by way of a reasonable compromise, the birth of the 'dream' to, say, the writings of the Slovenian Protestant movement protagonist Primož Trubar in the 1600s,[5] or more rigorously still, to the early articulations of the demand for the autonomy of the Slovenian lands within the Habsburg monarchy in the mid-nineteenth century.[6]

To be a Slovene means that one has to be in full possession of three prerequisites: Slovenian origin in pseudo-biological terms; the Slovene language; and Slovenian culture. Having just the latter two is not enough to pass as a Slovene.[7] Again, the difference between leftist-libertarian and rightist-conservative views is but a nuance, and essentially involves a slightly different perception of linear historic time. The former would concede that having a non-Slovenian parent or ancestor is no big deal, and that in time such an admixture of non-Slovenianess fades out; the latter increasingly believe that Slovenianess is a genetic category, that 'amalgamation' does not fade out, and that Slovenes as a biologically and culturally unique community existed at least a thousand years ago. Consequently, cultural uniqueness is a function of biological uniqueness, so that Slovenia is primarily seen as being a state dedicated to pure Slovenes, and the preservation of such biologically pure Slovenianess. This view would seem to be supported by Article 3 of the Slovenian Constitution.[8] Thus, politicians on both sides of the spectrum expressed their exhilaration at the passing of the Law on Slovenes without citizenship outside Slovenia in 2006, which requires those who are potentially eligible to present: 'documentation to prove their Slovenian origin'. This legal requirement has been boiled down from the draft bill provisions which expressly forbade candidacy for the status of a Slovene without citizenship to non-Slovene spouses and adoptive children of those eligible who were, in an uneasy accord with a notorious historic precedent, required to prove their ancestral Slovenianess over five preceeding generations.

In order to understand what generates and makes possible the coexistence of such linear discourses on blood and history, and the discourses on disempowerment that are in the same breath, both cyclical and fatalist, one should turn to the more permanent topics in the national debate on the self. Preferably, it should be topics that were generated at the very beginning of the story of independent Slovenia that remain open to this day, and that persist as formative of the 50–50 division that characterises both the Slovenian parliamentary partisan arena and the body of voters. They should be of such nature and duration that one can see them as constituting the core of the debate on the national self in Slovenia. Our choice here is made up of three separate, if tightly intertwined debates, namely: on national reconciliation; the concept of a dying autochthonous nation; and on the state of the social sciences and humanities in Slovenia. All these issues were articulated during the revolutionary 1980s not only as the key points in favour of Slovenian statehood and independence, but also as the very core issues of Slovenian existence as a nation. The mother of all issues that determines which team one is in, the leftist or the rightist, is that of national reconciliation.

National reconciliation

During the late 1980s, the Slovenian philosopher Spomenka Hribar (Hribar 1987: 74–103) quite forcefully advanced a thesis she had first articulated in 1982 (Hribar 1982[1990]) that in order to build a democratic society on the ashes of the old totalitarian regime, Slovenes needed to come to terms with the so-called Civil War that had taken place both during, and within, the Second World War. Just after the war, the then regime extra-judicially executed and buried in unmarked mass graves several thousand collaborationists. Hribar felt that the mutual killings during the war as well as the final massacres were two extreme aspects of the same chain of events that called for a clear articulation of the historic truth, universal piety for the dead on both sides, and the acceptance of the fact of the then division within the nation. The three elements are prerequisite for the national reconciliation, as the latter:

> ... not only concerns Slovenes and us as Slovenes, but concerns us as human beings in our human/national habitus, and in our humanity. However, without reconciliation and civil society, we will be unable to exist as people, and unable to persist as a nation. (Hribar 1987: 100; all emphases original)

Reconciliation, she continues, is an alternative to the Communist Party's prejudice of avant-gardism that is the source of all hatred;

reconciliation is also 'the "soil" from which will sprout love and remembrance' (101); it essentially entails an 'acceptance' of our history:

> [Reconciliation] enables us to see the revolutionaries as well as counter-revolutionaries, in the end, as miserable 'sons of the same mother', meaning, that we see and accept them primarily as people (of a certain epoch). This of course does not mean we have to accept their ideologies! To err is human, but errors cannot be accepted and perpetuated. However, refusing the ideologies does not mean excommunicating their bearers; we have to differentiate between the person and the ideology. I believe that reconciliation, understood and lived in this way, offers the opportunity to break the chain of hatred which endangers the motherland in its foundation. (Hribar 1987: 102; all emphases original)

The three prerequisites for national reconciliation Hribar identified were and remain to this day to be understood to mean historical revisionism, incessant bone-hunting, and the impossibility of achieving forgiveness: a perversion that Hribar's customarily highly subjective and emotional style of argumentation[9] did not help prevent. While the first two represent perhaps universal enough phenomena in postsocialist societies that Katherine Verdery, for instance, summarises as being 'something more', the transitional surplus value involving: 'meanings, feelings, the sacred, the ideas of morality, the nonrational – all ingredients of the "legitimacy"' (Verdery 2000: 25). Indeed, both Spomenka Hribar and her husband, philosopher Tine Hribar, insisted on the 'sacredness of all life' in their argumentation, the latter is more intriguing in that it either categorically equates 'acceptance' with 'forgiveness', or poses the latter as the prerequisite for the former. Needless to say, there ensued an endless debate on who is to ask forgiveness first, who is to accept it, whether it should be mutual, and whether the gestures already offered were enough, thus ensuring that the debate cannot end. The only argument in circulation, seemingly extraneous to the bipolar opposition is equally categorical and exploits the generation gap: the young people have nothing to do with it, and are not interested in the disputes of their forebears, therefore we should in their interest, or at least they themselves should, forget all about it and move on.

Meanwhile, the divide between the believers in the Communist Partisans of the Second World War and those that supported the collaborating Home Guard actually plays the role of the primary diacritic in the left/right positioning of the political parties, and the body of

voters. Political and civil initiatives and debates abound around questions as to whether or not members of the Home Guard and their offspring should be eligible for the kind state compensation that becomes
the victims of the war; and this can cause public turbulence as when,
say, the Supreme Court annulled the trial of Bishop Rožman, staged in
1946 by the Communist Regime under accusations of active collaboration.[10] Today, as in the time of the Second World War, the opposition
is primarily between those right-wingers and some Catholics who are
perceived as being pro-Home Guard, and the pro-Partisans and non-
Catholics who are deemed as being left-wingers. During the Second
World War, as in the inter-war period, the opposition was between conservative Catholics and leftist socialists and communists; before the
First World War, as had been the case since at least the mid-nineteenth
century, the opposition was between Catholic pro-clericals who were
anti-German and the liberals who were essentially anti-Catholic and
pro-German.[11] In the last three years, the divide has been between the
latest incarnation of political righteousness, the followers of the current
Prime Minister Janez Janša, and those against his rather evangelically
disposed party and government. This tradition of confusing confessional and political programmes with ethno-national goals has been
perpetuated, or at least simulated in the current left–right polarisation.

That forgiveness is not just impossible, but simply an irrelevant concept worthy of exploitation, and a meaningless course of action to take,
is a heresy that no one on either side of the debate is prepared to consider. That the Partisan-Home Guard controversy is, far from being the
ultimate peril of Slovenianess, but, rather its indispensable constituent,
only adds the insult of impiety to the injury of the misery of 'sons of
the same mother'. To observe that the current left–right division is the
continuation of what was not a civil, but a localised confessional war
during the Second World War, a war that raged from the beginning of
political Slovenianess as its primary agent of cohesion, would go down
as immoral. To suggest that Slovenianess, as any other imagined community, is nothing more than the incessant talk about the national self
rather than mythical millennial histories, racist exclusivism and folklore
is offensive as it belittles the national sentiment. To insist that a nation
state in the shaping of the national interest could profit from a different
basis for primary social cohesion than a simple 50–50 confessional split
is anti-Slovenian. To suggest that the events of the Second World War
certainly do not call for forgiveness, but rather for an analysis of their
consequences for the living, is sacrilege: sprinkling salt on the wound is
obviously more functionally indispensable than healing it.

The dying autochthonous nation

Slovenes are slowly dying out. Few people in Slovenia have any serious doubts about that. It has become both a truism and a dogma; on this issue, the differences between the left-wing and the right-wing are minuscule. The former believe that Slovenes are endangered, but will somehow survive if only they are careful to preserve 'our language and culture', and cultivate 'national pride' more. The rightists believe that too, but they also believe that, had the Communists not massacred the Home Guard, 'we' would have a population in excess of 4 million today. Also, they would just as soon not leave it to chance in the future. Since the 2004 elections, both the government and the Catholic Church, often jointly, invested considerable effort into awareness-raising campaigns and concrete measures to increase fertility.

Not every citizen's and resident's fertility, though, for while it is widely accepted that the overall population of Slovenia, having surpassed the 2 million mark in 1991, fell back on the infamous political issue of the so-called 'Erased',[12] and passed the mark again in 2004, it is steadily increasing in number. Of grave concern is the 'fact' that the fertility of 'real' Slovenians is in catastrophic decline. Professionals and laymen alike insist on the following narrative, that autochthonous Slovenes have been experiencing declining birth rates since at least the early 1980s when the reproduction rate fell below 2.1 children per woman (Josipovič 2005). Immigrants, by contrast, especially from the other 'former' Yugoslav republics have exhibited disproportionally higher birth rates. Because of this, immigration is clearly not a solution to the dire demographic problem as foreigners are certain to bring not only more children, but also unfair competition for jobs, while making impossible demands on the already crumbling systems of social solidarity. Furthermore, alien languages and cultures would be certain to slowly displace the Slovenian language and culture. Because of the smallness of the Slovenian nation, the integration of newcomers in any substantial number is virtually impossible. On top of this, the number of people who speak Slovene as their mother tongue is declining steadily from one census to another, not only in the neighbouring countries where the historical process of bordering severed them from the national mainland nearly a century ago, but also the language is declining in Slovenia itself; a situation that allegedly proves the absolute imminence of the vanishing of Slovenianess and the Slovenian nation. All meticulous demographic analysis and evidence to the contrary (cf. e.g. Josipovič 2004, 2005; Kneževič Hočevar 2004) is essentially ignored. Again, attempts at explaining that spatial provenance, linguistic repertoires, cultural practices and social discourse on communal history do not easily translate into Slovenes by blood, the purity of the Slovene language, Slovenian folklore and millennial histories, would fail not only in lay arenas, but increasingly in academic ones as well. To explain that a vast proportion of living Slovenes have ancestors from non-Slovenian spaces, and that perhaps a fair share, if not the majority, of living Slovenes may not be the biological offspring of Slovene speakers of, say, the sixteenth century, is unfathomable. To insist that migration is a process that was always happening and will very likely not stop happening, but that in order to problematise it in terms of blood and culture, one first needs an exclusivist nationalist ideology is, bafflingly, read as a statement praising the value of such national ideology. The history of past centuries is seen as a steady process of the distillation of pure Slovenianess from amorphous mobs, confused identities, impure ethnic admixtures and the domination of foreign state formations. With statehood, Slovenianess reached, or should have reached, its all-time purest form and composition that is, alas, threatened with extinction.

This idea of absolute purity, referred to as 'autochthony', has also become a piece of Slovenian constitutional terminology. The term 'autochthony' was first introduced into the Slovenian Constitution towards the end of socialism and then adopted by the current constitution of 1991. Autochthony specifically refers to the state-protected Italian and Hungarian minorities to be found in the border regions of Slovenia, and to those Roma populations that have been protected by law since 2007.[13] The term has also been applied to Slovenes living in neighbouring states. However, since independence, autochthony[14] has also become a household term that may be frequently found in both absurd and comical contexts, whereby anything from people, local rock bands and breeds of chickens or goats to local granite or wood is spoken of and commercially advertised as being autochthonous (cf. Janko Spreizer 2006). With reference to the comical nature of this usage, the Constitutional Court is currently faced with an impossible dilemma, for while the term forms part of the basic legal vocabulary of the state, the Court is no longer able to decide what being autochthonous really stands for, and which criteria a population should meet before being deemed autochthonous, within the context of the 1991 constitution, in cases of discrimination on the grounds of ethnicity and race.

In its wisdom, the Court decided to hand this hot potato back to the communities that are recognised as being authochtonous by the constitution, and a number of laws. They have to determine themselves what the criteria for autochthony are, and how they plan to abide by them in determining and recruiting membership.[15] As yet, this glaringly obvious proof that the notion of autochthony is as legally defunct as it is humanly absurd (Šumi and Josipovič 2006) has failed to stir any political initiative to discuss it, much less to refute it.

In all the wide-coalition governments led by the LDS, the ministry and governmental office for Slovenian affairs has always been delegated to the party that was furthest to the right in the coalition. The left generally exudes the sentiment that questions on the nation and nationalism are not quite cosmopolitan enough and are better left to the political right with its strong affiliation to the Catholic Church. This over-relaxed attitude towards nationalism may have been one of the most general and long-term mistakes of the LDS governments, and consequently, the ultimate reason for the defeat of leftist parties in 2004.

Social sciences and humanities in peril

As Janša's Social Democrat Party of Slovenia (SDS) is the first right-wing party in the history of independent Slovenia to have won the parliamentary elections, it is only natural that under the present coalition, the concern for Slovenianess has become one of the highest issues guiding all the work of the government. This means that nationally financed academic research offers the clearest picture of how this government has set out to make the people, and especially academics, live by these principles of Slovenianess, and how the academic community is understood to have a duty of reproducing such principles in a manner not unlike that in which academics were expected to produce 'scientific socialism' in the former SFRJ.

The first symptom of this process appeared in the form of the thesis that Slovenia cannot hope to sustain the 'entire' range of all existing sciences and disciplines, but would have to prioritise.[16] The priorities were, not surprisingly, reminiscent of the former socialist times and their obsession with industrialisation; what was needed was a way in which the natural sciences could stimulate the development of modern technologies. Less explicitly vocalised was the fact that a more-or-less constant budget for the natural sciences, meant less funding being made available for the social sciences and humanities, and as a consequence, the social science and humanities programmes of public universities were forced to substantially reduce their enrolment. True to the dogma of a 'dying autochthonous nation', the social sciences and humanities

were widely understood as having one sole purpose, namely to help preserve Slovenianess, and as such, they should limit themselves to topics
that objectively supported this cause.

Aside from the annual call for applications for basic, applied and post-
doctoral research, the government issues at least one additional tender
sponsored by all ministries that calls for, in the style of the CE's framework tenders, predetermined thematic research. The selection procedure is also based on anonymous peer review procedures, but with a
distinctly local flavour. Thus in 2005, the basic and applied research
call was refereed by foreign scientists of Slovenian origin who were
transported to Slovenia and sequestered for the selection process in
Slovenia's top hotels. In 2007, one of the three referees for each project
evaluation was a layperson whose job was to determine whether the
proposed research was useful for the 'common people' of Slovenia, and,
by extension, for Slovenianess. A quick analysis of the national tenders for research funding, issued since early 2005[17] demonstrates that
Slovenian history, Slovenian folklore and Slovenes outside Slovenia are
the most generously financed forms of research. Critical, analytical and
comparative work is all but banned. Furthermore, since 2004, researchers in (Roman Catholic) theology have particularly benefited. Most
notably, the Franciscan Family Institute that receives ample donations
from large, state-owned enterprises seems incapable of failing to win
any of the national tenders for research money. While the Institute's
priorities seem to lie in what are obviously diagnosed as the main problems for the social sciences in Slovenia – namely, low fertility, the highest suicide rate in the EU, epidemic alcoholism and rampant domestic
violence – the Franciscan Family Institute is, given that it is licensed for
both counselling and research, steadily winning national dominance
in all branches of social work, demography, sociology and, by natural
extension, the studies of ethnicity and nationalism.

The current government inherited and affirmed the long-held belief
that the most accurate and prestigious evaluation devices of scientific
output are commercial indexing and the referencing products of ISI
Thomson Inc. All the more so as the only true, 'exact' scientists, those
in the natural sciences and technology, get to publish hundreds of the
so-called 'original scientific articles', that is multi-authored technical
reports on experimental procedures. Since there are, sadly, also other
kinds of scientific production which are more difficult to classify and
evaluate, the state Public Agency for Research (ARRS) commissioned a
special group of academics chiefly recruited from the Slovenian Academy
of Arts and Sciences to devise an appropriate bibliography-evaluating

system. It is called SICRIS[18] and is an instrument that the ARRS will exclusively rely on in assessing the scientific excellence of individual researchers, projects and programme groups. It takes into full account the widely acknowledged dogma according to which there are, especially in the humanities, many fields of research that are important only to Slovenes and the preservation of Slovenianness that will not translate, and cannot get published, abroad as they simply are not of any interest to foreigners. A vast range of such exclusive research pertains to the Slovenian language and dialects, especially as regards the problem of their lexicological and grammatical purity; to Slovenian lore and mores and folklore and ethnology in general; to Slovenian history, art history, literary history, and the like; to Slovenes in the neighbouring countries, and the diaspora; and to Slovenian political history and culture. In short, all these fields require an underlying discourse that only Slovenes fully possess and can partake in. The purpose of these studies is to sustain Slovenianness, not to analyse it. Analysing Slovenianness, as stated above, has become implicitly immoral: while most Slovenians probably think so, leftist politicians included, the present government certainly unscrupulously heralds its belief that the 'humanities' are essentially intended to 'help the national cause' (cf. also Močnik 1999: 115), while any social sciences, worthy of the name, should be supportive of the state and nation.

The SICRIS bibliographical system, while enshrining the ISI Thomson indexation, establishes a wide selection of Slovenian periodicals that are of special importance for the academic support of the national cause. A number of confessional, informational and popular publications were elevated to the status of academic press. By definition, anything that an academic institution publishes became unquestioningly scientific, including reviews and the bulletins of professional associations. These institutions, naturally, primarily publish the works of their own members and employees, so that running an in-house journal and/or a book series has become a truly profitable activity for authors and publishers alike, since the latter also live on a state budget. Furthermore, all reviewing procedures are simplified to the point of parody, entrusted to the author's best friends and nearest colleagues, or completely absent. One can publish up to five or more 'original scientific articles' in an in-house periodical annually, and gain far more points than by publishing a piece in an internationally acclaimed and fully peer-reviewed periodical. Anything will do: a chapter from a book published years ago; a stash of field or study notes; autobiographical musings, moralising tracts, travel notes, addresses delivered to the lay public, perfunctorily augmented newspaper pieces or a previously published article with a new title. Nobody will read it, nobody will review it and nobody will comment on it. Much the same goes for book-length publications: one can become an author or a co-author, editor or co-editor of a scientific monograph simply if the publishing house says so. A slightly less-valued type of publication is the so-called professional monograph: anyone who can put together more than 50 pages (in any format) and publish them anywhere, as long as it is not obviously fiction, will have accomplished a third-highest-rated scientific product. The system quickly made people aware of the system: introductions to edited volumes or editorials in reviews do not bring points, so it is better for them to give their works any title that does not spell out 'introduction': in this way, the piece will pass as, say, a 'short scientific article'. Conference proceedings carry no value; therefore one must carefully turn them into edited volumes and avoid making any reference to their origin being a conference or symposium that may have initially brought all the authors together.

Points, of course, bring eligibility to compete for national projects. A thousand points in the past five years make one eligible automatically. It is not that everybody is so keen to do research: rather, that winning a national project is the prerequisite for having a salary. In Slovenia, full-time researchers in public institutions are legally on a par with the state bureaucracy and public employees. Unlike them, however, these researchers are required to win their entire salary on the market and through tenders. University tutors have it slightly better as between 80 and 100 per cent of teaching is financed; however, establishing private universities and faculties has become something of a national sport as the state will also finance private schools up to 80 per cent. The current government recently moved towards the full financing of private schools. Any initiative to establish a private university, or even a public one, is typically led by a local, world-famous senior academic who wishes to assemble under their wing all their academic underlings, ex-students, political friends and, not at all infrequently, their closest kith and kin.

The SICRIS system is neither an accident nor a mistake. It is based on a peculiar understanding of the purpose of knowledge production. It is upheld by an absurd financing system that gave birth to spontaneous mafia-like informal organising. It is also based on the most corrupt uptake of the national interest: Jonathan Swift's quip about patriots as scoundrels is here played out to the full, as the informally organised groups around their academic godfathers sell exactly that: hastily manufactured pure Slovenianess and patriotism. Arguing against the dogma on exclusive knowledge of the nation's essence is equally as unacceptable to the political and academic left as it is to the right; it is tantamount to high treason, invites morally scandalised reactions in both professional and lay circles, and is likely to bring a naive researcher into disfavour with the powers that be, especially those currently entrusted with handing out the national research budget. Open adversity to, and criticism of, the system is sparse and slow in coming as it is obvious that a critical mass within academia actually thrives on the situation (Cf. e.g. Šumi et al. 2008). As for the rest, of course, 'nothing can be done': as any half-baked or openly fraudulent state system is thought of as essentially something to cheat, outsmart and adjust to, not strive to expose and do away with. If you oppose it, you are just querrulous; if you outsmart it, you are a hero.

Post-colonial symptoms

Slovenian nationalist ideology, since the early 1990s, narrates a history and diagnoses a present that essentially constitutes a traumatised post-colonial society. For 1,000 years (indeed, until only ninety years ago), Slovenes have lived enslaved and endangered in a not-so-benevolent Germanic empire, only to be included within another hegemonic kingdom, and after that an oppressive communist regime, their national consciousness awakened late and under the considerable pressure of imminent extinction. The Slovenian language was deemed inferior and only turned into a versatile written code less than 150 years ago. Slovenes possess knowledge about their past and their being or essence that is both sacred and secretive and must be carefully protected and nurtured. Slovenes, especially the 'true' or 'pure' Slovenes, are few in number and are threatened by their low fertility, and the fear of both immigrants and culturally powerful neighbours alike. Above all, the Slovenian nation is low in national self-esteem and lacking in national pride.

It does not go against this national ideology to publicly recognise that Slovenes live in a generalised, all-encompassing predicament, a kind of structural paralysis (Gearing 1971)[19] that allows them to clearly see the problems, while prohibiting any kind of active solution. On the contrary, it is popular to say so. Slovenians seem to clearly recognise the traumatic effects of this state of affairs, and will quote epidemic alcoholism and other substance abuse, the highest suicide rates in the EU, enraged and dangerous driving and rampant domestic violence as proof of this. Curiously, all this implies the need not for an analysis of the present, but for a deeper search into the nation's past, folklore, uniqueness, pureness and autochthony. It is also not unusual to hear that Slovenia is a province and that Slovenians are provincial and backward; like the rednecks from the *Vorstadt* [suburbs]; and the question is how to preserve the national essence while making the nation more cosmopolitan at the same time. Slovenes also have a very low opinion of their own 'national character'. All the classic writers, Primož Trubar included, numerous poets and literary figures, contemporary singers, sociologists and philosophers who are held in the highest regard, alongside the folk wisdom that many a proverbial common man or woman have produced, and still produce the well-known diagnoses of the Slovenian inclination towards envy, maliciousness, pettiness and a tendency to intolerance for everything and anyone who rises above the average. When asked, virtually every Slovene, irrespective of age and other circumstances will agree that living in Slovenia easily becomes stifling and that one needs to 'get out for a breather' from time to time. What comprises a transgression, however, is to suggest that things should be analysed, and changed: this belittles the grandeur of the national plight, and to belittle it is a danger to national survival per se.

As said before, publicly voiced analysis of a phenomenon like ethnic belonging or nationalist ideologies (within Slovenianess) is, in itself, immoral as it dissects the sacred and is read as a (malevolent) view from without. In a classroom setting, explaining the differences between, say, the Barthian uptake on ethnicity as opposed to that of Anthony Smith is consistently read as an inventory of shortcomings in the Slovenian national character and consciousness. The few students who grasp the theoretical plane of analysis will henceforth express a personal disillusionment with their own Slovenianess and, curiously, the belief that deconstruction is not a mere analytical tool, but the actual substitute truth for Slovenian nationalism. Likewise, senior specialists in ethnic studies (regardless of their political persuasion) will take Barth (1969) to have said that the 'culture stuff' is the generating layer of ethnicity; and that Anderson's (1983) notion of imagined (national) communities stands for the indisputable fact that a nation is a truly 'organic' system in the Durkheimian sense. All this goes to show that there exists a systemic and well-interiorised disbelief that something as personally felt and lived, something so precious and sacrosanct, something so often nearly lost, so often fought for, and still so threatened with extinction as Slovenianess could be a social figment, a flimsy thing born in, and sustained by, social relations, but must have a palpable, 'real', essentially material substance. All theorising and modelling, including saying that

things that have been 'socially constructed' are not flimsy and imaginary, but absolutely real, simply falls short of explaining it and is dismissed as unimaginable and somewhat insulting.

Science, the social sciences included, is generally understood as being
a quest for the Truth, not for models of reality. This magnanimous
uptake on the mission of the social sciences produces, seemingly paradoxically, a kind of ecumenical, pro-harmonious disposition towards
social problems and debates, and the ability of the social sciences to
deal with them: things are a little bit white, but also a little bit black,
and predominantly of course, grey. Truly esteemed senior academics
will exploit this position not as analysts, but as wise elders, in their
writings and speeches. Slovenes firmly believe that the truth of anything at all lies in the middle between a categorical denial and categorical acceptance.[20] It is precisely the extra-analytical and the downright
commonsensical that will fascinate both the professional and the lay
public as being truly professional and scientific: it looks very suitably
entangled, complex to the point of being better not to be messed with,
and difficult to master, even as an inventory, all of which sustains the
belief that true social science is essentially mystical, preferably a type of
psychologising with a flair for the unfathomable, bigger than life – as is,
indeed, the very essence or being of Slovenianess, and truly professional
only when not leading to any diagnoses, let alone decisions.

Quickly adopted, however, are the symptoms of all manner of
Western conceptual talk, except that in the Slovenian academic and
political digest, ethnic groups become the equivalent of 'national
minorities' (exclusively those that are recognised constitutionally), the
ethnic boundary, the '(unjust) state border', ethnic belonging and the
'national consciousness' (Šumi 2001). Structurally identical domesti-
cation of meaning befalls, as mentioned above, to Hribar's notion of
national reconciliation. The acceptance of a history is read as the issue
of forgiveness, and the problem of piety the sequence of apologising.
In the same vein, in both lay and professional discourses, 'legality' is
universally understood as 'justness', 'equal rights' as 'equal entitlement'
and 'democracy' as 'pure Slovenianess'.

Having noted that Slovenia presents a clear-cut case of post-colonial
symptoms, let us briefly inspect them in a perspective organised so as to
clearly expose the existing styles of leadership. Slovenia's leadership sets
are, while completely devoid of any kind of aristocratic trait or grace,
perceived as feudal in their imperviousness to responsibility, and are of
short duration as they are created by, and dependent upon an allegiance
with one or the other, the 'traditionalist' or the 'progressivist' bloc in

power; all, however, agree on the sacred and secretive national being or essence that constitutes the entire universe of their dialogue, and sees any potential third voice as a transgression, as coming from outside the perimeter of the community. The two blocs are led by ostensibly 'charismatic' leaders, an adjective that has, in Slovenia, come to mean not a visionary or a person of morally superior character or extreme qualities, or at the very least a person of overpowering charm and energy, but someone who can consolidate a critical mass of uncritical supporters zealous on the issues that underpin the 50–50 division. These leaders oppose each other on a political and interpersonal plane in a manner that frequently supersedes any type of political opposition by far and borders on interpersonal hatred. The latter is a mark of the forcefulness of righteous persuasions they represent, and is functional in feeding the public's aforementioned schizophrenic perception that there is an unnamed 'true game' behind the visible and the declarative. According to Močnik (2000):

> In this schizophrenic public consciousness, one could see the definitive sign of the religious structure of contemporary politics. Since there are no ideological differences, the pseudo-political discourse concentrates on 'persons' who are, in turn, presented in the manner of a hagiographic discourse. We think we are reading political news, but we are in fact reading the lives and times of the saints. We think we are watching a political chronicle, but are in fact watching the Acts of the Apostles. In real saints, schizophrenia is covert within a narrative streamlined through time: before they become saints, they were sinners just like us. The more they sinned early on, the greater their sainthood later on. The political lives of saints, however, lack this sequencing in time, as all whose lives are narrated are saints. They are beatified because they are part of the *nomenklatura*: they have already risen to sainthood, but still sin. Their schizophrenia therefore is not covert, but the structure is nevertheless hagiographic.

A complementarily organised perspective should cast an eye on the public that, in turn, gazes upon these leadership styles and repertoires. As said before, to secure a position of authority, especially in a public career that should be based upon professionalism and neutrality, one is well advised never to present a view on Slovenianess that can be interpreted as being external to the national community, and to hone to perfection commonsensical wisdom rather than stark professionalism. This stance is mirrored in the arena of the general public, albeit in a more down-to-earth fashion: the behaviour of the political leadership is seldom judged against a goal, a programme or an aspiration: these are met with ready-made cynicism. Rather, they are judged in comparison with the competing pole's record. In a clearly Mafioso manner, all corporate bodies, political parties and public and private institutions, even down to the level of alternative programmes in kindergartens, are seen as clearly 'belonging' to one or the other pole, one or the other prominent godfathers, either through consanguine or politically congenial lineages. Being knowledgeable about these lineages is an essential part of local social intelligence. Gossip on belonging is rampant and reminds one of classical anthropological accounts of small-scale postcolonial tribal societies. It would seem that while people seldom talk to each other, they do incessantly talk about each other. Again in what seems to be a paradox, this 'talk-about-everyone' approach produces small, enclosed circles that never seem to communicate directly. A governmental office will, for example, commit itself to organising a public event, and will publicly lament that they lack specialists for the topic. They will, as a rule, be unaware that, perhaps just a block away, there is an entire institution filled to the brim with exactly the sort of specialists they need. However, it will take a chance acquaintance, and a judgement that these people out there are 'OK' in a political and familial sense, before any professional contact will be innitiated. In a similar manner, any public institution will strive to build its own cadres across a wide span before it will consider linking up with another institution for anything, whether it be from cleaning or accounting to professional cooperation. On an interpersonal level, these enclosed circles are anything but stable; rather, they are in a constant personnel flux that is most often triggered by what looks like interpersonal disagreements on the basis of a principled dispute, but is structurally in fact a small-scale war of dominance. Thus it is difficult to follow who is currently allied to whom, and who was so until yesterday, but is no longer: another challenge for anyone aspiring to perfection in local social intelligence.

The actors in these personnel-shifting disputes will fall short of any structural understanding of their positions: they will most likely personalise the evil, which is not difficult: in Slovenia, as in any small tribal community described in anthropology, one is not judged on what one actually says or does, but rather on what is rumoured about one. Since the beginning of the mandate of Mr Janša's government, these ethnographically idyllic circumstances have been, demonstrated on the national scene with what can be described as a disillusioning clarity for the interested onlooker.

To the analyst, perhaps the most pressing question is whether this period of the first right-wing government in independent Slovenia means a radical consolidation of the constituent 50–50 national divide, and, if so, what makes it so opportune.

The inability to heal: A social stratum gone national

Our final question, therefore, is: Why are these self-perpetuating structures so diligently, and hopelessly, maintained in Slovenia? At the beginning of this chapter, we posed three questions: What kind of state has Slovenia become? Is Slovenia's period of transition over? Is Slovenia a Western democracy? Obviously, the answer to the first question is that: Slovenia is a state that continues to accommodate a heavily traumatised, post-colonial society. It can be described as a secluded island, a 'Garbo nationalism' (Zimmermann 1995),[21] or a reservation that is organised around a fiercely maintained, highly idiosyncratic insider discourse. As for the third question, our answer is by definition a negative one. So, Slovenia is not yet a Western democracy. However, an answer to the second question about Slovenia being considered as a Western democracy can at least be attempted.

In September 2007, over 500 journalists published a petition stating that the entire media industry was subject to censorship and political pressure. They accused the prime minister of limiting the freedom of the media, and expressed their deep concerns, given that Slovenia was about to preside over the European Union:

> What kind of message is given to the citizens of the EU when they are under the presidency of a country where pressures on journalists are self-evident and in which an authoritarian mode of governing is growing stronger, at the expense of democracy and the freedom of press? Such a presidency is a worrisome omen for the present, let alone for the future of the European Union.

The letter was distributed to several hundred addresses in the EU, including all member state governments. In response, on 19 November 2007, the prime minister staged an all-night soliloquy in parliament in which he presented numerous instances of the negative disposition of the press towards his party, government and his own person, and accused the petitioners of a lack of national loyalty. He believed that, instead of trying to clear the air at home, they were turning to foreigners and openly shaming Slovenia even as the latter was preparing to preside over these same 'foreigners'. While the prime minister would be more than justified to doubt the general state of professionalism of Slovenian journalists; he focused instead on the attacks against his person, party and government, and used these issues, in a dramatic manner, to demand a vote of confidence from parliament that his coalition should remain in total control. It completely escaped him that, in order to maintain the face of democracy, he should have refrained from commenting on the press in the first place.

Likewise, Slovenia's membership in and presidency of the EU – this bright goal of Slovenian independence – was presented as a plot of 'we Slovenes' facing the 'foreigners' with whom one is on one's best behaviour: a stance that was, in turn, presented as a matter of natural consensus of all Slovenes, and the main purpose of the Slovenian national interest.

The above episode was but one in a series of attempts by the present government to fight what they perceived to be the 'sick condition' of Slovenianess. Their mandate was preceded by the aforementioned Assembly for the Republic by a few months. This forum set out to comment and act upon all the historical and social woes referred to above. The forum launched the new *mot essentiel* of the coalition: 'relaxedness'. Obviously inspired by (yet another) Heideggerian notion of *Gelassenheit* [calmness] (cf. Vezjak 2007), 'relaxedness' stood to mean the final end of Communist oppression (of which the LDS governments had been but a continuation). This realisation of true democracy, or true Slovenianess meant the release of the creative energies of all. It also meant a newly found nationwide *joie de vivre*; a radical change in the proverbial Slovenian melancholic disposition of character, in other words, the end of 'structural paralysis'. What was released in great proportions, however, was an unrestrained public and not-so-public campaign against people perceived as belonging to the 'other bloc', peppered with racism, personal disqualifications and moralising harangues, and a flood of changes of personnel in the entire public sector that has since been referred to as Prime Minister Janša's 'tsunami of the cadres'.

Although expected and contextualised on the grounds of the immediate political circumstances of the Slovenian public, Prime Minister Janša's government may have merely contributed the latest round to a historic series of events that have marked political Slovenianess since its beginnings in the latter half of the nineteenth century. The permanency of the 50–50 division is, in this light, much less a matter of either Slovenian 'national character' or 'plight' than the consequence of repetitive, very nearly rhythmic instances of the decapitation of incipient national elites. The 1920s brought a radical reshuffling after a bloody war and the dissolution of the Habsburg Empire. Twenty years later, in the 1940s, this was succeeded by a second radical reshuffling; this time in massive proportions. During the 1970s, the original Communist elites were first substantially challenged; and, during the 1980s and 1990s, their successors had to radically reorient their priorities and techniques, and accept the sharing of political space with the incipient ideology of heterogeneous elites. If anything, Prime Minister Janša's 'tsunami' merely happened a little early, given the twenty to thirty years rhythm of these decapitations.

The historical origins of political Slovenianess were located in class consciousness rather than national consciousness within the Habsburg Empire. Slovenian speakers were a more-or-less homogenised stratum of the Empire's population, who were to be found predominantly in an agrarian sector made up of small-scale owners. There was virtually no nobility exploiting Slovenian cultural repertoires, and very few middle classes of any kind before 1940. In the aftermath of the Second World War, the remnants of the German, Italian, Jewish and Slovenian middle classes (i.e. those with substantial ownership of land, industries, and real estate) were ferociously eradicated, expelled or disowned. The 1980s witnessed the triumph of a 'civil society' (cf. Pupavac 2006: 119) that was hardly backed by any substantial power or resources other than intellectual; it can be said that despite its ride on the wave of the Europe-wide anti-communist drive, the Slovenian demolition of the old regime was essentially a grass-roots movement whose commitment to political democratisation, and the institutionalising of a Western-style democracy, was truly believed in by only a thin layer of the leadership of Slovenian 'civil society'.[22] Consequently, in the early 1990s an uneasy feeling spread, that the proverbial Slovenian 'structural paralysis' style of communal and political existence was an invincible 'culture' in Marshall Sahlins' sense: no matter what the formal nature of the political system, be it feudal, capitalist or communist, the pendulum of change will invariably lose its momentum in short order and bring Slovenianess back to its paralysing equilibrium; indeed, 'nothing ever changes'; 'everything remains the same' (and 'nothing can be done about it'). The fact that new things will quickly begin to happen in old ways was variously attributed to the general corruptibility of any new thing per se, to the inertia of 'communism', the effect of 'Balkanisation', 're-Catholicisation', a 'serfdom mentality' and so forth, depending on the bloc affiliation of the speaker. Again, repetitive stabilisations into 'paralysis' were not, and are not, seen for what they obviously are: a structural necessity of the viability of the Slovenian national community.

While the above history is seen as a dramatic and heroic national 'plight', structurally it is little other than a history of continuous and radical efforts at preventing class differentiation within Slovenianess. Historically, perhaps the most consistent corroborator of the class uniformity of Slovenes has been the Catholic Church – incidentally, also the big winner in the ongoing denationalisation processes of property. All historic formations and attempts at social stratification were in retrospect labelled essentially anti-Slovenian. The nineteenth-century liberals were ostensibly pro-German; the Second World War Partisans were pro-Russian (and before that, part of the Jewish-Communist conspiracy). The post-1945 communist elites were distinctly anti-bourgeois and increasingly pro-pure-Slovenian despite their sworn working-class internationalism; the post-1990 LDS was seen as being pro-communist, or rather a post-communist continuation, especially with the notion of a Balkanising element. The common denominator of these incipient elite-eliminating sequences, and the internal logic of this political history, is the eternal 'return' to a (re)conceptualisation of a variant of pure Slovenianess. Presented as the 'good or justified nationalism' of an ever-endangered national community, it displays every trait of the merciless grip of class-solidarity on its members, a drive that produces social consequences on a par with a number of post-colonial situations, and sharing with them a number of discernible symptoms.

As we draw into the argument the post-colonial but not the class-solidarity mechanisms that no doubt exist in many a Western national community as well as in an equally merciless way, the critical difference in play is the claim to ethnic national distinction. Just like Slovenianess, post-colonial populations lay critical claim to a difference in origin: it is the critical criterion of the 'deep well of history' that distinguishes the construction of the ethnic, impassable difference, from any difference that does not lay claim to origin, the cultural or passable difference (cf. Šumi 2001, 2004). At least in Western societies there exists the uniform notion that class difference is minuscule and can be surpassed in each individual's life path. Indeed, there is in place the ideology that presents breaking away from one's class of birth as a life goal in terms of education, equal opportunity and meritocracy, and a pseudo-legalistic system that bases the very gist of democracy as a political system in this allegedly systemic possibility. 'Ethnicity', on the other hand, even when carefully presented in terms of 'culture', for example,[23] rather than in any of the plethora of pseudo-biological terms, is seen as a matter of origin, ancestry and histories so wide apart that they do not join either in the relevant past or the foreseeable future. The notions of 'class' and 'ethnicity' as they are lived and understood in the Western experience and folk theories obviously exist in a state of paradox: while the pseudo-biological ascription of 'ethnicity' is obviously empirically much more porous and much less of an obstacle to climbing the social ladder in a Western nation state than the ideology would have it. The mark of 'social class' is empirically much more rigid and forbidding in terms of individual advancement, despite the ideologies of democracy that sustains it.

There are many arguments in favour of the thesis that Slovenianess is indeed a case of a 'social class gone nation'.[24] Since class differentiation such as one could envision it as akin to the process of the splitting of cells to form diverse colonies is prohibited and stifled in regular intervals, the social differentiation necessary for a meaningful social dialogue, even such as it exists in Slovenia, is created in the approximation of what one could compare to an internal cancer growth. In Močnik's words (2002), the political layer sprouts: 'clientele networks that spread like cancer', but remain, unlike global capitalist elites, 'a horde of profiteering individuals constantly at war with each other':

> An anthropological hypothesis would have it that [they are] a polysegmented assembly with hierarchical clans whose internal cohesion is assured by a little bit of bribery, and a little bit of blackmail. They are only able to back their mutual interests in a negative way, against the rest of society: for instance, with a high degree of mutual tolerance.

There is no doubt that a living community that depends on imagining its boundaries needs to maintain standpoints and opinions that exist within an entire spectrum from complete accord to total denial. In Slovenia, this spectrum is reduced to the 50–50 equilibrium; precisely because the fanning-out of issues and opinions is starkly controlled. The inner splitting and growth, however, is astounding even in the most formal aspects of national organisation: thus for instance, Slovenia's 20,000 square kilometres and 2 million people are divided into no less than 210 counties (which also means 210 mayors and 210 county councils), and are threatened to be further compartmentalised into ten, fourteen or more regions. Out of a total of 838,005 employed people in Slovenia, in January 2007, more than 150,000 worked in the public sector.[25]

Finally, what does all this mean in terms of democracy and transition, the latter standing primarily for the reintroduction of capitalism? Recently, many theoreticians and commentators have argued that since the end of the Cold War it has become increasingly obvious that capitalism can exist and prosper in virtually any kind of social system – the very notion of globalisation testifies to that. Picking up on the issue and commenting on contemporary China, Žižek (2007) demonstrates the fallacy of the inseparability of the conceptual duo, capitalism-democracy, and poses the fatal question: what if (Western-style) democracy is no longer: '... a condition, and the agent of the economic progress, but an obstacle to it?' (Žižek 2008: 7). All possible objections as to the validity of this question and its underlying premises (What is progress? What is the economy outside social relations and values? What is democracy, and where does it actually exist and function?) sound merely pedantic in the face of another possibility, that Western democracy is but a historically localised phenomenon of state-homogenised population conglomerates, that have existed since the late nineteenth century.[26] In other words: what if the economy, neo-liberalism and globalisation are, when it comes to the form and quality of societal relations, just imprecise names for global Slovenianisation? This example of a social stratum gaining the political status of a nation state in a whim of the historic unfolding of events that came to its national sovereignty, in other words, the solidification of its communal perimeter, with unbreakable mechanisms of social stratum, and a class-like enforced solidarity ready-made?

Notes

I would like to thank Janine Wedell for several sessions of very elucidating brainstorming on the post-socialist condition; to Braco Rotar and Taja Kramberger for sharing their views on Slovenian national formation and history; and to Damir Josipovič, Duška Kneževič Hočevar, Hannah Starman and Cirila Toplak for their data, insights, ideas, comments and suggestions offered upon reading the earlier drafts of this piece.

1. In Slovene, the plebiscite question employed two adverbs: *samostojen* (literally, 'self-standing') and *neodvisen* (literally, 'independent'). No less than 93 per cent (1,361,738) of the total registered voters (1,457,020) took part in the plebiscite, of which 1,289,369 voters voted in favour of independence. Data taken from the Election Committee of the Republic of Slovenia's official report published in the Official Gazette of the RS, No. 2/1991.
2. Following the reshuffle of the rightist coalition parities, Janez Drnovšek's first government fell and was replaced by the government of the new

Coalition of Slovenia led by Andrej Bajuk, from 3 May until 17 November 2000. These six odd months were the only interruption in the twelve-year run of the LDS-dominated governmental coalitions, from 1992 to 2004.

3. The DEMOS (Democratic Opposition of Slovenia) coalition of the political parties formed after 1989 came to power after the first multi-party elections on 8 April 1990 with 54 per cent of the votes cast across the so-called parties of the communist continuity. The main task of this government was to prepare Slovenia for secession from Yugoslavia. The DEMOS government fell in April 1992, whereupon the LDS began its twelve-year rule.

4. Lojze Peterle (b. 1948), the candidate supported by the ruling party and all other rightist coalition partners, was prime minister of the DEMOS government, and minister of foreign affairs between January 2003 and October 2004, and June and November 2000. Since 2004, he has been one of Slovenia's seven MPs in the European Parliament. Danilo Türk (b. 1952), the candidate supported by the Social Democrats (SD), the strongest opposition party, and the Zares party, an offshoot of the old LDS, had an early academic career in law, and has been affiliated with UN diplomacy since the mid-1980s. The peak of his diplomatic career was when he held the position of the UN Assistant Secretary-General for Political Affairs between 2000 and 2005. As such, he enjoyed little popularity as he was hardly known to the electorate. He won the elections in the second round by no less than 68.3 per cent of votes after the third candidate, Mitja Gaspari, ex-finance minister and Central Bank Governor, was eliminated in the first round. Gaspari's voters obviously transferred their preference to Türk in the second round. Peterle's defeat was widely interpreted as a popular vote against his governmental policies.

5. In 2005, Slovenian citizens had 500 lawsuits filed in Strasbourg's European Court of Human Rights that pertained to the breach of Article 6 of the European Convenant on the protection of human rights and basic freedoms (the right to fair trial), and Article 13 (efficient court procedures in the home state). In 2006, Slovenia was obliged to pay the plaintiffs €84.800 in damages and €23.840 in trial expenses. These expenses pertained to only 24 out of 500 cases filed (cf. e.g. http://24ur.com/bin/article.php?article_id=3073141; www.mladina.si/tednik/200551/clanek/nar-profil--ursa_marn/).   In response to the European Court's opinion that the right to fair and timely trial is seriously breached in Slovenia, the current Minister of Justice Lovro Šturm devised and launched Programme Lukenda in 2005, named in honour of the first plaintiff to win his trial in Strasbourg, the miner Franjo Lukenda, in order to speed up court procedures (cf. e.g www.mp.gov.si/si/novinarsko_sredisce/novica/browse/17/article/744/2118/?cHash=2e50d49a16).   The success of the project, however, remains uncertain, as there are simply too many dysfunctions in the judicial system.

6. Primož Trubar (1508–1586) was a Slovenian Protestant reformer, the founder and first superintendent of the Protestant Church of the then Slovenian Lands within the Hapsburg Empire. He wrote the first books in Slovenian, the *Catechismus* and *Abecedarium* (printed in 1550, in Tübingen).

7. The Slovenia United programme dates back to the revolutionary year 1848. It demanded that Slovenian speakers from all Slovenian Lands of the Habsburg Empire unite in a separate kingdom under the monarchy.

8. For a more detailed analysis of definitions of the 'Slovenianess' of an individual that are widely shared by both lay people and social scientists that specialise in the home tradition of ethnic studies called the Slovenian national question, see Šumi 2001.
9. The Constitution clearly states, in Article 3, that: 'Slovenia is the state of all its [female and male] citizens', but also, that it is: 'founded on the inalienable right of the Slovenan nation to self-determination'. Furthermore, Articles 5 and 64 specifically name such persons who can enjoy special political rights in Slovenia. These are Hungarians and Italians along the Slovenian borders, and Slovenes without citizenship, all of whom are described as people with 'autochthonous' rights. The position of Slovenes without citizenship is determined by a special law that the Constitution refers to, which was passed in 2006.
10. In her concluding paragraphs to the cited essay, Hribar (1987: 103) formulates her reconciliation theses in terms of a personal revelation amid utter despair over the Communist monopoly on the truth: 'Is death really the only way out from this closed circle? ... Is it impossible to live peacefully and normally without being humble as a serf, and mute? The doubts, the suffering! Then, a kind of self-defence spontaneously rose in me: It cannot be so? It is not possible that it can **only** be so! ...'
11. Grigorij Rožman (1883–1959) was inaugurated as Bishop of Ljubljana in 1930. A zealous anti-communist and anti-Semite, he pledged loyalty to the Italian occupation forces in 1941, and celebrated a mass for the Home Guard prior to their oath of allegiance to Hitler at the Central Stadium in Ljubljana on 20 April 1944. In 1945, he fled to the British zone in Austria, then to Switzerland, and subsequently died in Cleveland, USA. In 1946, he was tried *in absentia* at the military court in Ljubljana on charges of collaboration, found guilty and sentenced to eighteen years' forced labour and ten years' suspension of civil rights. On 1 October 2007, the Slovenian Supreme Court annulled the sentence on the basis of procedural mistakes, and returned the case to the District Court of Ljubljana.
12. The doyen of Slovenian politics and academia, Dr France Bučar, ex-partisan, law professor, first Speaker of the Parliament, one of the authors of the Slovenian Constitution, made a similar summary of Slovenian political history in his interview (Veselinovič and Žerdin 2008). His career is exemplary of a 'critical mind' with shifting loyalties that nevertheless remains insistently within the confines of the national debate on the self, as will be discussed below.
13. The term 'Erased' (*Izbrisani* in Slovenian) pertains to 18,305 people of former-Yugoslav provenance who were, until 26 February 1992, residents of Slovenia. On that date, the Ministry of Interior of the Republic of Slovenia transferred them to the status of foreigners. These people, predominantly of Serbian origin, failed to file for Slovenian citizenship in the prescribed time following Independence. The error of the state, however, was in the fact that the register of residents included citizens only, a state of affairs that the Constitutional Court recognised as illegal in 1999. Despite this verdict, the problem remains unresolved, and was meanwhile taken to the European Court. The Erased remain the central issue at the heart of the massive Slovenian disregard for basic human rights that is most often quoted in European as well as US State Department and NGO reports.

14.   *Zakon o romski skupnosti v Republiki Sloveniji*/The Roma Community Act was enforced in March 2007.

15.   The term is nearly interchangeable with the Slovenian variant, *samobitnost*, literally, something possessing an exclusive 'being/essence of its own', which carries a pronounced sentimental elevation. A corroborative term is also *narodna bit*, the 'nation's being/essence', another common expression very likely domesticated for public usage from Heideggerian readings of the current prophets of Slovenianess.

16.   Decision No. 844 of the Constitutional Court, 1998. Official Gazette of the RS, No. 20/1998: 1308.

17.   The actual president of the Slovenian Academy of Sciences and Arts, Dr Boštjan Žekš, systematically advances the thesis that Slovenia cannot hope to sustain so much science, and so many sciences. A mathematician and physicist, Dr Žekš is categorically much more in favour of the hard sciences and technology than the arts and humanities. See, for instance, Bošnjak 2005 (www.delo.si/index.php?sv_path=43,49&so=Delo&da=20051103&ed=0&pa=18&ar=bd3302cbf7b68a33fe78b86770368b8f04&fromsearch=1).

18.   The SICRIS (Slovenian Current Research Information System, http://sicris.izum.si/default.aspx?lang=eng) is an integral database listing research organisations, projects, programmes and of course researchers. The special feature discussed above is the so-called 'representative' bibliographies drawn from the national bibliographic service COBISS (www.cobiss.si/) database that lists all published works of registered researchers. Thus for instance, the COBISS database currently lists 261 documented works to my name, while the SICRIS database quotes a meagre eight as being representative. I am completely at a loss to explain why these works are listed and not others.

19.   Frederick Gearing has authored one of the earliest works on ethnicity with his book *The Face of the Fox*, in which he describes the 'unbelievability' (of the Fox in the eyes of their non-native neighbours) and of the all-pervasive 'structural paralysis', the insistence that things remain as they always were, that the Fox seemed to insist upon. Although clearly Eurocentric in its stance, his is a classical description of a traumatised post-colonial communal stasis.

20.   Commenting on the brief episode of Bajuk's government, Rastko Močnik (2000) positioned the 'demagogical value' of the mythology of professionalism in the midst between the political right and left: 'The state is ... imagined as a boat: it can tilt to the left and to the right, but it will sail best when upright. In this middle position, there lies what is called "professionalism".'

21.   The last US Ambassador to Yugoslavia, Warren Zimmermann, coined this phrase in regard to the Slovenian stance in the then post-secession negotiations: Slovenes were said to practise a 'just-leave-me-alone, (Greta) Garbo' style of nationalism.

22.   Although this piece cannot lay claim to a geographically broader or comparative analysis, similar histories may have been the lot of all Yugoslav constituent 'nations and nationalities' since the mid-nineteenth century, and perhaps of some of Eastern Europe's ex-Habsburg nations as well. The Balkan Wars of the 1990s could therefore be seen in a light devoid of the

standard 'inter-ethnic' interpretation, should one undertake to examine the class aspect of post-1989 situations in respective Yugoslav republics.

23. This essentially goes to say that the recent sociological observations of folk perceptions of ethnic difference in Europe from 'racial' to 'cultural' may not be extremely well thought out. Whether people put their faith in the colour of the skin as a main impassable difference, or demonise 'cultural' difference (in religion, ideology, communal ways of life, or even in the popularised versions of the Huntingtonian 'civilisation') is irrelevant from the point of view of how these racisms behave socially. All these perceptions are imbued with the notion of a categorical non-compatibility, the notion that is critical for the formation of categorical, impassable, ethnic difference.

24. Slovenian historians certainly corroborate this perception: the Slovenian 'national question' as it unfolded by the end of the nineteenth century is uniformly seen as a sort of irregularity, historical luck, a victory in the face of near failure (for a summary in lay terms, see Zajc 2006). The majority of historians, however, see this 'luck' in terms of 'fate' rather than 'chance', thus preventing themselves from a meaningful structural analysis.

25. Data are from the webpage of the Statistical Office of the Republic of Slovenia, www.stat.si/novica_prikazi.aspx?id=771.

26. This is a reference to states that had to come to terms with a well-diversified population in terms of social classes and their diverse interests, consciousness and goals (and means of disciplining their members), to begin with.

11
No Monuments, No History, No Past: Monuments and Memory

Božidar Jezernik

Public monuments, that is to say, statues or groups of statues designed in memory of a specific historical event or person and placed in a public space, form an important – perhaps even necessary – inventory of the modern nation. In addition to schools, museums and theatres, they represent the official culture of a particular state, and help to construct the collective memory of its inhabitants. By presenting specific personalities and events they determine which among them are of broader social significance, and thus are influential in determining how individual social communities evaluate their own history. 'Until recently,' suggests David Lowenthal, 'most monuments were exhortations to imitate the virtues they commemorated; they reminded people what to believe and how to behave' (Lowenthal 1985: 322).

The Ancient Greeks, for a 'memorial' used the word μνμείο, which derives from the word μνήμη, which means 'memory' (Wenham 1977: 17). Similarly, in Latin, the word *monumentum* (hence the Italian and Spanish word *monumento* and the English and French *monument*) is linked to the word *moneo*, 'I recall', while the German expression *Denkmal* is associated with *denken*, 'to think' (Brown 1905: 18; see also Čopič 2000: 17). The link between *spomenik* ('monument') and *spomin* ('memory') is also evident in Slovenian and in other Slavic languages.

A monument to a specific person or event, placed in a public space, serves as a materialisation of the social memory of a particular social community; this is, indeed, a fundamental element of the identity of individuals and society. Without memory, we do not know either who we are or from where we come; and if we do not know this, then we also do not know where we are going. At the same time, however, the monument and the space in which it stands are both living their life in changing times. With the new generations they share a changing political fate: historical changes may have as a consequence a change in the symbolic significance both of the monument and of the person it represents. Political symbols, namely, reflect and represent the prevailing ideology and its changes, therefore, particularly following revolutionary upheavals, it may well happen that particular monuments no longer harmonise with the altered historical and ideological context within a specific social environment.

Symbolic links with the past

As a rule, resurgent national and ethnic alliances require symbolic links with the past which serves as a living spring supplying the essential elements of national mythologies (see Lowenthal 1985: 396; 1996: 58). During the nineteenth century, Slovenian nationalism was emphatically apolitical and concentrated its efforts on the cultural field, giving priority to men of letters such as the 'first Slovenian poet', Valentin Vodnik (1758–1819), 'foremost Slovenian poet', France Prešeren (1800–1848), and the 'creator of the Slovenian written language', Primož Trubar (1508–1585). The famous American war correspondent, William Shirer, who visited Ljubljana on 10 March 1938, called it 'a town to shame the whole world'. He said that Ljubljana was 'full of statues and not one of them of a soldier. Only poets and thinkers have been so honoured' (1988: 95). Shirer cannot have realised that the Slovenian liberal bourgeoisie were using culture as part of a strategy to assure people who had no political definition before 1848 that they did, indeed, enjoy a national identity. Likewise, it seems, he jumped to conclusions about Ljubljana's statues before he had seen all, for up to the end of the 1880s the most popular statue in the city was that of the Austrian field marshal, Count Radecký (1766–1858). Marshal Radecký had close links with Slovenia: he was married to Countess Franziska Strasold, a native of Carniola, and inherited considerable property there; he thus acquired Carniolan citizenship in 1807. Marshal Radecký was very popular with Slovenian soldiers who placed full reliance upon him. His exploits were celebrated in folk songs like, for example:

Radecký is a real gentleman,
he will prevail every time, everywhere... (Lampe 1892: 324)

In 1852 the people of Ljubljana erected a life-size statue of Count Radecký in marshal's uniform in Zvezda Park. Six years later, the municipality decided that this statue was not really a worthy monument, because it was only a cast. They therefore commissioned the famous Viennese sculptor Anton Fernkorn to produce a bust of Radecký. The full-length statue was stored in the municipal depot where it remained until it was re-erected in front of Tivoli Castle in 1882. The costs of restoring the monument were not insignificant but with it Ljubljana regained its first representative public monument and its citizens were fond of it.

The ideals of official memory must be enacted in ceremonies and commemorations if they are to last (Shackel 2001: 660). Accordingly, Radecký's monument was made a focal point for many events and acts that extolled the capital of the Duchy of Carniola and symbolised its loyalty to the Habsburg crown. On the other hand, this ceremonial role also made the monument a venue for various merry bands of students who played many night-time pranks there. In one of these, they piled all the benches in Zvezda Park one on top of the other around the Radecký's statue, making a ladder onto it. Two of their number climbed up and sat astride each of the old Austrian field marshal's shoulders and slapped his face from either side. The rest of the company made an appreciative audience. Of course they all ran away when they heard the police coming (Tuma 1937: 62).

Public memory is more a reflection of present political and social relations than a true reconstruction of the past. As conditions change socially, politically and ideologically, the collective memory of the past also changes (Teski and Climo 1995: 2). That is why after a revolutionary coup, certain monuments no longer fit the new historical and ideological context of a society. The demolition of such monuments is usually an aspect or even a trigger of historic change. When democratic systems were introduced into most European countries the old symbols of monarchy were discarded (see e.g. Firth 1973: 328–367). The most spectacular example of the demolition of old monuments and the erection of new ones took place when Bastille was stormed in 1789, marking the beginning of the French Revolution. Correspondingly, Radecký's destiny as a Slovenian hero was short-lived. During the night of 30 December 1918, two 'patriots' pulled down the statue in front of Tivoli Castle and the same night his bust was removed from Zvezda Park.

Displaying the past

While a succession of 'national monuments' constantly changed the appearance of nineteenth and twentieth-century Ljubljana, their principal function was to forge the new collective identity supposedly handed down by history. The main stages in this identity were, first, modernisation led by the Slovenian liberal bourgeoisie, and second, half a century later, communist revolution. Both were radical breaks with history.

Nationality is a political phenomenon, especially when it is used in a struggle for power with the others who are identified as culturally alien (Mach 1993: 14). If the proponents of national 'awakening' were to construct Slovenian nation, they had to stand for something, culturally and politically: this inevitably meant distinguishing Slovenians from the non-Slovenians, and building a wall between them. Thus, for instance, even 'Carniola's biggest son', Anastasius Grün (Anton Alexander Graf Auersperg), as the nineteenth-century historian Peter von Radics (1885: 19) termed him, became a stranger in a land where his family lived for centuries; today he is almost completely forgotten.

Accordingly, 'national monuments' did not simply put history on display; they were instrumental in creating a particular kind of history for the public and were lending that history their own legitimising stamp and justifying the claims of the Slovenian elite. They gave the outward appearance of a new image of Slovenian community, a community with a particular historical mission and rights in relation to other groups. The men of letters were valuable not only as symbolic proof of Slovenia's place in the family of civilised nations, but also as symbols of transcendence, able to displace attention from political conflicts within the group and project them on those outside it. The developing Slovenian bourgeoisie, which was not strong enough to compete with its German rivals, endeavoured to contain the German *Drang nach Ost* with the support of their 'brethren', the (Southern) Slavs. As a Slovenian member of the Yugoslav Committee in London during the First World War, Bogumil Vošnjak, put it: 'The Slovenes are Jugoslavs. Their fate is inextricably bound up with that of all other Jugoslavs, and there can be no future for them apart from the rest of their race' (Vosnjak 1917: 29).

It was mainly political ambitions that made Mayor Hribar join those in favour of the erection of the monument to the Austrian emperor Franz Joseph I (1830–1916). In 1895, the year of the great earthquake, when the emperor visited the devastated city, the city authorities of Ljubljana decided to erect a monument in the capital of the province as a 'visible and permanent expression of gratitude for the emperor's kindness in visiting them' (Hribar 1903: 1). In 1903 a competition was launched which only Slovenian and Croatian sculptors could enter and which was won by Svetoslav Peruzzi. Peruzzi's design for the monument was very simple: a bust of the emperor and a kneeling female figure representing Ljubljana were placed on a prismatic pedestal.

Many contemporary experts maintained that the city authorities, that is their committee, opted simply for the cheapest offer which was, as *Slovenec* (The Slovenian), the daily with the largest circulation, put it on 7 January 1904, 'not monumental at all'. On 8 March 1904 the same newspaper complained bitterly:

> We are a small nation with an unfortunate fate. Adversaries will not recognise our literature, and now we are about to put a weapon in their hands ourselves, so that they can also reject our art, by refusing a good work that would be our pride – and by erecting statues that will speak of our poverty to the future generations. It would be better if we engraved all our monuments with the following words: It is miserable, because such a meagre sum was allotted for its making! Art is no exception: aut Caesar aut nihil!

The unveiling of the emperor's monument was lavishly celebrated in the presence of the representatives of ecclesiastic, secular and military authorities, the Ljubljana municipal council, the fire brigade, the philharmonic and the wardens of the judicial administration. A military brass band played. The event was also attended by Prince Bishop Jeglič, who was 'repelled' by the thought of finding himself in the company of 'supporters of the Liberal Party', but he could not risk 'appearing unpatriotic' (Jeglič 1908: 47).

The following year, the emperor's monument in front of the court featured significantly in the election campaign. On 17 April 1911 Dr Šuštaršič addressed a rally of the Slovenian People's Party in the Union Hall. According to a report summing up his speech in *Slovenec* the following day, monuments were a clear indication of the impact of the Liberal Party in Ljubljana:

> Just look at the emperor's monument! If I were the government, I would prohibit such a monument to our emperor. (Hear, hear! It's a scandal!) This monument shames the emperor! (Hear, hear! It is true!) Is that the emperor? I once knew an old porter who looked like that 'emperor,' placed by the Liberals in front of the court. (Laughter.) If our grandchildren see that monument, they will get a completely false idea of what our emperor looked like. One of the first proposals to the future municipal council is to remove the 'emperor's' statue that now stands in front of the court, and place it in the museum. In Hribar's corner in the museum! (Loud laughter.) A sign will have to be placed below the statue that will say: This

'emperor' was made in Ljubljana when Ivan Hribar was the mayor. (Very loud laughter.)

Another public monument to Emperor Franz Joseph I was erected at Ljubljana Castle during the First World War to mark the emperor's eighty-sixth birthday. In the circumstances, the monument instilled even profounder patriotism. On 18 August 1916 *Slovenec* issued a long report on the celebration in Ljubljana and the unveiling of the emperor's monument, which took place 'without special pomp but with profound inner emotion and great pride. Yes, pride in the fact that we are Austrians, sons of a country that lovingly cares for all its nations like no other.' The mayor of Ljubljana, Dr Ivan Tavčar, placed the monument in the municipal care and stated in Slovenian and German:

> On behalf of the provincial and diocesan capital of Ljubljana I declare that our municipality hereby takes this monument, erected on its land, into its care and I pledge that the city will until the end of time lovingly and conscientiously guard this symbol of dynastic loyalty of the population of this duchy.

As argued by Shackel (2001: 657), public memory associated with highly visible objects is constantly reconstructed, changed and challenged. Accordingly, 'the indescribable joy' which filled Slovenian hearts during the First World War dried up as soon as hostilities were over: anonymous patriots tore down both imperial monuments.

Redefining the past

The First World War left masses of dead and wounded. The bloodbath ended in major changes to the geopolitical map of Europe, one of the most visible of which was the collapse of the Dual Monarchy. This put an end to any gratitude towards the emperor: it was decided that the monument should be pulled down and replaced, in 1926, with a monument to Fran Miklošič (1813–1891), who was regarded as the greatest grammarian of the nineteenth century. This famous scholar of Slavonic languages was particularly popular among Slovenians after the war because during his lifetime he had worked for the union of all Slovenians and for linguistic equality in schools and offices. But the elders of Ljubljana, for reasons of economy, decided simply to set the bust of Miklošič on the pedestal which had originally supported the memorial to the emperor, whose name was obliterated. The stonecutter chiselled a new inscription. What remained on the pedestal of the Miklošič memorial were two imperial eagles and the kneeling woman holding the coat of arms of the city of Ljubljana in one hand and in the other a laurel wreath which she raises towards the figure above her. On the back of the memorial is a bas-relief of victims of the earthquake in 1895 (Čopič et al. 1991: 84).

After the disintegration of Austria-Hungary, the greater part of Slovenian territory was incorporated into a new state, the Kingdom of Serbs, Croats and Slovenians, which united the majority of the southern Slavs. In a country shared with their Slav compatriots, Slovenians found it easier to breathe, for after many centuries of domination they were free from Austria-Hungary, now referred to as the 'prison-house of nations'. They concluded with satisfaction that the new state had not only liberated them from a 'centuries-long yoke' but had also made their ancient dreams come true. The deep emotions of the people around this time found their expression in a monument to a man who symbolised the realisation of their dreams, King Peter I (1844–1921), called the Liberator. Equestrian monuments were considered as the most appropriate mark of respect that can be paid by a people to their sovereign (see e.g. Cleghorn 1824: 170). The monument was to last for 'all eternity' and was therefore cast in bronze and erected in front of the town hall.

After the death of King Peter, the throne went to his son, Alexander I (1888–1934), who transformed the Kingdom of Serbs, Croats and Slovenians into the Kingdom of Yugoslavia, so earning the title 'the Unifier'. As stated in 1940 by Josip Pipenbacher, president of the Committee for the Erection of the Monument to the Noble King, Alexander the Unifier had 'decided to build what had been the dream and wish of all noble Yugoslav men for centuries, that is the national unification of all Yugoslavs' (Maleš 1940: 7). He, too, merited a monument and one was erected in his honour in Ljubljana. The execution of the monument was entrusted to the most distinguished Slovenian sculptor, Lojze Dolinar, who was well prepared for the public tender for the erection of the monument in Ljubljana, having already made detailed studies of an equestrian figure when he received the commission for the earlier monument to King Peter. He had studied the image of the horse for many years, attempting to create a perfect harmony between its shape and that of the rider, and producing an accurately sculpted form. Although made in the style of already obsolete European models, the sculpture was admired by all. Its height, six metres, on top of a four-metre pedestal made it 'the greatest monument in Slovenian territory' in its dimensions and its artistic merits (Maleš 1940: 19).

The equestrian monument to King Alexander I was unveiled on 6 September 1940. In the year of the erection of the monument to the Chivalrous King, Europe was already engaged in a new war. On 6 April 1941, without warning the Axis forces attacked the Kingdom of Yugoslavia from different directions and its army capitulated soon afterwards. Occupied Yugoslavia was divided among the aggressors. Slovenian territory itself was parcelled out to three occupying forces (Germany, Italy and Hungary), while the capital, Ljubljana, found itself in the zone occupied by the Italians. Though astonished by the 'high level' of culture they encountered there, they found Ljubljana, to the discontent of its inhabitants, not big enough for the equestrian monuments. On 3 July 1941, High Commissioner Emilio Grazioli himself made an attempt to appease the representatives of Slovenian political circles who were present at the session of his council by explaining that the monuments to the 'Serbian' kings would be kept in a museum as 'works of art' (Grazioli 1941: 2). In fact, both monuments were pulled down by the Italian occupying authorities during the summer of 1941. They performed this part of their 'cultural mission' thoroughly: one night in early August, the pedestal of Alexander's monument was destroyed with a concrete crusher, and the stones and rubble were taken away in a lorry (Šnuderl 1993: 108, 132, 140). The feelings aroused in the inhabitants of Ljubljana by this act were noted by a contemporary in his diary:

> Nobody knows if the matter will be brought up again. But by pulling it down, they have offended Slovenian national feelings, not dynastic ones. The statue was beautiful and served as a decoration. It was ours. Its removal is a blow to Slovenians. Why was it in the way? Would not it have been better for them if they had left it, with a fine smile on their lips, in generous awareness of their power and force? This way, they performed the act of a weakling and lost all sympathy. (Šnuderl 1993: 132)

Controlling the past

When the war was over, royal monuments had already become the artefacts of a seemingly distant past. The first Yugoslavia, which had in the meantime been identified, like its Austro-Hungarian predecessor, as a 'prison-house of nations', was replaced by a new state which proposed the final solution to social and national problems. The colossal undertaking was, of course, impossible without new heroes. The result was an increase in memorial sculpture, with an extensive new programme of monuments to the national liberation struggle and the socialist revolution. Three of the giants of the period were offered up to eternity in bronze and marble in the city: Josip Broz Tito (1892–1980), Boris Kidrič (1912–1953) and Edvard Kardelj (1910–1979).

The monuments, made of 'eternal' materials (bronze and marble) that were supposed to last until 'the end of human history' lived to tell their tale for a mere half century. This short period of time sufficed to show Tito's Yugoslavia to be a state in which the national and social questions were not resolved. When Yugoslavia disintegrated, monuments to its heroes received special attention: one of the first official acts of the new Slovenian government was to remove photographs of Josip Broz Tito from government offices; his statues were also promptly done away with. The full-length statue carved in white marble which stood in the entrance hall of the Slovenian Parliament House until 1990 when it was taken to the depot of the City Museum. The famous full-length figure of Marshall Tito made by Antun Augustinčić in 1947, a cast of which stood in front of the then Museum of People's Revolution, was removed 'for cleaning' in 1990, – and never brought back. Meaning that for the leader of the second Yugoslavia there is no place – even in the Museum of Contemporary History.

In 1995, the procedure for the removal of 'monuments to the labour movement, national liberation struggle and the construction of socialism' were initiated by the city council. These would eventually lead to the elimination of monuments to Boris Kidrič and Edvard Kardelj who were central to the socialist revolution, 'in the name of which thousands of Slovenians had been murdered'. Those proposing the move pointed out that the removal of these two monuments would not mean their destruction but merely the 'clearing of the public areas in question' and putting them 'into a place where history is preserved, a museum' (Kovačič 1996: 30). Or, according to a statement made at the meeting of the city council by a contemporary Slovenian writer and poet, Jože Snoj, 'the monuments to criminals and dictators must finally be removed from public areas and placed in a museum to serve for the studies of historians and art historians' (quoted in Žolnir 1996).

The proposal to remove the Kardelj and Kidrič monuments triggered an extremely lively debate. The main Slovenian daily newspaper *Delo* even started a special column, 'Monuments Yes, Monuments No' on the letters to the editor page. Many contributors agreed with the proposal, claiming that 'even in the former Soviet Union, the communist monuments to Stalin and other criminals have been removed' (Stibrič 1996: 16).

But, on the other hand, many passionately opposed 'such vandalism', especially former partisans, who strongly objected to the destruction of monuments to their wartime leaders.

A nation without history

According to Vošnjak, who was a politician himself, it has been 'the fate of history to be exploited by politics' which uses historical facts 'to furnish arguments for the exigencies of political life' (Vosnjak 1917: 155). Serving as a tool in the hands of politicians history became past politics remembered, or perhaps even more frequently forgotten, for present causes.

During the nineteenth and twentieth centuries, public monuments in Ljubljana were erected with the object of rendering present and visible that which was absent and invisible: Slovenian history. While public monuments in Ljubljana were time and again explicitly declared to be means for the commemoration of historical personalities and events, and elites were well aware of the power of remembrance, they were no less conscious of the supremacy of oblivion. Unable or unprepared to confront the monuments of past epochs, the protagonists of political changes regularly destroyed them. They saw public monuments as a mere tool with which to reconstruct the Slovenian past as linear and straightforward story connecting the present with the mythical past. This reconstruction of the past went in line with George Orwell's syllogism: 'He who controls the past controls the future; he who controls the present controls the past' (Orwell 1984: 34).

By using the past in the service of their future aims, Slovenian elites made use of history as a conflict between good and evil that contained a purpose that led it inevitably to an end (see e.g. Plumb 1969: 98). In this scenario, today's heroes ('we are like them') created by political change not only repeatedly displaced the old ones as yesterday's villains ('we are not like them') but also exorcised the memories of what had hitherto been celebrated as a 'glorious age'. When the First World War ended, all monuments in Ljubljana that were expressions of Austrian patriotism were removed. During the Second World War monuments that were an expression of Yugoslav patriotism were demolished. Finally, after Slovenia became an independent republic the new authorities got rid of Tito's monuments. The predecessors of the Slovenians are thus deprived of centuries of common Austrian history and decades of common Yugoslavian history.

12
Belgrade–Ljubljana–Brussels
Slavko Gaber

Introduction

In January 2008 Slovenia assumed the Presidency of the European Union, and, in its mandate it coordinated the ratification process of the *Treaty on the Functioning of the Union*, which is interpreted by some as a European constitution.

For those familiar with developments in Eastern and Central Europe, in the 1990s, this development might have seemed to be a strange contradiction. How is it that 'secessionist' Slovenia, which less than twenty years ago had wanted independence, and had wanted to leave multinational Yugoslavia, was, in 2008, presiding over an even bigger, more complex multinational entity?

Where did this change come from? Did a change take place in Slovenia's attitude towards the nation, nation state and trans-national entities? Is this change the result of the new democratic standards that prevailed during accession to the European Union, or is it just the logical consequence of secessionist nationalism? These are the questions that will be addressed in this chapter.

Where did Slovenian nationalism disappear to?

In 2003, just a few days before the signing of the *Accession Treaty to the European Union*, the citizens of Slovenia voted on accession and the referendum result demonstrated an overwhelming support for joining the EU.[1] In order to qualify for EU entry Slovenia had amended its constitution, a month previously, thus including the *possibility of transferring part of its sovereignty* to a supra-national organisation. Article 3a of the Constitution of the Republic of Slovenia thus states that: 'Slovenia may...by international treaty, ratified by the National Assembly with a two-thirds majority of the votes, transfer the execution of part of its sovereign rights to international organizations'. Furthermore, in the discussions a proposal that Slovenia must have the right to withdraw from such associations was rejected.[2]

At first glance, this decision seemed to contradict the decision adopted by Slovenia at the beginning of the 1990s that resulted from the political developments of the 1980s. In 1987, circles connected with the *Nova Revija* magazine had claimed that: 'a significant number of Slovenians wish at present to be free not only from foreign nations but also from nations related to them too' (Hribar 1987: 26). This claim was seen in Yugoslavia as: 'a threat to the territorial integrity of the Socialist Federal Republic of Yugoslavia', and was perceived as a call for an 'independent state within a confederal union' (Ramet 1999: 32). As such, the subsequent *May Declaration* formed the hypothesis of an 'asymmetric federation'.[3]

When, in September 1989, Slovenia declared constitutional amendments, including one legalising the right to self-determination and the right to secession,[4] it triggered a reaction from the entire 'federal machine' and the Serbian political elites even '... called on Serbian enterprises to boycott the Slovenian market' (Ramet 1999: 33). Responding to the call: 'Serbian enterprises cancelled orders for Slovenian goods and services, and terminated all forms of economic cooperation' (Ramet 1999: 33).

Yet, in September 1989 secession was still described by essentially all Slovenes 'as a "last resort", if all else should fail' (ibid.). One year later, with a stronger Milošević, a weaker central government and the world superpowers[5] supporting the centralist orientation of Belgrade, a referendum was called in December 1990. The inhabitants of Slovenia were asked whether they wanted to stay within Yugoslavia or to become an independent state. The turnout was unexpectedly high and the vote for independence even more so.[6] They voted for 'Ljubljana' and against Milošević's 'Belgrade'. Many of those in liberal circles were worried by the perceived rise in nationalism that this decision represented.

Less than fourteen years later the citizens of the Republic of Slovenia again went to a referendum; 89.6 per cent of them voted in favour of surrendering part of their sovereignty and entering the European Union.[7]

In a period of approximately fifteen years, the citizens of Slovenia had travelled along a narrow road from the gradual formation of a demand for independence, through the decision to create a sovereign nation state, to once more transferring an important part of their sovereignty to a supra-national entity. Although it seems that we are dealing with a nationalistic move on the one hand and giving up what is 'national' on the other, the large majority of Slovene citizens were convinced that the referendum of 23 March 2003 was the logical consequence of moves begun by Slovenia at the beginning of the 1980s.

The question whether or not a nation that had risked armed attack to obtain sovereignty and, according to some, had even triggered the war in the former Yugoslavia,[8] had unthinkingly 'exchanged [the embrace of] Belgrade for that of Brussels' is an intriguing one. Yet for us the particularly challenging question is the logic that combines nationalism, democracy and European integration. Is it possible that Slovenian 'nationalism' changed into an overwhelming need for cooperation and association? Is it possible that it was not simply a nationalistic and undemocratic drive that drove Slovenia and some other nations out of Yugoslavia? What was it then that destroyed Yugoslavia? How could one define the relationship between nation, 'national', 'supra-national' and democracy?

Liberal democracy and the lack of 'deep structures'

By looking at the decision on independence – to obtain national sovereignty – on the one hand, and the decision to transfer part of its sovereignty to the European Union on the other, we will try to throw light on the role of democracy and 'standing up for national sovereignty' as the two crucial driving forces behind the transformation of Slovenia.

I will try to demonstrate, using concepts of *common and differentiated citizenship*, that there is no contradiction in the seemingly irrational and schizophrenic decisions by the citizens of Slovenia. Nationalism is not the problem per se. It seems that it is far more problematic that we treat nationalism by definition as undemocratic and irrational.

The 'end of history' as the victory of liberal democracy and nationalism

The fall of the Berlin Wall gave new momentum to liberal democracy. Enthusiasm related to this 'historic sign' of 'final victory' is still best expressed by Fukuyama:

> ...a remarkable consensus concerning the legitimacy of liberal democracy as a system of government had emerged throughout the world over [the] past few years as it conquered rival ideologies...More

than that ... liberal democracy may constitute the 'end point of mankind's ideological evolution' and 'the final form of human government' and as such constitute the 'end of history'. (1992: xi)

The victory of liberal democracy also presented a hope for the final victory of common citizenship. As liberals we believed that: 'citizenship defines the floor on which all members of human society stand. Ideally, this means all humans just like that' (Dahrendorf 1990/1997: 28).

It nevertheless soon became evident that people did not find much that was attractive in Dahrendorf's definition of citizenship as something that: 'all human beings have in common, in order to set people free to be different' (ibid.: 29). This remained true even if we added the concept of active citizenship or 'constitutional patriotism'.[9] Dahrendorf asked himself why this was so. In his answer he claimed the absence of ligatures was the reason for unrest. Citizens were *without answers to questions of belonging and meaning.* He argued that:

Individuals need an inner compass to guide them, and for the compass to work there have to be magnetic fields outside, which enable us to distinguish between north and south, right and wrong, desirable and undesirable course[s] of action ... Chances are incomplete as long as they are merely options. Only if certain deep structures ... are added, do they become chances with meaning, life chances. (Dahrendorf 1990/1997: 30)

And in the 1990s two deep structures returned: *nation* and *religion.*

Knowing that 'nation' was back on the agenda, Dahrendorf was, like many of us, unable to find the sources of identification only in liberal democratic values (such as liberty, democracy, the rule of law and justice). And yet at the same time he was embarrassed by demands for the right to 'self-determination' (ibid.: 26).

His position is in this respect quite similar to the position of a number of Western politicians at the end of the 1980s and in the first half of the 1990s. Dahrendorf belongs to a milieu in which common citizenship had prevailed for some 200 years, and many theoreticians and members of the political class tried hard *not to reflect* on elements that did not fit in with the pattern of *common citizenship.* At the beginning of the 1990s the 'blind spot' of liberal democracies covered the claims of groups, especially ethnic groups, for special rights.[10] With the rebirth of demands for nation states, a common undifferentiating citizenship became inadequate. Still, instead of reconceptualising citizenship many turned to the thesis of 'despair and the quest for certainty' (Dahrendorf 1994: 16) as the reason for moving towards the 'national'. According to Dahrendorf the reason for a return to the 'national' is the unlikelihood that citizenship (democracy) would actually offer anything to the citizens. 'For many in the former Communist countries of Central and Eastern Europe and elsewhere, it sounds almost cynical to call the 1980s the decade of provision. Provision, choices, economic and otherwise, are exactly what they did not have what they have now'[11] (ibid.). A lack of expanding provisions resulted in: 'confusion, despair and the quest for certainties ... People want to know where they belong, and they want to belong to familiar and homogenous groups, not to the Czech and Slovak Federal Republic but to Slovakia' (ibid.). Within the realm of this conceptualisation, any correct 'national' path which falls short of outright independence is considered to be irrational.[12] In this light: 'the prospects of citizenship are put at risk' (ibid.: 17). Dahrendorf is at this point far 'behind' the 'liberal nationalists' (Harty and Murphy 2005: 48) that re-emerged during the 1990s. His position was one of the: 'common view that liberalism and nationalism embody hostile if not entirely antithetical ideals ...' (ibid.: 53). According to Harty and Murphy, critics of nationalism have been inclined to conceptualise nationalism as: 'a form of irrational tribalism, an inherently divisive and violent political doctrine' destined to 'sacrifice the interests and well-being of the individual to those of the nation ...' (ibid.).

Milošević: The pillar of common citizenship and rationality?

The very enthusiasm for the end of history, alongside a misrecognition of common citizenship as the only form of liberal democracy, and a black and white conceptualisation of nationalism combined to cause blindness towards a proper understanding of post-socialist nation-building in Yugoslavia.

In addition, the reunification of Germany provided a clear example of the return of the demands for a nation state, and was considered proof of the wisdom of the great powers and their capacity to understand the trends of a changing world as integrated.[13]

Out of a fear of nationalism most authors pointed too quickly to group rights as antidemocratic claims. In one of the forums discussing Yugoslavia, Flenley found that: 'nationalism [was] obviously a theme which permeates all the articles' (1993: 4). He praised the authors for providing 'stimulating insights into why nationalism has become the dominant ideology in the region' (ibid.). Today it is clear that: '... the liberties of all individuals, regardless of their national origin, are defined as the constitutive principle of a modern state' (Golubović 1993: 76). But on the other hand, those who count only on individuals[14] or claim that a 'nation state as the locus of sovereignty is by definition in opposition to a democratic state which should be based on citizenship, and not on ethnicity' (ibid.), do not address the complex relationship between nation and democracy.

We can agree that at that time: 'the discourse of nationalism had succeeded in hegemonising intellectual debate' (Bowman 1993: 37). Yet it seems that the equalisation of representative democracy co-constituted the structured blindness of the time.

At the end of the 1980s, together with the concept of representative democracy: 'citizenship became a fashionable concept all over the political spectrum' (Dahrendorf 1994: 12).

It is becoming evident that through a fear of the dominance of nationalism we sometimes even contrasted the 'national' and the 'democratic' without pointing out that by forming nation states we can also strengthen democracy. On a number of occasions we overlooked the fact that although aggressive nationalism was linked with the debate on the 'national', the 'national' was often linked to demands for the democratisation of society, the provision of special rights for individual ethnic groups and other minorities, and for human rights as well.

The 'nationalistic' debate on an asymmetric federation, for example, took place in Slovenia in parallel with the debate on preventing human rights violations in courts in Yugoslavia. Mass protests against the violations of the basic human rights by Kosovar Albanians were just one of the many clear signs of this connection. In Slovenia calls for the right to self-determination ran in parallel with the process of establishing a representative democracy.[15]

The 1989 amendments to the Slovenian constitution covered two processes that were unacceptable to the old regime. Alongside demands for the right to self-determination, social movements strengthened their demands for human rights. Furthermore, all started with the demand for the right to the freedom of speech, with the fight to remove Article 133 of the Penal Code, which infringed the right to public expressions of opinion.[16] These were followed by demands for the freedom of choice and the freedom of organisation. The gradual strengthening of demands to establish a set of human rights culminated in the demand for a representative democracy, through a multi-party system. For Slovenia, at least, it seemed possible to state that the demands for greater national autonomy – right up until the demands for a confederative solution – went hand in hand with demands for a representative democracy.[17]

Perhaps the most glaring difference between Slovenia and some of the other republics of the former Yugoslavia lies in this very point. The powerful civil-society movement that in part turned into political parties at the end of the 1980s and was predominantly liberal in orientation prevented an exaggerated swing to the right and hence towards nationalism, which would lose the connection with democracy.[18] By 1992, a coalition dominated by a centre-left party had already come to power.

The coexistence of the nation state and democracy

Our main thesis is that Slovenia demonstrates first and foremost that the coexistence of the 'national' and democratic is possible and that it is even possible for one to strengthen the other; and secondly that a reconceptualisation of citizenship rights is required to understand what is actually going on in Europe today.

It is rightly said that democracy has often been the victim of nationalism; it is also true that modern democracy 'has been closely connected to the nation state' (Touraine 1994: 99).

The inner tension of the nation state 'between *ethnos* and *demos*' (Dimitrijević 1993: 51)[19] is potentially productive. Slovenia, as in the cases of Canada, Spain, Belgium and the United Kingdom (Kymlicka 2001), demonstrates a possible productive relationship of this tension. The main distinction is not therefore between state and nation state, but within the concept of a nation state and its relationship to democracy. In Touraine's opinion democracy is 'connected to a certain comprehension of the nation-state and is in conflict with another' (1994: 99).

It seems that the idea that the 'sort of nation-state we have seen to date would continue to exert a strong structural force' (ibid.: 29) remains valid.

The dissolution, break-up and disintegration of Yugoslavia – for all three of these occurred – already in Slovenia's case demanded conceptualisation which, while accepting the concept of common citizenship, reaches beyond it. The contradiction between individual and group rights is in this respect crucial to an understanding of relations between nation formation and democracy.

Common citizenship and group rights

The claims and demands of (groups of) citizens and the crises we have faced over the past decade support the theoretical claim that we are facing a process of the expansion in citizenship rights.

It seems though that Waldron justifiably emphasised the emergence of a ' "new generation" of human rights' (1993: 339). While Young has claimed that: 'group differences cut across individual lives in a multiplicity of ways' and that this 'can entail privilege and oppression of the same person in different respect[s]' (1990: 42), Waldron observed that the greatest pressure was arising out of demands for the special treatment of the questions of representation, the rights of women and those of different ethnic groups.

After the implementation of the so-called first generation of citizenship rights ('free speech; religious liberty; the right not to be tortured; [and] the right to a fair trial ...' (Waldron 1993: 5)) and second-generation rights, chiefly socio-economic rights, we are obviously facing demands for the implementation of a third-generation of rights. They have a 'non-individualistic character ...' and 'are the solidarity rights of communities... They include minority language rights; the right to national self-determination; and, the rights that people may have to diffuse goods, such as peace ...' (ibid.: 5).

No doubt claims for a new generation of human rights brought numerous dilemmas to the surface. The first set of them raises the fear that the rise of group-based claims will 'further erode the sense of shared civic purpose and solidarity' (Kymlicka 1998: 168). In line with such a fear even Rawls shared the opinion that the: 'organization of society on the basis of rights or claims that derive from group membership is sharply opposed to the concept of citizenship' (ibid.: 167).

Yet the thesis according to which the concept of differentiated citizenship is a contradiction in terms is obviously overstated, and 'differentiated citizenship... defined as the adoption of group specific, poly-ethnic representation, or self-government' today presents a reality which is in some form or another recognised by 'virtually every modern democracy' (ibid.: 167–168). Modern democracies neither recognise certain forms of differentiated citizenship by mistake, nor do they find themselves in a position to avoid it. In Spain, Macedonia, Kosovo, Belgium, Northern Ireland and Bosnia and Herzegovina there is a need to protect fundamental human rights and to point out that citizenship is a 'forum where people transcend their differences and think about the good of all citizens' (ibid.: 168); however, beyond a certain point there is also a need to admit, for example, that in Macedonia a third of its population is ethnically Albanian, and that in addition to common citizenship rights they want special rights in the field of education.

Ignoring such facts can lead to civil disobedience, ethnic clashes and finally also to war. On the other hand, a country can benefit from introducing 'asymmetrical federalism'. Canada, which grants Quebec powers not given to other provinces, is one example (Kymlicka 1996: 156). Belgium is another, and Slovenia, where members of the Italian and Hungarian ethnic minorities have special rights in the fields of education, culture and special representatives in the national parliament, is yet another. In all these cases the special rights increased rather than diminished the sense of citizenship.

To reflect the changes in citizenship and citizenship rights, it seems right to support, at least in principle, the idea of the combination of *common citizenship and differentiated citizenship* where the latter approach complements the former.

Common citizenship is here defined as: 'the first generation' of citizenship rights (Waldron 1993), which can be described as: ' "the civic element of citizenship" – comprising the rights necessary for individual freedom and the institution most directly associated with the rule of law and the judicial system – and "the political part of citizenship" – comprising the right to participate in the exercise of political power' (Barbalet 1988: 6).[20]

Special representation rights

By accepting the concept of *differentiated citizenship* as supplementary to *common citizenship* one is confronted with a second set of questions.

The debate on *special representation rights* is at least as old as the debate on representative democracy. As a matter of fact we could claim that the classic (Burkeian) concept of representative democracy as the representation of citizens emerged from the confrontation with delegates of individual groups or classes of the population. Representative – citizenship – democracy is founded on the assumption of representing the whole nation without being tied to any class or individual party or group of voters. This assumption is clearly defined in the majority of modern constitutions. It is written in Article 82 of the Slovenian constitution too. However, in reality the tension between classic concepts of citizenship and classic representation has never been resolved. The political structures of contemporary bicameral parliaments where the upper chamber often represents specific professional groups and local entities (provinces), and where the lower chambers of parliaments provide different kinds of representation – for example, the representation of minorities, gender quotas, and so forth – point to the fact that the tension between the general and particular or group representation is written into the structure of liberal democracies. The omnipresent perception that the 'political process is "unrepresentative", in the sense that it fails to reflect the diversity of the population' (Kymlicka 1996: 157), does not relate just to the issue of 'presence' (A. Phillips 1995, 1996). It ultimately highlights the desire of a people, or groups of people, for a delegate model of democracy.

Accepting group rights as legitimate does not mean facing the question of 'inclusion or not', whether or not to allow the presence of group interests in decision-making in the parliamentary democracy. The real questions are:

- Where? (in the lower or upper chamber);
- How much power should we give to group interests? (presence only or something more);
- Which groups represent an entity entitled to representation in parliaments? etc.

Furthermore, at the edge of the spectrum of group rights in the political field we face the question of self-governance and the rights of self-determination. For many liberals, even for nationalists, it is on the other side of acceptable.

Rawls, Rorty and Dworkin all stay on the 'safe' side of common citizenship (comp: Harty and Murphy 2005: 59–60). If poly-ethnic and representational rights 'can promote social integration and political unity, self-government rights pose a more serious challenge to the integrative function of citizenship' (Kymlicka 1998: 174). Self-government presupposing the right to self-determination is not only the 'most complete case of differentiated citizenship' (ibid.: 175). The possible and actual concern for the interests of one's own nation in a multinational state is thus regarded as something in which it 'is not clear that … [it] would support solidarity and cohesiveness in a liberal society' (Lehning 1998: 233).

In line with the common citizenship strategy for dealing with cultural pluralism, many multinational or at least multi-ethnic states wish to circumvent the actual and mostly justified demands for the rights of self-government and replace them with the right to cultural-pluralism. Yet self-determination is not only about cultural distinction but is 'in the first instance … a claim to autonomous institutions of self-government (that) provide nations with the laws, priorities and policies' (Harty and Murphy 2005: 80). Kymlicka emphasises that the use of a common citizenship strategy which believes that multinational states can be organised without a self-government strategy only 'aggravates alienation among national minorities and increases the desire for secession' (1998: 176). Contrary to Rawls' expectation that common citizenship promotes the political virtues of reasonableness and a sense of fairness, a spirit of compromise and a readiness to meet others halfway: 'common citizenship may in fact threaten these virtues' (ibid.: 176).

The case of Yugoslavia in the past shows what can happen when the authorities, with the help of the world's powers, believe that the concept of common citizenship counter-positioned to group rights (national rights) becomes the guardian of democracy, while federalisation, confederalisation or even the emergence of new states are, by definition, instances of 'balkanisation' and 'tribalisation'. Today the new arrangements for Northern Ireland, and for Serbia, Montenegro and Kosovo demonstrate that one should be aware that: 'claims to self-government are here to stay, (and) we have no choice but to try to accommodate them' (ibid.: 178).[21] However, it may seem odd that although the right to self-determination is not by definition an element of integration, it can, building on common citizenship rights, prevent secession and certainly, if taken seriously, even prevent war.

It is crucial to recognise ethnic rights as playing a positive role in the framework of citizenship rights, and to see them as provisions and entitlements. They are not something to be afraid of like the return of the Real into the sphere of the symbolic organisation of the modern Western world. Habermas emphasised that: 'the nation state provided both the infrastructure for rational administration and the legal frame for free individual and collective action' (1994: 21); moreover: 'the nation state laid the foundations for cultural and ethnic homogeneity on the basis of which it then proved possible to push ahead with democratization ... The nation-state and democracy are the twins born of the French Revolution' (ibid.: 22). Although the same author suggests that the modern concept of the nation state as a 'loosening of the semantic connections between national citizenship and national identity, takes into account that the classic form of the nation state is at present disintegrating' (ibid.: 21). The fact remains that, even in the process of forming the European Union, 'the sort of nation-state we have seen to date would continue to exert a strong structural force' (ibid.: 29), but it would be in the form of differentiated citizenship or in the form of 'multinational citizenship' (Harty and Murphy 2005). It also seems that we will see ethnicity in different combinations reaching a form of 'nation sub-state' as in the case of Scotland, Catalonia and Wallonia through the nations of

Great Britain, Spain and Belgium, all the way to the supra-national European Union.

Ljubljana–Brussels

With the above concepts in mind it is easier to understand that Slovenia in declaring independence decided not only for the right to 'make choices about culture' (Harty and Murphy 2005: 79), but that the citizens of Slovenia also voted for a representative democracy – for the rule of law, human rights and for their right to make their policy decisions in accordance with their interests and conceptions. While in Yugoslavia the 'Milošević' type of politics wanted to control the right of assembly, freedom of speech, the free organisation of political parties, and to restrict normal economic and cultural development, Slovenia decided for an independent state that from the start offered special rights to national minorities in the constitution (Article 64).[22]

At the same time, at the end of the 1980s the inhabitants of Slovenia decided first in favour of the right to *self-determination*; second for *representative democracy* and with that the respect of human rights; and finally, but consistent with the first and second, in favour of *European integration*. It is thus not surprising that, in June 1991, parliament declared that: 'The Republic of Slovenia has proclaimed its sovereignty and independence and has thereby assumed actual jurisdiction over its territory. Consequently, Slovenia as an international, legal entity, in the full sense of the term, and in conformity with the principles of the unification of sovereign states in Europe, seeks association with other states, membership in the United Nations Organization, membership in the European community and participation in other alliances of states or nations' (*Declaration of Independence*, 24 June 1991).

Combining *self-determination, representative democracy and European integration*, at the end of the 1980s Slovenia started a discussion on the future of Slovenia and Yugoslavia. One important reason for going further with self-determination than its inhabitants had expected in 1989 is that the former Yugoslavia was unable to accommodate the need for an internally conflicting but stimulating tension of the three.

The result of the referendum of 23 March 2003 was clearly just the logical conclusion of the expectations and concepts from the 1980s. Self-determination, human rights, democracy and membership in the European Union are intertwined and very far from being contradictory per se.

Notes

1. The turnout was 60 per cent, of which 89 per cent voted in favour of Slovenia joining the European Union.
2. The parliamentary deputy Franc Cukjati proposed a new third paragraph to Article 3a of the Constitution that would read: 'The withdrawal from an international organization or defense alliance shall be determined by a similar process to that which applied on accession'. The Expert Commission of the Constitution Commission did not support Deputy Cukjati's proposal.
3. The basic points of the 1989 *May Declaration* included demands for a 'sovereign state for the Slovenian nation' and 'independent decision-making' on relations with other Yugoslav nations. Ramet credits Mitja Žagar with the idea of *'asymmetric federation'*. Žagar on the other hand claims it for both himself and Peter Jambrek. 'At one of the round table discussions in the spring of 1988...the idea was raised during a discussion on the Canadian federation and Quebec's special position within it, that the same principles of "asymmetry" could also be applied within the Yugoslav federation – to regulate the position of individual republics as sovereign national states. During the discussion Prof. Peter Jambrek and I (M.Ž.) both spoke on the issue' (Žagar 1990: 382)
4. 'The Socialist Republic of Slovenia is a constituent part of the Socialist Federal Republic of Yugoslavia on the basis of the lasting, integral and inalienable right of the Slovenian nation to self-determination, which includes the right to secede and accede.' (Constitutional amendment no. X to the *Constitution of the Socialist Republic of Slovenia, Uradni list SRS*, no.32/89.)
5. The United States in particular.
6. At the plebiscite on 23 December 1990, Slovenian citizens voted for a sovereign and independent country. Voter turnout at the plebiscite was 93.2 per cent, with 88.2 per cent voting for an independent and sovereign Slovenia.
7. Of interest from an analytic point of view is the fact that support for joining NATO was significantly lower – though still high at 66 per cent.
8. 'Nobody was surprised at the declarations of independence by Slovenia and Croatia. But everybody was surprised at the audacity with which Slovenes moved to transform their independence from the rhetorical to the real...Now in a lightning maneuver the Slovenes had in a few hours changed the borders of Yugoslavia, which had been stable for half a century, a hundred miles to the east. It was the first act of war' (Zimmermann 1999: 143, 142).
9. Here he quotes Habermas and his defence of patriotism as a feeling of pride and belonging 'to your country (democracy) as an actual type of state that one may be proud of due to the high democratic standards'. However Dahrendorf believes that 'constitutional patriotism remains *Kopfgeburt,* a thing of mind, not of the heart' (ibid.: 33).
10. Group rights are suspicious by definition: 'The practical problem with all so-called collective rights is that someone has to claim them on behalf of others ...' (ibid.: 26).
11. It is telling enough that their positive or negative thesis of provision (selfishness) was one of the main arguments related to nationalism within

socialist anti-nationalist ideology. Claiming the right to self-determination was judged as a 'completely inappropriate and unacceptable social action' (Urbanič 1987: 34).

12. Fukuyama calls the path towards liberal democracy a transition in consciousness 'that can take a variety of irrational forms before it is transformed into universal and equal recognition' (1992: 207). Examples of irrational forms are religion and 'nationalism' (ibid.).

13. The German understanding of the situation in Yugoslavia and early recognition of the independence of new states is probably attributable to a far more articulate conceptualisation of their own reunification. Germans understood unification as the right of a nation to self-determination. Zimmermann here too demonstrates his weak understanding of the relationship between globalization, differentiation, nationhood and democracy when he writes that erroneously equating the Slovenian right to self-determination with that of the Germans: 'may have been the key factor in the German Foreign Minister Hans-Dietrich Genscher's tenacious decision to rush the independence of Slovenia and Croatia' (1999: 146).

14. Libertarian enthusiasm (although rightly emphasised) was blind to other important forms of identity and it is demonstrated in the concluding sentence: 'Society, which has imposed the so-called general will as a substitute for considerations and inclinations of individuals, now needs strong individuals' (Gaber 1993: 63).

15. The 1989 May Declaration in addition to the above claims for the rights of the Slovenian nation also claimed: 'respect for human rights and liberties – including political pluralism'.

16. 'Whoever shall in writing, by pamphlet, drawing, speech or in any other manner call for or incite the overthrow of the rule of the working class and workers, for anti-constitutional changes to the socialist self-management social system...shall be punished by a prison sentence of one to ten years' (Penal Code SFR Yugoslavia, *Uradni list SFRJ* 44–654/76).

17. Calls for fundamental human rights – the line taken by the *Mladina* magazine – were only seriously affected around the time of independence, during the brief war and during the first two years of independence when the country was fighting for international recognition, encountering economic difficulties, accepting around 80,000 refugees from the former Yugoslavia and with a war raging not far away. During that period there was the threat of a takeover within the centre right (the group centred around *Nova Revija* that won the 1990 elections) by totalitarian elements connected with extreme nationalism. Limiting women's rights to abortion, restrictive refugee policies, and the anti-constitutional treatment of inhabitants without citizenship were clear signs of such a danger. The treatment of inhabitants without citizenship was undoubtedly the worst mistake from the period of establishing the nation state.

18. See *Abortus – pravica do izbire?* (Abortion – the right to choose?) (1991).

19. When claiming that one should take a closer look at the 'warning of ethno-nationalism that can be drawn from legal provisions', Dimitrijević takes as an example Article 3 of the Slovenian Constitution, which states: 'Slovenia is a state of all its citizens, based on the permanent and inviolable right of the Slovene nation to self-determination.'

20. Marshall talks about three parts or elements of citizenship: 'I propose to divide citizenship into three parts...I shall call these three parts, or elements, civil, political and social' (1950: 10).
21. 'It has been calculated that 8000 miles of new borders have been created in Central and Eastern Europe alone since 1989' (Giddens 2007: 202).
22. Today it became clear that Roma population rights need further elaboration, especially in the light of Roma rights violations in past two years.

13
Hypercapitalism As the Replacement of Old Nationalist Fears

Renata Salecl

Slovenians are often asked how do countries which used to form part of Yugoslavia react to the fact that Slovenia still seems to draw profit from the undeveloped south, in the sense that today's capitalists have simply replaced former communists in taking control over the less developed countries of the former federation. This state of affairs would seem to be particularly surprising given the nationalist struggles that we have witnessed in recent years. Nevertheless, it is too soon to say that capitalism might present a cure for nationalism. As this chapter will demonstrate, capitalism has always been wise to incorporate national feelings into an ideology which primarily tries to increase profit as well as play on the various fears that people may have about their well-being. In the way people react to fears there also seems to be very little difference between the developed West and post-socialist countries.

A couple of years ago, when the anthrax panic erupted in the United States, the media in Slovenia suddenly reported a number of cases of fake anthrax. For some days, the media alerted the public to the dangers of strange letters containing white powder that were being sent to public institutions. The drama was soon over, however, when it became clear that someone was just making a hoax by sending fake anthrax. Nonetheless, in the way the Slovenian media reported these anthrax scares one could identify concern coupled with some kind of narcissistic exultation. When these anthrax cases became the primary news story of the day, it was as if this tiny country was becoming an equal of the powerful America in the expression of its fears. Since Slovenia itself had suffered a brief war after seceding from former Yugoslavia, there was also a lot of identification with the victims of the attack on the World Trade Center. Slovenians (and Bosnians even more so) remembered that they had been through moments of suffering when their whole perception of the world and their own personal safety had collapsed. But how can we read together the genuine identification with the victims of September 11 and the emergence of fake anthrax in some post-socialist countries?

After September 11, Thomas L. Friedman[1] reported on the sympathies that lots of Middle Easterners felt towards America by saying that: 'America is not something external to them; people carry around pieces of it in ways often not articulated.' At moments of disaster, it is nowadays fashionable to express solidarity by pointing out how when certain violence is inflicted we are all victims. During the war in Bosnia, Western intellectuals liked to say, 'We are all Bosnians.' And after the violence in America, it was fashionable to state that this was a general attack on the spirit of democracy and the values of the civilised world. What does it mean when we say that we are all victims? Although such an expression might seem the highest form of identification with the actual victims, it betrays a certain lie and a distance in it. Freud had already been trying to figure out how people identify with one another,[2] and his famous example was of girls in a dormitory who might start crying when one of their friends receives a sad letter from a lover. Freud's point was that these girls do not simply identify with the pain of their friend – what triggers their crying is that they identify with *ein Einziger Zug* (a single trait) in the girl who got the letter, which is linked to her desire to be loved. The other girls are also concerned with questions about their love lives; in other words, they also want to be loved by someone. And when their friend receives the sad love letter, the other girls identify with this single trait of the girl – her desire to be loved by her boyfriend – so they are sad that they too might not be fulfilled in this desire. So when Friedman said that people are carrying around pieces of America in ways often not articulated or when someone might have said, 'We are all Americans' – in other words, 'we are all victims' – this should be understood as another example of the identification with a single trait. It is not that one can easily feel the pain of someone who has been the victim of the attack: what we identify with is the fact that we can all be victims of such an attack.

It is very hard to truly identify with the pain of the other in the meaning of understanding what another is going through, what kind of fantasies he or she has had shattered and what kind of perception of the world he or she has built after a traumatic event. When we identify with the pain of the other, there is often an imaginary dimension at work, and we perceive that what has happened to another could also happen to us.[3] In this case we perceive the suffering other as a mirror image of ourselves. If this kind of identification relies on a certain narcissistic relationship, there is yet another type of identification that supports this first imaginary one. Lacanian psychoanalysis places a particular importance on the symbolic identification through which people feel compassion for each other. Symbolic identification involves a dimension of the Ego Ideal – a point in the symbolic world in which the subject lives, that presents an ideal with which the subject may identify. Let us say that in democratic societies compassion and generosity are such ideals with which people might easily identify. When they identify with the victims of violence, they cannot directly identify with the pain of another; they might rather identify with the ideal of compassion in such a way that they find a particular satisfaction in observing themselves as compassionate, caring and generous. In this case, it is as if the subject steps out of their self and observes their actions from the position of the Ego Ideal with which they identify.

In the places where there was no serious expectation that they might come under terrorist attack, one can also observe a particular kind of symbolic identification with the victims of September 11, which can also be understood as a desire to belong to the Western world. This desire was especially present in the way some Poles reacted to the news that a number of their compatriots had been killed in the World Trade Center. At first the news was that there were dozens of Poles killed there, but when later the number became much smaller, some people in Poland almost reacted with disappointment: it was not that people secretly wished the death of more Poles, but rather that they very much wanted to 'belong' and to be counted as being one of the important European nations. Some Poles perceived having significant casualties in the World Trade Center as being a way to get the symbolic recognition of being equal to those Western countries that had lost a considerable number of their people. Post-socialist countries have this desperate desire to jump on the train of the developed world and at the time of the terrorist attack in America, their governments perceived that it was necessary to be as quick as possible in offering support to America, even if the latter might never need their direct help. But at the same time, the public felt uneasy about the American obsession with war, its constant search for new enemies and its ignorance towards the developing world. While the post-socialist countries can often be quite pathetic in their desire to belong to the First World, the latter may also demonstrate some considerably extreme ignorance towards the former.

This game of seduction that goes on in both directions between the West and developing countries is most obviously visible in the art world.

Artists in the developing world who try to be recognised in the West often fail in this attempt. Ilya Kabakov nicely described the tension between the Western art world and non-Western cultures by pointing out that the Western art world is like a fast train that travels through different countries. In these remote places, people stand on the platforms and hope that they will be able to catch the train. However, the train rarely stops, and even if it does stop, there are no places on the train. Some people nonetheless succeed in climbing onto the train and then desperately look for empty seats. When a seat by chance becomes free and the person sits down, the fellow passengers look at the newcomer with disdain and comment: 'Why did you not sit down earlier. And why did you look so desperate – you should have a smile on your face! We are always happy to get new people on board.' Precisely the game global capital is playing in today's post-socialist world. And with regard to the September 11 attack, Slovenia as well as other post-socialist countries very much wanted to be perceived as the passengers on the right train. Being on the right train, however, does not involve simply expressing compassion for the victims of terror, but also a desire to be favourably treated by the drivers of the train – in other words, global capital.

Former Yugoslav countries are, together with the rest of the post-socialist world, quickly transforming themselves into the consumerist type of society that is predominant in the Western world. Urban development has followed the ideals that American society introduced decades ago. In the post-socialist states we may observe the dying off of the old cities and towns and the emergence of huge shopping malls on the outskirts of the cities, where people now spend most of their free time. The search for money and profit seems to have overcome old nationalist divides. But again, we notice that it is the developed north that is reacting quickly in the new circumstances and thus introducing the new global capitalism into the rest of the Yugoslavia. However, the response towards this new form of cooperation is mixed. When, for example, large Slovenian firms open shopping malls in Serbia and Bosnia, these are often accepted with great joy by the local population. However, when a Slovenian firm tried to buy a decayed vacation complex in Croatia, this caused great nationalist opposition among the Croats.

Capitalism per se has been embraced in the post-socialist world with both joy and anxiety. What is the logic of this anxiety? When, after September 11, we are constantly told that we live in the new age of anxiety, our first impression is perhaps that this is related to the proliferation of possible catastrophes such as terrorist attacks, the collapse of the financial market, strange illnesses, ecological changes, the possibilities of new wars and new developments in science. However, it would be arrogant to say that contemporary society actually experiences more anxieties than our predecessors. They too had to deal with wars and conflicts, poverty and many more illnesses that radically shortened people's lives. If, therefore, anxieties with regard to possible catastrophes might not be so different today than in the past, then the anxieties that very much pertain to contemporary society are linked to the new feelings of insecurity on which contemporary capitalism capitalises itself. Insecurities have always been the vehicle of the capitalist labour market; however, in post-industrial society we can observe changes in the subject's self-perception, which have in turn been affected by the transformations of the social symbolic order.[4]

Consumerist society seems to be thriving on the particular feeling of inadequacy that people are commonly experiencing today. To grasp the power of this feeling one only needs to look at any women's magazine or the style section of a daily newspaper. What we find in such publications, apart from advertising and reports on the latest fashion, cosmetics and celebrities, is advice. We live in times characterised by survival. Therefore it is not untypical to come across articles about: 'The single girl's guide to survival'; a mother's secret diary on how to survive childbirth (since 'Having babies does terrible damage, especially to the fashionably forty-something mother'), advice on how to survive being in or out of a relationship, advice on diet and exercise, and so forth. Of course, advice radically changes over time, so that, as one health advice column claims, until recently 'we have become neurotic about getting enough sleep, but the new research now suggests that the less we have, the longer we'll live'.[5]

To summarise this, such magazines offer a cocktail of advice and prohibitions that finally tastes like guilt. If the 1990s ideology followed the commands of 'Just do it!' and 'Be yourself!'[6] today, it seems that the new motto that the media promotes is: 'No matter what you do, you will do it wrong, but it is better that you follow our advice and try again'. The 'Just do it!' ideology relied on the idea that the subject is 'free' in the meaning of being a non-believer in authorities and someone who can be fully in charge of changing his or her identity as and when he or she pleases. Today it looks as if we are living in times when people have woken up and acknowledged their limitations in such pursuits. However, it is not that we have finally realised that we are not self-creators who can reject the old authorities (such as religion or the state) and make out of ourselves a work of art which is not limited by any cultural or even biological restraints; it is rather that the very ideology of 'Just do it!' instead of offering unlimited optimism opened the doors for a particular kind of anxiety. This anxiety is linked to the very idea that today we have the freedom to create a self-image in which we will appear likeable to ourselves. However, people today more than ever before experience all kinds of traumas related to their body image, and as a result are suffering from anorexia, bulimia, excessive exercising, an obsession with plastic surgery, or a shopping addiction. What is so horrifying in the possibility of making a work of art out of oneself, in which one should be free in creating our lives the way we supposedly want to? Why does the very freedom that we supposedly have in making choices in our lives account for an increase of anxiety?

When I recently visited Lithuania, I often heard people commenting that they feel they are not accustomed to making choices in their lives and that, in contrast to the Americans, who seem to know how to handle choice, they are overwhelmed by it. This observation pertained not only to the choices of consumer products, but also to choices about the direction of one's life. However, Americans too are talking about a so called 'tyranny of choice'.

How is this so-called abundance of choice[7] operative today? The past twenty years were dominated by the ideology that people would be happier and better off if they were constantly shopping for the best deals. On the one hand we got the huge emergence of new products, manufacturers and providers to choose from, but on the other hand, the idea of choice also became an end in itself. Some social scientists started to talk about the 'tyranny of freedom' in today's world, since consumers are forced to make choice even on things they never envisioned they could have, and did not even want to have, any power over. An example here is the choice of the electricity provider. This choice has incited quite an anxiety among consumers, since as a *New York Times* article explained: 'the anxiety over energy is exposing something even deeper in human wiring'.[8] It is not only that people do not want to constantly be perceived as autonomous, rational consumers: 'when it comes to electricity, a mysterious and dangerous thing that is also the foundation of modern living, Americans are just a little afraid to be alone'.[9] People are supposedly anxious for two reasons: first, it seems that no one is in charge in society any more, and second, the freedom of choice actually does not give more power to the consumers, but to the corporations. A person shopping around on the Internet for the best price on a product, for example, gives the corporations a chance to collect valuable data about the consumer's desires and spending habits. What provokes anxiety for a person therefore seems to be both that no one appears to be in control, and that those who do exert control (the corporations) do so in a hidden way.

When people speak about anxiety today, they also invoke the idea that they are now asked to make choices about their sexuality, marriage and childbearing that used not to be regarded as choices in the past. But the more choices there are, the more it appears possible to achieve an ideal result in every case. This seems to be the case not only for people who are continually changing their long-distance telephone service in the hope that they will find the best deal, but also for those searching for a love partner. If we look at the proliferation of self-help books devoted to love, it becomes clear that love especially provokes anxiety today and that people are searching for all kinds of guidance to alleviate this anxiety. In today's consumerist society, searching for a partner follows a similar logic as buying a new car. One first needs to do an extensive research of the market, then check all the qualities of the desired 'object', insure oneself with a pre-nuptial agreement and after some time exchange the old for the new, or in order to minimise the hassle decide to go just for a short-term lease.

While on the one hand the subject is perceived to be a self-creator, that is a subject who can make out of him or herself what he or she pleases and who no longer relies on old authorities such as family, religion and the state, on the other hand the subject has lost the 'security' that the struggle with the old authorities often brought about. The shift that has happened in the subject's perception of themselves and of his or her place in the social symbolic network, which incited new anxieties that subjects have in regard to their body image and their role in society at large are very much linked to the way capitalism functions today. Paradoxically, the ideology of consumerism also offers 'solutions' on how the subject should deal with his or her anxiety. It even seems that anxiety is the very motor of the marketing politics that dominates today's consumerist society.

Psychoanalysis and marketing share the same knowledge that desire is always linked to prohibition. Freud was quite cynical about this fact and pointed out that where cultural prohibitions did not exist people invented them in order to keep desire alive.[10] And Lacan was quick to follow, stating that the subject would never want to have a sublime Thing unless the symbolic law was to prohibit access to it. With regard to consumer goods it is well known that we desire and cherish them more if they are expensive and hard to get. I will never forget the enjoyment in the eyes of the Serbian student I met in Belgrade who told me he obsessively cleans his one pair of Nike sneakers as he hopes to have them for a number of years.

The new philosophy of the brand makers is that they do not try to prevent their logos being stolen and copied in the Third World. If a Turkish manufacturer, for example, makes copies of Nike sneakers, Nike will not try to prosecute him for copyright violation. Since Nike is primarily concerned with the dissemination of their logo, they take the fact that someone copied their product as just another advertising campaign. Another well-known strategy in creating 'addiction' to consumer goods is that Nike and similar brands like to throw their excess products into the poorest neighbourhoods, like the Bronx in New York, and thus keep the young consumers attracted to their goods.[11]

If desire is linked to prohibition, does the fact that some companies nowadays give away products for free kill the desire? Paradoxically this does not happen since today's capitalism does not simply rely on selling goods, but on the creation of a certain imagery which people can identify with. In this context, the aforementioned feeling of inadequacy plays a strong role in the way marketing operates today. However, the problem is not that the media offers to people some images of success and beauty with which they want to identify, and since they cannot come close to this ideal, they feel inadequate. For some time now the fashion industry, for example, has been convincing consumers that they should not follow fashion advice and try to make themselves into someone else, but should rather find what is unique in them and with the help of fashion just accentuate it. Early advertising, at the beginning of the twentieth century, which tried to use psychoanalytic knowledge, often tried to promote an identification of the consumer with an authority. The advertisers' guess was that the consumer 'nearly always purchases in unconscious obedience to what he or she believes to be the dictates of an authority which is anxiously consulted or respected'.[12] In those times, marketing thus tried to convince people to look and behave like someone else, in other words, to identify with an authority. While people today still look for role models (for example, in the entertainment industry), advertising is nonetheless playing much more with the idea that that people will try to find in their products much more than is actually in them and not simply follow the dictates of the market. However, this new marketing strategy creates a lot of unease for consumers, since what actually provokes anxiety for the subject is not the failure that he or she cannot be someone else, but rather that he or she cannot be him or herself.

How is this anxiety channelled in today's consumerism? Numerous studies have recently analysed the change in capitalist production where instead of material manufacturing being of the foremost importance the marketing of a particular image has become the main concern. In this new culture of capitalism, it is crucial that suppliers and users replace buyers and sellers; markets are now managing ways for networks and ownership to be replaced by access. Since the production costs of goods are today minimal and the market is so saturated with goods, the economy depends less on the individual market exchange of goods and more on establishing long-term commercial relationships.

For companies, the most important thing is the creation of a lifelong relationship with its customer in order that they may become his or her supplier over a lifetime. The manufacturers thus invest most of their energy in developing trusting relations with their customers and try to figure out what the future desires of the customers might be without the customers knowing that they might actually want or need these things. The example here might be that of a manufacturer of nappies who provides home delivery of their product and soon after the parents get the first delivery of the nappies, they start buying all other baby goods from this provider. When the baby grows up, the provider will then offer goods for toddlers and later for adolescents. (One can imagine that the manufacturer might at some point also offer free psychoanalytic advice on how to raise children.)

On top of establishing a trusting relationship, manufacturers more than anything try today to sell an image or, better, a lifestyle. Let us take the example of so-called 'designer coffees' sold at Starbucks or Coffee Republic. In these places what is sold is not simply coffee, but a particular type of experience: nicely designed places, which offer a cosy, homely atmosphere with a politically correct intellectual touch. One thus gets ecologically informed messages on how the coffee has been produced and even the explanation on how by buying this (expensive) coffee one helps the poor people in Columbia. On the one hand, the consumers of such expensive coffee are offered a symbolic space in which they appear likeable to themselves, but, on the other hand, they get the protection from the outside world – especially from the poor.[13]

Today's hypercapitalist society is making a long-term shift from industrial production to cultural production, in which cultural experiences are more important than goods and services. Jeremy Rifkin points out in his book *The Age of Access* that we are entering a so-called hypercapitalism, or better cultural capitalism that relies on the 'experience' economy in which each person's own life becomes a commercial market: 'Global travel and tourism, theme cities and parks, destination entertainment centres, wellness, fashion and cuisine, professional sports and games, gambling, music, film, television, the virtual world of cyberspace, and electronically mediated entertainment of every kind are fast becoming the centre of a new hypercapitalism that trades in access to cultural experience'.[14]

In this context, businesses guess about the 'lifetime value' of their customers, when they try to assess how much a subject is worth at every moment of his or her life. And economists speak about the change that has happened from the commoditisation of space and material into the commoditisation of human time and duration. The prediction is that in the future almost everything will be a paid-for experience in which traditional reciprocal obligations and expectations – mediated by feelings of faith, empathy and solidarity – will be replaced by contractual relations in the form of paid memberships, subscriptions, admission charges, retainers and fees. The guess is that in the new era, people will purchase their very existence in small commercial segments, since their lives will be modelled on the movies so that 'each consumer's life experience will be commoditised and transformed into an unending series of theatrical moments, dramatic events, and personal transformations'.[15]

Rifkin summarises these new trends by pointing out that:

> In the new network economy what is really being bought and sold are ideas and images. The physical embodiment of these ideas and images becomes increasingly secondary to economic process. If the industrial marketplace was characterized by the exchange of things, the network economy is characterized by an access to concepts, carried inside physical forms.[16]

An example here again can be Nike, the company that truly sells only image. This company has no factories, machines or equipment, only an extensive network of suppliers, so-called production partners. Nike is only a research and design studio with a sophisticated marketing formula and distribution system.

Another important point is that if what mattered in industrial society was the quantity of goods, in post-industrial society this is replaced by quality of life. That is why we do not buy goods any more, but access them in time through, for example, leasing and franchising. It looks as if capitalism is losing its material origins and is becoming a temporal affair which is linked to the fact that customers do not so much need things, but just their function. In this context, the customer becomes a client and partner who needs attention, expertise and, most importantly, experience. (It is interesting how psychoanalysis is also replacing the name 'patient' with 'client'. And one wonders if some clients are doing analysis as some kind of a new experience they want to buy.)

Still another crucial element in our new society is the new take on community. Companies are thus desperate in creating communities for their clients. In many company manuals one can thus read about the four stages of how one deals with clients: first comes so-called 'awareness bonding', which makes the consumer aware of the new product or service; second is 'identity bonding', when the consumer starts in a particular way to identify with the brand; third is the 'relationship bonding', when the consumer establishes a particular attachment to the brand; and fourth is 'community bonding', when the brand maker keeps consumers satisfied by organising specific events and gatherings, or at least by sending birthday cards to the clients. In Slovenia, for example, the company American Way, which organises a chain for the home selling of various products, strongly encourages the building of a new community and thus organises family meetings of its members and so forth.

A particular marketing strategy that some brands of casual clothing use plays on an illusion of equality, which helps to mask class divides in today's world. Poor people shop in shops like Gap in order to appear middle class and the rich shop there in order to appear more 'normal'. Such brands also seem to erase gender differences in clothing, which changes the old divides in how men and women tend to choose their clothing. As Darian Leader points out, women usually search for what no one else has, while men want to buy clothes that everyone else is wearing.[17]

In sum, we are witnessing a transformation in the nature of commerce from the selling of things to the selling of images and the creation of communities. The idea behind this change is that people more than anything want to appear likeable to others and to themselves and also very much want to 'belong'. Now that old types of community, such as families or cultural groups, are in steady decline, by becoming subscribers, members and clients people acquire access to a new type of community. However, behind this attempt to create new communities is the perception that the totality of people's lived experience needs to be transformed into commercial fare. It looks as if human life itself becomes the ultimate commercial product. And some warn that when every aspect of our being becomes a paid-for activity then the commercial sphere becomes the final arbiter of our personal and collective existence.

The rapid emergence of capitalism thus provoked all kinds of new fears which had replaced the old ones that existed under communism.

In many post-socialist countries where global capitalism mostly brought richness to the elite and misery to the majority of the population, the fear in the face of global capital also opened old nationalist identification and paranoia about intrusive Western capital. Here, too, we can observe the phenomena that danger seems to be always coming from the outside.

In such a perception of fear, East and West are not so different from each other. If we look back at the times of the greatest tensions between America and the Communist states, we can observe how both parties perceived fear as related to the danger coming from the outside, and an answer to this fear was a raft of conspiracy theories. In the 1950s, in America there was a great fear of communist conspiracy; in one particular way this was reflected in the horror films of the time. Communism was perceived as a parasite that could invade the social body or as a deadly bacterium that could come into every pore of society. Horror films pictured the danger coming into society from the outside either in the form of extra-terrestrials or some strange external phenomenon that captures humans and replaces them with alien doubles as happens in the film *Invasion of the Body Snatchers* (Don Siegel 1956). The social paranoia of that time also centred on the fear of being brainwashed through communist ideological indoctrination, which would involve various forms of psychological control. At the same time, the Communist East feared the infiltration of the foreign spies and the ideological control coming from the West in the forms of bourgeois consumerism and entertainment.

In the late 1970s and early 1980s, a radical change happened in the perception of fear when the object of fear became more and more located inside society and especially inside the human body. Communists thus started being afraid of the enemy within in the form of the dissidents and the youth movement. In the West, the emergence of the HIV virus radically changed the perception of danger and the human body became the ultimate place where the enemy can attack. In the past two decades, immunology gained enormous power and the studies of the dangers of bacteria and viruses attacking the human body often use the military jargon of the 'wars within'. Similarly, one can observe changes in Hollywood horror movies: the films like *It Came from Outer Space* (Jack Arnold 1953) were replaced by *They Came from Within* (David Cronenberg 1975).

Over the past decade it looks as though the virus had replaced the bomb as the ultimate danger to human beings and the body became perceived at the same time as a possible victim and as a great warrior against this internal danger. But after September 11, it looks as if the virus and the bomb started to act together and follow a very similar pattern. Terrorists seem to be very similar to the viruses and bacteria – they are at first invisible, then they suddenly erupt in one place or another; afterward they hide again and one never knows how they multiply or what mutations they make after they come under attack. As bacteria became resistant to antibiotics, terrorists, too, seemed to resist the warfare that was supposed to annihilate them.

This simultaneous danger coming from both the outside and the inside has in a particular way been reflected in the struggles in the past decade that shattered the former Yugoslavia. The first paranoia about alleged Albanian separatists, who under Milošević's regime were renamed as terrorists, centred on the stories of Albanians trying to poison food in the army. Later, Milošević's great ideological victory was that he was able to create enormous support for his nationalist politics by continuously inventing new enemies and was able to keep alive the fear that there is some ultimate threat to the Serbs. The perception that violence is like a virus which unexpectedly attacks a community has also been the theme of the film *Before the Rain* (Milce Manchevski 1994), which depicts the nationalist tensions between Albanians and Macedonians. Here the idea of violence as the virus ultimately covers up the political dimensions of the conflict.

After September 11, the American government has been keeping the fear of new, potential attacks alive by continuously reminding the public of the unpredictable danger that can come from hidden terrorists. Some have even observed a pattern in the way the government uses hints about potential new attacks. In the first months after September 11, new warnings came every three weeks, just before the weekends. One is tempted to guess that some psychologists might have advised the government to keep the public alerted to possible danger, so that the public would continue with their patriotic support of the government's foreign policies. In the way the media speculated about probable new targets of attacks, one can also discern a particular pattern. There almost seemed to be competition among the media over who would figure out another possible place for attack. One of the first ideas was that Disneyland might be such symbolic target. Since Disneyland is such an ultimate American fantasy, one is not surprised that America envisions that an attack on this place would inflict a particular symbolic wound into the American's self-identity. Other envisioned places of attack, however, all centred on the body being the target of violence through contaminated water, air ventilation or food poisoning.

If at the time of the divide between capitalism and communism the enemy had been clearly perceived as someone coming from the outside, now, with globalised capitalism, the enemy is like a wandering terrorist (who in its elusive character strangely resembles the anti-Semitic image of the dangerous wandering Jew), while at the same time the inner antagonisms that mark Western capitalist societies are perceived in the guise of viral dangers. Here we need to remember that in the former Yugoslavia, Milošević kept power for so long precisely because he was able to constantly invent new enemies.

Milošević in the last years of his life played the role of an anti-American hero who at the same time condemned NATO's military actions in the Third World and presented himself as the politician who has only been fighting terrorism all along. Milošević's 'success' has been that under the guise of constantly finding new potential enemies and thus keeping the fear alive, he was able to introduce radical economic and political changes in society without the majority of people paying much attention to them. In guise of these changes, it has been most ironic that after Milošević's fall, Serbian politicians wanted only to charge him for his financial manipulations and not for his involvement in war crimes. Bush's government, under the guise of fighting terrorists and bacteria, also introduced radical economic and political changes that went unnoticed by the public. When people feel uncertain and afraid they look for clear images of their enemies.

Returning to the problem of the former Yugoslavia, one can observe that some perceive the rapid introduction of Western capitalism as a success, while others perceive this as a failure. However, in this distinction between success and failure, corporations seem to have outsmarted the public again and thus introduce a new marketing logo: Success in failure. How great success in failure can be, we may learn from the example of Coca-Cola and its advertisement entitled 'Life tastes good!' In the TV clip we see a boy visiting his grandfather who asks him how his studies are going. The young guy responds that he is taking a year off. Then the grandfather enquires about the last girlfriend and the grandson admits that he already has a new one. The grandson then asks how his grandmother is doing and the grandfather informs him that she has moved in with their friend from the bridge club. At this point both men salute themselves with Coca-Cola and we are reminded that life tastes good.

This advertisement very much depicts the reality of today's family life, where the stability of relationships is a thing of the past. Things have changed for the young and the old. But now the advertising depicts what used to be perceived as failure (not studying at school, break-ups of relationships) as just a change and continues by reminding us that life is good anyhow. Contemporary consumer ideology is constantly convincing us that the subject is just a work of art, that 'being' has given way to 'becoming', and that the new self is just an unfolding story continually being updated and re-edited. Such re-editing can also be observed among corporations who today struggle for continuity and thus want to create an image about themselves that will pass into the future and be present in as many places as possible. Both individuals and corporations thus try very much to achieve some kind of immortality. However, here we need to remember Kierkegaard's famous saying that more horrible than death is actually the possibility of immortality.

Notes

1. *The New York Times*, 18 September 2002.
2. See Sigmund Freud, 'Group psychology and the analysis of the ego' (1921[1985]), *S.E.* 18.
3. More on this in R. Salecl, *The Spoils of Freedom: Psychoanalysis and Feminism after the Fall of Socialism* (London: Routledge, 1994).
4. This point is further developed in R. Salecl, *On Anxiety* (London: Routledge, 2004).
5. *The Sunday Times, Style* magazine, 15 September 2002.
6. For the analysis of how the ideology of the 'new money and being yourself' was linked to the success and failure of the 1990s dot.com businesses, see T. Frank, *One Market under God: Extreme Capitalism, Market Populism, and the End of Economics Democracy* (New York: Anchor Books, 2000).
7. The inability to make decision is referred to also as buridantis. See, www.oprah.com/health/omag./health_omag_200101_reinven.jhtml
8. See *The New York Times*, 27 August 2000.
9. Ibid.
10. See S. Freud, 'Group Psychology and the Analysis of the Ego', in *The Pelican Freud Library*, Volume X (London: Penguin, 1985). Paradoxically it was Freud's nephew, Edward Barney, who became seen as the father of public relations. His book, *Propaganda* in 1928 promoted advertising as the primary mode of communication. As a representative of Lucky Strike, Barney became known as the person who helped to break the ban on women smoking in public. His marketing strategy was to organise a group of women contingent of women to ostentatiously puff 'torches of freedom' during a parade.
11. See N. Klein, *No Logo* (London: Flamingo, 2001).
12. J. Lears, *Fables of Abundance: A Cultural History of Advertising in America* (New York, Basic Books, 1994): 139, 208.
13. Recently, there has been a boom of such coffee places in Japan. The consumers there explain that in the past after work-hours they used to frequent bars and tea houses in order to avoid going home, but now they go to Starbucks

because it feels more like home. Of course, this fake 'home' is a calm oasis without the screaming children and nagging spouse.

14. J. Rifkin, *The Age of Access* (New York: J.P. Tarcher, 2000): 7.
15. Ibid.: 29.
16. Ibid.: 30.
17. See D. Leader, *Why Do Women Write More Letters Than They Send? A Meditation on the Loneliness of the Sexes* (New York: Basic Books, 1997).

14
Revisiting Involvement and Detachment: Yugoslavia As an Object of Scholarship

John B. Allcock

'Hang on to your objectivity!'

I begin by quoting from the concluding paragraphs of the paper I delivered to the conference on 'Yugoslavia: Antagonism and the Construction of Identity' in August 1992:

> Shortly after the civil war engulfed Croatia I decided to telephone two families with whom I have had long-standing friendships in order to find out if they were still safe. After some difficulty I managed to contact both of them. The difficulty was understandable. One family, which lived near the Borongaj barracks in Zagreb, had been intermittently in the air-raid shelters. The other had been evacuated from Dubrovnik and had found refuge with relatives in Montenegro. I asked each of them if there was anything I could do for them – more as a token of my good will than in any expectation that I would be able to help. Although members of different ethnic groups, by coincidence they both said exactly the same thing to me that evening: 'Hang on to your objectivity'.[1]

'Hang on to your objectivity.' The spirit in which I want to continue this discussion is not one of vindication – asserting the claim that 'I did just that!' It is not one of self-criticism – making a public confession of the extent to which I might have failed to live up to this aspiration. My purpose is to explore what I believe I have learned during the period of the break-up of the former Yugoslav federation which might enable us to advance our understanding of what is involved in the pursuit of academic detachment.

Certainly the problem of involvement and detachment has been a controversial one throughout the past decade. Accusations of partiality have been made loudly and publicly. Brendan Simms' review of British foreign policy with respect to the region is probably the most noteworthy case in point.[2] Perhaps closer to home in relation to the community of academic social science is Carole Hodge's pamphlet on the supposed pro-Serb lobby in Britain.[3] One might add to these examples – although I do not think that it is appropriate on this occasion to indulge in wholesale 'naming and shaming'. (I do 'have a little list', in the words of W. S. Gilbert – but probably we all do.) In general terms Robert Hayden has summed up the problem well:

Protracted international conflicts often produce more partisans than scholars; if truth is the first journalistic casualty of war, objectivity is the first scholarly one. Academic debates of the former Yugoslavia are as polarized as those surrounding the creation of Israel or the partitioning of Cyprus, with criticism of a study often depending more on whether the work supports the commentator's predetermined position than on the coherence of its theory and reliability and sufficiency of its arguments.

Subjectivity, involvement, engagement and partisanship are chronically disseminated throughout the field, distorting priorities and imposing a political framework on academic debate.[4]

'Hang on to your objectivity!' Very well, but exactly *how* is one to do that? Two possibilities come to mind. Does one achieve this by an act of will? Is objectivity like Lee Strasberg's 'Method acting'? You spend some time working yourself into the mindset and motivation of an objective person. Is it a matter of adopting the academic equivalent of Norman Vincent Peale's 'power of positive thinking', repeating to oneself the mantra 'I must, I can, and I will be objective!'?

Does the assurance of objectivity, on the other hand, depend upon our always selecting the middle option – the 'Third Way' – between competing alternatives? Max Weber has already warned us of the inadequacy of this 'optimistic syncretism':

It can, to be sure, be just as obligatory subjectively for the practical politician...to mediate between antagonistic points of view as to take sides with one of them. But this has nothing whatsoever to do with scientific 'objectivity.' *Scientifically the 'middle course' is not even truer by a hairsbreadth*, than the most extreme party ideal of the right or left.[5]

This approach has been singled out rightly by Simms as an indication of the lack of objectivity, where it reduced the position of the British government to 'even-handedness' in relation to the conflicting 'factions' in the Bosnian War. In his view it was precisely this determination to steer a middle course which betrayed the government's failure to achieve an objective understanding of the issues.

If in neither of these two directions, then, in what does the key to objectivity, or detachment, lie?[6] I believe that for social scientists the goal of objectivity is important. In pursuit of this goal, not surprisingly, I believe that it is appropriate to begin with some remarks about the work of Norbert Elias, whose collected essays on the subject of 'involvement and detachment' remain one of the most important contributions to reflection on this topic.[7] Although I admire the work of Elias, I believe that he does not answer adequately the question of exactly how objectivity is to be defended and advanced. We need to move beyond Elias: and it is to that end that this chapter is primarily directed. I illustrate my argument by reference to some aspects of the academic study of the Yugoslav region over the past ten years; but it will be useful to approach this concrete task (parodying Elias) by means of a 'detour via abstraction'.

Norbert Elias on 'involvement and detachment'

Three important points might be said to provide the basis of Elias's approach to 'involvement and detachment', with which it will be helpful to begin.

In the first place, what is under consideration here is *a continuum of positions between notional extremes*, and not a simple binary choice:

> One cannot say of a person's outlook in any absolute sense that it is detached or involved... Only small babies, and among adults perhaps only insane people, become involved in whatever they experience with complete abandon to their feelings here and now; and again only the insane can remain totally unmoved by what goes on around them. Normally adult behaviour lies on a scale somewhere between these two extremes.[8]

Our pursuit of objectivity does not oblige us to choose between infantilism and insanity! Neither individuals nor the groups to which they belong can be identified without qualification as involved or detached, either in general or in relation to any particular issue. As

Robert van Krieken insists in his study of Elias, what distinguishes his position is:

> ... a rejection of *both* the concept of 'truth' as absolutely distinct from 'falsity' *and* a relativistic conception of knowledge, in favour of the concept of a greater or lesser 'object adequacy' in human knowledge, lying somewhere between 'involvement' and 'detachment'.[9]

Second, Elias emphasises the importance of appreciating that neither involvement nor detachment are states of individual psychology. A distinguishing feature of the social sciences is the fact that as observers we are simultaneously and necessarily implicated in the action we study:

> [Social scientists] cannot cease to take part in, and be affected by, the social and political affairs of their groups and their time. Their participation and involvement, moreover, is itself one of the conditions for comprehending the problems they try to solve as scientists...

The problem confronting those who study one or the other aspects of human groups is how to keep their two roles as participant and as enquirer clearly and consistently apart and, as a professional group, to establish in their work the undisputed dominance of the latter.[10]

To the extent that it is possible for individuals to be said to be either involved or detached, it is a matter of their being supported within a matrix which is social and cultural in character – particularly that of their membership of the profession of science.

Third, a good deal of Elias's argument is addressed to the false tendency to take a model of 'scientific method' based upon an idealised image of the way physics works, and to regard this as providing a guarantee of our capacity to achieve scientific detachment.[11] 'Scientific method' can become, in this view, the equivalent of a kind of talisman. This stance is erroneous for several reasons. It is often in danger of falling back upon the voluntaristic understanding of the problem, whereby all that individuals need to do is to 'believe and be saved'. If this is so, then to be 'scientific' is little more complicated than 'pulling one's sock up'. More significant and more interesting, perhaps, is his affirmation that we need to recognise the fact that different types of system require analysis according to different types of model, not all of which are amenable to judgement by the same standards.[12] Uncritical and unconditional commitment to a single ideal of scientific method *is itself a form of involvement*, which subordinates our actions to the satisfaction which they give us rather than their ultimate effectiveness. We feel good about being 'properly scientific', even if that goal is achieved at the cost of advancing our understanding of the social world. Objectivity is advanced, however, by our being honest and clear-sighted about the specific characteristics of the social world, which is our field of study, in place of an ideological scientism.

Elias's argument is both helpful and unhelpful, with respect to my goal of hanging on to objectivity.

It is helpful in that it reassures us that we do not have to strive for the unreachable (and indeed, undesirable) goal of complete freedom from commitment. Who among us is not in some sense and to some extent partisan in relation to one or another of the peoples or regions of the former Yugoslavia? Perhaps only those who could be described as 'Yugonostalgic'. Who would be left if we had to renounce all of our loyalties to friends or to country? In this respect, Elias's notion of the 'detour via detachment' is helpful. We are all situated along his continuum of positions, moving towards greater 'object-adequacy' and detachment, although perhaps at an uneven pace.

Furthermore, his emphasis upon the importance of the collective endeavour of science is helpful, in that we do not need to take upon ourselves as individuals, unaided, the intolerable burden of responsibility for objectivity.

I find Elias's attack upon a simple-minded scientism, based upon the model of physics, to be very helpful. We do not need to beat ourselves over our heads with our failure to live up to an irrelevant ideal of 'pure' science.

He is rather less than helpful, I find, when it comes to telling us positively what we can do or should do. What Saint Norbert offers us is a *via negativa*, which enjoins renunciation. There is a monastic rule which requires us to renounce our indulgence in the sins of involvement. It leaves far from clear, however, the picture of how we should live in the service of detachment. The problem is compounded by two factors – by the central position which the 'double bind' occupies in his field of attention, and by the sheer scale of his historical canvas.

Naturally, as social scientists, we are impelled into the study of particular problems because they *matter* – not only to us personally, but within our *milieu* more generally. Our 'emotivity of response', as Elias puts it, has the effect of placing us in a double bind, which works to undermine our potential for achieving the level of detachment which might make for a more object-adequate address to the problem:

> High emotivity of response lessens the chance of a realistic assessment of the critical process and, hence, of a realistic practice in relation to it; relatively unrealistic practice under the pressure of strong

effects lessens the chance of bringing the critical process under control. In short, inability to control tends to go hand in hand with high emotivity of response, which keeps the chance of controlling the dangers of the process at a low level, which keeps at a high level the emotivity of response, and so forth.[13]

Furthermore, I am impressed, one should perhaps say daunted, by the historical scale of Elias's treatment of these issues. It is important to be clear that his concern is not identical with Weber's discussion of value-neutrality as an issue of method in the social sciences. Elias's remit is better described as a sociological history of human knowledge. He used to describe a part of his introductory lectures in sociology at Leicester as the provision of a 'bird's eye view of human history', and this is expressive of the scope of his discussion of the movement towards greater 'object-adequacy'. 'Elias' discussion of involvement and detachment (Mennell insists) is not narrowly concerned with the problem of "objectivity". It raises the whole problem of the long-term development of human knowledge and the place of the sciences within it.'[14] If the grandeur of his account of the process of detachment matches that of his analysis of the emergence of the monarchical state in medieval Europe in *The Civilizing Process*, then clearly the individuals involved in it can hardly be expected to grasp the wider significance of the events in which they are involved, let alone to 'put their shoulder to the wheel of history', in Lenin's celebrated phrase.[15]

Given the apparent intractability of the 'double bind' problem which undoubtedly afflicts the social sciences, compounded by the sense of the relative historical insignificance of any contribution which we might be able to make to the larger enterprise of the advancement of human knowledge, there is a temptation to lapse into despair. Is there actually anything that we can do in order to ensure that we do hang on to our objectivity? I want to reply to that question with a tentative 'Yes'.

Serendipity

In part this chapter grows out of my own earlier attempt to answer this very question. My answer (offered to the conference of August 1992) hinged upon the idea that, when one examined the course of academic study of Yugoslavia in Britain, it was a striking feature of that development that detachment seems to have been enhanced *accidentally*, in several ways. I developed the idea of a 'detour via *involvement*', to convey the sense that (albeit imperfectly and haltingly) there were reasons to celebrate the achievements of scholarship in this area, even though these were entirely serendipitous by-products of the specific character of people's involvement in the region. Three illustrations of this 'detour' were explored, whereby it might be claimed that British scholars had (at least relatively speaking) advanced the cause of a more detached understanding of Yugoslav affairs.

> I compared the avowedly pro-Yugoslav activities of British academics with the failure to engage at all which had characterised their French colleagues, whose lack of engagement with the study of the region arose from General de Gaulle's detestation of the regime which had executed Draža Mihailović.

Which is the more 'involved' historical account of the war (I asked)? Is it the engagement of British historians in the construction of a historical narrative which met the standards of professional historians despite its possible incompleteness or one-sidedness, or the almost total silence of the French?[16]

My second example centred on the tendency of British students of Yugoslavia to be drawn into the field as a result of their own commitment to socialism. Despite the unquestionably involved stance this entailed, I argued that:

> Yugoslavia did have a genuinely important role in relativising the claims to historical inevitability of the Soviet model. It held out the possibility of there being contradictions within socialist systems, and gave a critical edge to the appraisal of real socialism within the Soviet bloc to an extent not often appreciated by westerners.[17]

Finally, I examined my own experience, and the 'Yugophile' position which might be said to have characterised my own work. I pointed out that the specific topics to which I had devoted attention as a sociologist all drew me into contact with groups or interests which could be regarded as relatively marginal in relation to the official model of Yugoslav self-managing socialism – agriculture, the private sector, tourism and women.

> Just as the relatively peripheral character of my academic interests, and the often marginal nature of my contacts, have given me a measure of distance from 'official' representations of Yugoslav identity in

the past, so my sense of what one might (perversely) call the 'coherence' of Yugoslavia gives me a standpoint or relative detachment from which to challenge the emerging common-sense wisdom of the present day.[18]

Although I stand by the case I made on that earlier occasion, I now find my own argument deficient, in retrospect, because it does leave the process of advancing detachment largely to chance. In all of the illustrations I took, the increment of detachment came about as an *unintended* consequence of the actions of those involved, and could only be recognised with hindsight for what it was. There is hope for our aspiration to produce knowledge which is more objective; but at the end of the day we still do not know what we might do to enhance our objectivity in a systematic way. How do we actually 'hang on to' our objectivity in a manner which does not depend entirely upon serendipity?

The 'State of Nature'

The greater part of my teaching career has been spent in an interdisciplinary department which included colleagues from philosophy. This exposure has been reflected in aspects of my own earlier work, and especially my engagement with the philosophical foundations of Emile Durkheim's sociology.[19] Recently I became aware of the potential interest of a philosophical contribution to clarifying our problem, in the form of Bernard Williams's study, *Truth and Truthfulness*.[20] A brief acquaintance with his work will be helpful in developing my argument.

The primary focus of Williams's interest is not the definition of the concept of 'truth', which has preoccupied so many of his colleagues in the past. Rather, it is what he calls the '*virtues* of truth – the idea that characteristically a certain *value* attaches to being truthful. He even refers at one point to the "passion for truth" '.[21] He sees the importance of truthfulness in human societies as best understood through the device of an imagined 'State of Nature'. This is not an attempt to provide a speculative reconstruction the distant past of the human race, but a 'thought experiment', which enables him to clarify in general terms the condition of a community in which truth-telling could get off the ground and be sustained. In this respect, he argues that truthfulness is necessarily rooted in the fundamental characteristics of any community which coordinates action and shares meaning through the medium of language.

'No society (Williams insists) can get by...with a purely instrumental conception of the values of truth.' Truthfulness cannot be 'entirely explained in terms of other goods, and in particular the value of getting what one wants, avoiding danger, mastering the environment, and so on'.[22] The values of *accuracy* and *sincerity*, which provide the foundation of his analysis, should be presumed to possess their fundamental character because without them no community engaged in 'cooperative communication' is conceivable. Paradoxically, our relationship to truth is one of involvement – we are *committed* to the 'virtues of truth' – but it is precisely our involvement in truthfulness that impels us towards greater 'object-adequacy' (to use Elias's phrase).

The problem with Williams's illuminating discourse, however, is that I wonder if it is not too optimistic. This is, of course, a *deliberately* optimistic work. The target of Williams's critique is the widely disseminated post-modern scepticism about the possibilities of truth which he sees as pervading the current intellectual climate, and the attendant spirit of helpless relativism. His attack, in this respect, is directed against what he calls the 'deniers'. He wants to affirm the idea that human truthfulness has a kind of anthropological foundation, in that it can be shown to be rooted in the necessary conditions of any successful human community.

Perhaps it is not too strong a statement to say that that Elias leaves me with a sense of despair. After all, in his discussion of the 'fishermen in the maelstrom', he never actually explains how the younger fisherman does manage to reach his more detached appraisal of his predicament.[23] The sense of complacency to which Williams is possibly prone, however, might be seen as equally unsatisfactory. I applaud his efforts to combat what is all too often the legitimation for sheer intellectual laziness. Nevertheless, if we are not careful, his optimism might do us a disservice, if it leads us to assume that, as with the hope that truth can be told, the aspiration for objectivity might be expected just to arise spontaneously, without any particular effort on our part. Surely the appropriate response to the injunction to 'Hang on to your objectivity' must involve more than just 'hanging on'!

Three possibilities

As I have already suggested, my discussion so far might be regarded as a kind of 'detour via abstraction'. In making some concrete suggestions about how it might be possible for us to 'hang on to our objectivity', I want to return to some specific aspects of scholarly engagement with the process of the disintegration of the former Yugoslav federation over the past decade. In that respect I want to suggest three important techniques that are available to all of us, which might assist us in our quest for detachment.

i) The deployment of theory   'The facts' are often made available through the work of good journalists; and if as social scientists all we have to offer is facts then our claim to any particular authority is limited. What we do as academics is to *frame the facts*; and we do so by the provision of explanatory devices which are typically known as 'theories'. These are logical structures which are independent of any specific bodies of data which they are expected to explain, and it is precisely these character-istics which give to theories their distanciating potential. This is what we have to offer the world – take it or leave it. I maintain that where we have managed to achieve and sustain a significant measure of detach-ment in our attempts to understand what happened to Yugoslavia, this has come about (at least in part) because of the effective deployment of theory. Conversely, where our understanding remains weak or con-fused, it is often because we have allowed our programme to be defined by criteria which have little or no theoretical interest.

A very positive example of the use of theory in Yugoslav sociology has been the work done on stratification. Despite attempts by the League of Communists to ideologise discussion of issues relating to inequality in Yugoslavia, a substantial body of material was accumulated by Yugoslav sociologists, documenting and analysing the nature and development of inequality in their own country.[24] This was achieved because Yugoslav sociologists were thoroughly au fait with worldwide discussion of the topic within the discipline, and it was against a professionally accept-able framework of theoretical discourse that they measured their work. I am sure that a high level of discursive penetration of issues relating to stratification was achieved in this area because, even where Yugoslav sociologists were compelled to play a kind of game in which the impli-cations of what they discovered were sometimes deliberately veiled by verbal tricks, they were effectively in command of sociological theory. This foundation has continued to provide the basis for the continuing production of high-quality work on the nature of social and economic inequality in the post-Yugoslav period.[25]

The success of sociologists from the region in this area contrasts remarkably with work on the sociology of tourism, which has remained descriptive, and embarrassingly under-theorised.[26] Here the pace and direction of questioning was set by the importance of tourism as an export sector, and the policy significance of sustaining and enlarg-ing it. Consequently academic treatment of the area was dominated by a crude 'cost-benefit analysis'.[27] The attempt by Simo Elaković to

introduce a Yugoslav academic readership to wider understandings
of tourism within sociology was not as influential as it should have
been.[28] Even where writers on this topic did indicate a familiarity with
the wider theoretical discussion in the discipline, they never succeeded
in utilising theory in order to give themselves any distance from the
definition of problems which was imposed by narrow and short-term
economic interest.

Whereas in Yugoslavia the primary danger to academic objectivity
lay in the elbowing-aside of theory by political and economic interest,
in Britain the greater threat in this respect has come from journalism.
One of the assets of *Academe* in Britain has been its openness to other
activities, such as journalism.[29] Nevertheless, there are some obvious
dangers of getting into bed with journalists. Above all, one runs the risk
that the academic agenda will be shaped by media concerns. In other
words, we run the risk of being seduced by journalistic criteria of news
value.

The factors which make for high news value are well documented in
the sociology of mass communication, and include inter alia a tendency
to focus upon elite persons. 'The more an event concerns elite people,
the more probable that it will become a news item,' write Galtung and
Ruge in their seminal exploration of this issue.[30] This 'personification'
of affairs, which is stimulated by the need of the media to provide readily accessible frameworks of meaning, constitutes a significant pressure
towards involvement, and is dangerously corrosive of detached social
science. This reaches its apogee, perhaps, in the absurd concentration on
the figure of Slobodan Milošević in the reporting of the Yugoslav wars.
The idea that it is possible to separate the politics of Milošević from his
context within the League of Communists, and the wider legitimation
crisis of the Yugoslav state, is a sociological absurdity. Unless one arms
oneself with theory, however, the pressures of media attention come to
identify the break-up of Yugoslavia to a grotesquely inflated extent with
the personality of this man – or perhaps worse, with the Macbeth-like
relationship between him and his wife.[31]

Without theory we are lost. With it we possess a resource which can
work for detachment and objectivity.[32]

ii) The resort to comparison One of the difficulties under which the
study of Yugoslavia laboured for many years was the problem of its supposed idiosyncrasy. There was at one time a commonly repeated tag
which described it as 'the graveyard of generalisations'. An entrenched
belief in the uniqueness of Yugoslavia came to be reflected in the reputation of those who studied the country for their 'eccentricity' (as

I termed it in an address to the Yugoslav Sociological Association in 1989).[33] Although that sense of eccentricity has gone, largely due to the dramatic way in which the country figured in news headlines over the past ten years, that vigorous interest for some time led to a problem, in that Yugoslav studies became too self-centred – occasionally almost solipsistic. As a corrective to this I want to insist upon the importance of *comparison*.

In the published version of my former chapter I adopted as a motto some lines from Leonard Cohen's song 'The Captain'.

> ...tell me, Captain, if you know
> Of a decent place to stand.
> There is no decent place to stand in a massacre;
> But if a woman take your hand
> Go and stand with her.

My intention in using these lines has been misunderstood on several occasions, so I want to take this opportunity to point out that Cohen's song does *not* say, 'if a women takes your hand go and *lie* with her'! My purpose in using these lines related to the point I made about the distanciating value of associating with people in marginal positions in society. I want to emphasise that point, in relation to my claim about the importance of comparison.

In a society as patriarchal as that of the Balkans, in almost any area of activity, a degree of objectivity can be achieved by means of the distancing device of listening to the point of view of women. (This does not mean that what you hear will be invariably more reasonable, as British soldiers will assure you who were confronted by groups of women in the Republika Srpska, attempting to block humanitarian aid convoys!) That point of view, and the experience it represents, often will be *different* and will relativise the dominant and predominantly masculine discourses.

By way of illustration, I offer an example from the historical research I did in preparing *Explaining Yugoslavia* (Allcock 2000). During the period of the Great Depression, when Yugoslavia's grain exports were hit hard, there was a debate in the Assembly about agriculture. A Serbian deputy, discovering that the export of eggs appeared to be more valuable for the country's economic health than the traditional export of maize, bewailed that fact that Yugoslavia's had become an 'economy of grand-mothers'! The raising of poultry was women's work, of lower status, and hence by definition of lesser economic significance. The fact that

Yugoslavia relied upon its grandmothers to stay solvent was a national disgrace. The woman who (metaphorically or literally) 'takes your hand' might well be a grandmother!

During the writing of *Explaining Yugoslavia* I found it extremely instructive to encounter works dealing with the economic history of the region written by scholars whose primary interest was the Habsburg or Ottoman Empires, not the Balkans.[34] Yugoslav writers had tended to take for granted the idea that the relative economic development of Slovenia had deep historical roots. Authors whose point of reference was the Czech lands, however, tended to see things very differently. More notably, the well-known Balkan proclivity for blaming their poverty upon 'five hundred years of Turkish night' appeared to be distinctly thin when put up against the research of recent economic historians of the Ottoman Empire.

There is in our area an insufficiency of work by social scientists such as that of Paul Stahl, on the 'household, village and village confederation in south-eastern Europe', which compels us to examine patterns and processes which extend across time and space.[35] Comparison can serve a particularly important function in that it assists us to judge the applicability of theory.[36] Historians have served us much better, generally speaking, in this respect, as histories of the Balkan region are relatively common.[37] In our search for objectivity we could be aided enormously by a greater willingness to follow their lead, and to rely more frequently upon comparative study.[38]

iii) The importance of discipline The need for 'discipline' is different from the need for theory. By 'discipline' I intend to call to mind the notion of *craft*. I have been encouraged to think about this issue, in part, by Bernard Williams's discussion (in *Truth and Truthfulness*) of the importance of 'making sense'.[39]

We are able to 'make sense' to each other, Williams tells us, at least in part, through *narrative*. A chronicle 'is simply a list of happenings in chronological order', whereas a narrative 'tries to make sense of something'.[40] It implies a story which connects these happenings to each other in some kind of order. What passes as an acceptable order will vary, of course; and there is no single order in which 'happenings' might possibly be linked into a story. What characterises 'disciplines' is the repertoires of conventions which control the telling of an acceptable narrative. It is this notion of the skilful deployment of these conventions to create a convincing narrative which I have in mind in speaking of a 'craft'. Williams's own attention is devoted to examining the attributes of the 'craft' of the historian, although he acknowledges that there can be others, such as psychological or sociological narratives, each of which is guided by its own body of conventions.

It is not that one is wrong and the other is right. Each discipline will have criteria which will enable its practitioners to recognise a story that is 'well told', in relation to the conventions which define the discipline. At this point we can see how this understanding of 'discipline' relates to theory. The concept of theory has to do with the *logical* structure of ideas within a given discourse, whereas the narratives which occupy Williams's attention have to do with the *rhetorical* form of that discourse. A theory stands up by virtue of its logical integrity. A narrative stands up by virtue of its rhetorical cohesion. It might seem to fly in the face of our normal approach to these matters to link directly rhetoric, which we habitually think of in terms of persuasion (an even of verbal trickery directed to that end) and objectivity. Nevertheless, I want to argue, drawing upon Williams, that in its sense-making function in the social sciences rhetoric is at least potentially an ally of objectivity, and not necessarily its ancestral sworn enemy.

In my own work recently I have been impressed by the importance of command of the craft of a discipline, and the ways in which that craft is differently constituted in different disciplines. For the second time, recently, I was approached by the International Criminal Tribunal for the Former Yugoslavia (ICTY) at The Hague, with a request to advise trial attorneys in the Office of the Prosecutor. This has brought home to me vividly the way in which the conventions of a lawyer's narrative of events may not be those of the sociologist. Both the lawyer (as prosecutor) and the sociologist (as expert witness) are committed to the pursuit of truth in relation to a given set of events. The story which the lawyer needs to tell hinges upon the need to determine the *individual responsibility* of a specific person who has been indicted for certain crimes. Which individuals, for example, were responsible for the Ahmići massacre of April 1993? It is this concept of 'responsibility' which gives meaning to the lawyer's story. The concern of the sociologist (qua sociologist), however, might have much more to do with establishing *structural patterns which have a causal bearing upon action*. In this respect, the nature of inter-ethnic relations in that part of West-Central Bosnia, and their changing significance within a situation of political conflict, might be of greater significance in imparting meaning to the story, than the personal responsibility of agents.

The story which the lawyer will develop must identify individual agents, and place them specifically in time and space in relation to events in Ahmići. That narrative must incorporate an attempt to establish the reasons for their actions. The sociologist is equally concerned with the truth of the matter as far as those facts are concerned. These could well be assembled, however, into a very different narrative, which might have to do, inter alia, with the general causes of the breakdown of the republic of Bosnia and Herzegovina as a state.

A second, and rather different, illustration arises in connection with the recent donation to the library of the University of Bradford of archival material from the collection of the American anthropologist Joel Halpern. Curious as to the nature of this material, and its possible utility, I spent an afternoon familiarising myself with its organisation, and dipping into some of the records which seemed potentially to have a bearing on my own work. Knowing Joel Halpern's studies of rural Serbia in their published form, I was fascinated to see the raw material from which these had been crafted.[41] I began to gain an appreciation of the process which had to take place in order to transform this enormous assemblage of data (public documents, statistics, personal memoirs of villagers, the anthropologist's own direct observations, and so on) into a narrative which might be useful in making sense of life in the Serbian village.

Lawyers, sociologists or anthropologists are not just thrown into this task of providing a sense-making narrative relying solely upon their own initiative, and making it up as they go along. The *conventions of narration* which are the property of their disciplines intervene as an intermediary between the initially chaotic mass of data and the narrator. The criteria as to whether or not the story is well told provide the means by which some distance is secured between the events and their narrator. They help, in other words, to ensure detachment – objectivity. The rhetorical conventions which define a discipline, therefore, are not reducible to the status of a decorative surface – a matter of mere style.[42] They are, in their sense-making role, and in their capacity for creating distance from the material, essential allies in Williams's quest for 'truthfulness', and my own pursuit of detachment.[43]

Conclusions

In the search for the means of detachment in our study of Yugoslavia and its successor states, I find that perhaps the work of Norbert Elias is too pessimistic, overwhelmed as he was by anxieties about the prospect of nuclear war, which dominated his time. Trapped within the double-binds created by our own emotional engagement with the world, he holds out the hope that social science will move towards a more 'object-adequate' understanding of our world – but only very slowly, and only if we are (like his 'fishermen in the maelstrom') by some undefined means able to avoid annihilation. Despite his Comtean faith in the capacity of sociology to link science and social policy, I do agree with him on one count. Sociology is not just *for sociology*. It is not an end in itself. My position on this is expressed very deliberately in the title of my recent book *Explaining Yugoslavia*.[44] (Note that I did not call it *Fixing Yugoslavia*!) As far as I am concerned, the realm in which we seek detachment is that of explanation. What to do as a result of our explanations I am content to see remain the territory of involvement.

Bernard Williams, on the other hand, is probably too optimistic. As a denizen of the Common Room at All Souls, his world is that of the civilised exchange of assertion, which is a long way from the ideological cockpit of the recent Yugoslav wars. His affirmation that we are already in possession of important tools of objectivity, in the form of the essential 'values of truthfulness', is certainly encouraging, and indeed serves its purpose of pulling us back from the brink of the hopeless relativism into which we might be tempted to fall as a consequence of Robert Hayden's observation with which I set out. I suppose that as we contemplate the task of analysing the course of events over the past decade, Williams's optimism is no small comfort.

My own earlier attempt to address the issue of involvement and detachment I now find inadequate. Whereas I stand by the points I made then, I no longer believe that we need to rely upon mere serendipity to advance the cause of a more detached understanding of our region. What I have offered in this essay is by no means the end of the story. It has been my intention, reflecting upon our engagement with scholarship relating to Yugoslavia and its successors over the past ten years, to underline the fact that we have already, in *theory*, in *comparison* and in *discipline*, significant resources which can serve the struggle to achieve a more detached, 'object-adequate' understanding of Yugoslavia and its successors. Our common endeavour to understand the events in the Balkans of the past ten years, though inviting our involvement and motivated by it, is not condemned to hopeless ideological relativism and partisanship.

Notes

Research Unit in South East European Studies, University of Bradford, Bradford BD7 1DP. Tel: +44 1274 233993. E-mail: j.b.allcock@bradford.ac.uk.

1. J. B. Allcock, 'Involvement and Detachment: Yugoslavia as an Object of Scholarship', *Journal of Area Studies*, 3 (1993): 144–160. The passage cited is from p. 158. I retain the friendships in question.
2. B. Simms, *Unfinest Hour: Britain and the Destruction of Bosnia* (London: Allen Lane, 2001).
3. C. Hodge, *The Serb Lobby in the United Kingdom* (Seattle: University of Washington, 1999), Donald Treadgold Papers in Russian, East European and Central Asian Studies, No. 22, September.
4. R. M. Hayden, *Blueprints for a House Divided: The Constitutional Logic of the Yugoslav Conflict* (University of Michigan Press, 2000): 18–19. Hayden adds: 'When one side in such conflict wins politically, it usually also wins academically, because analyses that indicate that a politics that won is, in fact, wrong tend to be discounted. Political hegemony establishes intellectual orthodoxy.' My thanks to Nick Glynias for drawing this passage to my attention.
5. M. Weber, *The Methodology of the Social Sciences* (New York: Free Press, 1949): 57). Emphasis in the original.
6. I shall treat 'objectivity' and 'detachment' (and also their antonyms such as 'involvement', 'engagement' and 'subjectivity') as synonyms here, for stylistic reasons. There may well be philosophical grounds for separating their meanings, but that discussion does not seem to be relevant to my concerns here.
7. N. Elias, *Involvement and Detachment* (Oxford: Basil Blackwell, 1987).
8. Elias, *Involvement and Detachment*: 3.
9. R. Van Krieken, *Norbert Elias* (London: Routledge, 1998): 137. See also S. Mennell, *Norbert Elias: An Introduction* (Oxford: Basil Blackwell, 1992): esp. 160.
10. Elias, *Involvement and Detachment*: 16.
11. Elias, *Involvement and Detachment*: esp. 21–26.
12. Elias is notoriously sparing in his use of footnotes. Nevertheless, it seems to be generally agreed that the direct object of his attack on this point is Karl Popper. Van Krieken, *Norbert Elias*: 140; Mennell, *Norbert Elias*: 159.
13. Elias, *Involvement and Detachment*: 48.
14. Mennell, *Norbert Elias*: 179.
15. See, N. Elias, *The Civilizing Process* (Oxford: Basil Blackwell, 1994). Volume II, 'State Formation and Civilization', chapter 2.
16. Allcock, 'Involvement and detachment': 151. Božidar Jakšić has suggested (in conversation) that a more convincing reason for French coldness towards the Yugoslav regime was Tito's support for Algerian independence. I am inclined to agree with him, but this does not undermine my original point.
17. Allcock, 'Involvement and detachment': 153.
18. Allcock, 'Involvement and detachment': 157.
19. I was responsible for editing the English translation of Durkheim's *Pragmatism and Sociology* (Cambridge University Press, 1983).
20. B. Williams, *Truth and Truthfulness* (Princeton, NJ: Princeton University Press, 2002). 'Objectivity' (or 'detachment') and truth are not identical, of course. (Apart from anything else, it seems to my inexpert philosophical eye to be possible to be both 'detached' and wrong!) They do seem to be

connected in important ways, however, as Williams himself indicates. See esp. p. 125, and in relation to the emergence of a more objective view of the past, esp. Chapter 7.

21. Williams, *Truth and Truthfulness*: 2.
22. Williams, *Truth and Truthfulness*: 59 and 58.
23. Elias, *Involvement and Detachment*: Section IX.
24. I have reviewed this material in part in *Explaining Yugoslavia* (London: Hurst, and New York: Columbia University Press, 2000): Chap. 7.
25. See, for example, M. Lazić (ed.), *Society in Crisis: Yugoslavia in the Early Nineties* (Belgrade: Filip Višnjić, 1995).
26. The text by Antun Kobašić, for example (*Turizam u Jugoslaviji* (Zagreb: Informator, 1987)), is straightforwardly descriptive.
27. Typical of this material is N. Andrić, *Turizam i regionalni razvoj* (Zagreb: Informator, 1980).
28. Simo Elaković, *Sociologija slobodnog vremena i turizma* (Belgrade: Savremena Administracija, 1989).
29. See my paper 'South-East European Studies in the United Kingdom and Northern Ireland', forthcoming in *Balkanologie*.
30. The *locus classicus* of this idea is: J. Galtung and M. Ruge, 'The Structure of Foreign News', *Journal of Peace Research*, 1 (1965): 64–90: reprinted in J. Tunstall (ed.), *Media Sociology: A Reader* (London: Constable, 1970): 259–298. See esp. pp. 265–267.
31. The worst example of this kind of thing which has come my way is S. Djukić, *Milošević and Marković: A Lust for Power* (Montreal and Kingston: McGill and Queen's University Press, 2001).
32. It is important to acknowledge, of course, that the selection of the wrong theory (or of poor theory) can just as readily obstruct our search for detachment.
33. J. B. Allcock, 'From the "Graveyard of Generalisations" to the Mainstream: Theorising Yugoslavia' (Jugoslovensko udruženje za sociologiju, Belgrade, 25–27 May 1989).
34. I have in mind, for example: L. Carl Brown (ed.), *Imperial Legacy: The Ottoman Imprint on the Balkans and the Middle East* (New York: Columbia University Press, 1996); D. Chirot (ed.), *The Origins of Backwardness in Eastern Europe* (Berkeley, CA: University of California Press, 1989); D. F. Good, *The Economic Rise of the Habsburg Empire: 1750–1914* (Berkeley, CA: University of California Press, 1984); H. Inalçik and D. Quataert (eds), *An Economic and Social History of the Ottoman Empire: 1300–1914* (Cambridge: Cambridge University Press, 1994).
35. P. H. Stahl, *Household, Village and Village Confederation in Southeastern Europe* (New York: Columbia University Press, 1986, East European Monographs CC). Of course, these days comparative study is possible which is based upon different states which were formerly part of Yugoslavia. I have in mind Diane Masson's recent *L'Utilisation de la guerre dans la construction des systèmes politiques en Serbie et en Croatie, 1989–1995* (Paris: L'Harmattan, 2002). In this respect I find Sabrina Ramet to be more persuasive when she is dealing comparatively with the relationship between religion and politics in Eastern Europe, than when she confines her attention to Yugoslavia.

36. A fine example of the mutually reinforcing utilisation of theory and comparison is C.-U. Schierup (ed.), *Scramble for the Balkans: Nationalism, Globalism and the Political Economy of Reconstruction* (London: Macmillan, 1999).

37. The names of Castellan, Crampton, Fine, Jelavich, Stavrianos and Stoianovich readily come to mind.

38. For many years I taught a course which examined the dramaturgical foundations of social action. In the course of that work I was impressed by the relevance of Bertolt Brecht's ideas about the importance of distanciation in the theatre. Although I see some important links between distanciation in his sense, and the role of comparison in the achievement of objectivity, any pursuit of this line of thought would be too great a distraction in this context.

39. This section of my paper draws in particular on Williams, *Truth and Truthfulness*: Chap. 10.

40. Williams, *Truth and Truthfulness*: 238.

41. The best known of these are: J. M. Halpern, *A Serbian Village* (New York: Colophon, 2nd edn, 1967), and J. M. Halpern and B. Kerewsky-Halpern, *A Serbian Village in Historical Perspective* (Prospect Heights, IL: Waveland Press, 2nd edn, 1972).

42. I have explored aspects of these issues further in a hitherto unpublished essay on the importance of metaphor in the methodology of the social sciences. Contemporary understanding of metaphor has moved away from the idea that it should be regarded as a mere decorative surface upon language, which in its essence remains essentially assertorial. Language is intrinsically metaphorical, and hence the idea that it might be possible somehow to set aside the rhetorical aspects of language use, leaving untarnished its truth-telling function, is founded upon a fundamental misconception. This approach finds a much earlier foundation in sociology in the writing of that unjustly neglected scholar, Kenneth Burke. See, J. R. Gusfield (ed.), *Kenneth Burke on Symbols and Society* (Chicago, IL: University of Chicago Press, 1989).

43. At this point it is appropriate to raise my concern with a kind of contradiction in area studies. The definition of one's field of interest in relation to an *area* can be an important aid to comparison. On the other hand, it can become a prison in which the terms are dictated by non-scientific, very involved, criteria and concerns. This can come about if resort to the focus upon an area is made *at the expense of* discipline. Why do South East European Studies constitute a proper area? There is a good justification for this approach in terms of the need to grasp a common historical and cultural heritage, and to focus our attention upon common structural concerns. Are we in danger here, if we are not careful, of falling into the trap of letting our agenda be determined by a kind of Orientalism, the parameters of which are defined by the idea of the 'Balkan' other? One of my recent concerns has been the possible dissolving of the boundaries of discipline, and their replacement by a rather unstructured amalgam which might be labelled 'cultural studies'. Elias's faith in the capacity of the community of science to enhance detachment actually depends upon our ability to operate within a discipline. These are clearly large issues which reach well beyond the reasonable scope of this paper, although they have been given

a vigorous public airing recently in discussion surrounding the aims of the Association française d'études sur les Balkans, and the future of the journal *Balkanologie*.

44. J. B. Allcock, *Explaining Yugoslavia* (London: Hurst, and New York: Columbia University Press, 2000).

Bibliography

Alfredsson, G., Ferrer, E. and Ramsay, K., *Minority Rights: A Guide to United Nations Procedures and Institutions* (London: Minority Rights Group, 2004).

Allain, M.-F. and Galmiche, X. *La question du Kosovo – entretiens avec Marie-Françoise Allain et Xavier Galmiche* (Paris: Fayard, 1994).

Allcock, J. B., *Explaining Yugoslavia* (London: Hurst, and New York: Columbia University Press, 2000).

Allcock, J. B., 'Involvement and Detachment: Yugoslavia as an Object of Scholarship', *Journal of Area Studies*, 3, 1993.

Allcock, J. B., 'From the "Graveyard of Generalisations" to the Mainstream: Theorising Yugoslavia', *Jugoslovensko udruženje za sociologiju* (Belgrade, 25–27 May 1989).

Anderson, B., *Imagined Communities: Reflections on the Origin and Spread of Nationalism* (London: Verso, 1991).

Andjelic, N., *Bosnia-Herzegovina: The End of a Legacy* (London: Frank Cass, 2003).

Andrić, N., *Turizam i regionalni razvoj* (Zagreb: Informator, 1980).

Anonymous, 'Cesarjev 86. rojstni dan v Ljubljani. Odkritje cesarjevega spomenika na ljubljanskem Gradu', *Slovenec*, 18 August 1916: 4.

Antias, F. and Yuval-Davis, N., *Women-Nation-State* (London: Macmillan, 1989).

Arsić, M. and Markovič, D., *Šezdesetosma: studenski bunt I društvo* (Belgrade: Istraživačko – Izdavački Centar SSO Serbia, 1988, 3rd edn).

ASNOM (1944–1994) (Skopje: Dokumenti, Arhiv na Makednoja, Matica Makedonska, 1994).

Balalovska, K. Silja, A. and Zucconi, M., *Minority Politics in Southeast Europe: Crisis in Macedonia* (Rome: Ethnobarometer Working Paper No. 2, 2002).

Barbalet, J. M., *Citizenship* (Milton Keynes: Open University Press, 1988).

Barth, F. (ed.), *Ethnic Groups and Boundaries* (Bergen: Universitatsforlaget, 1969).

Bates, H. R. and De Figueiredo, R. J., 'The Politics of Interpretation: Rationality, Culture, and Transition', *Politics Society*, 26, 1998: 221–249.

Bedard, T., *Participation in Economic Life: An Advocacy Guide for Minorities in South-East Europe* (London: Minority Rights Group, 2005).

Belić, M. and Borić, R. (eds), Centar za žene zrtve rata: Zbornik, (Zagreb: Ženski informativno-dokumentacijski centar i Centar za žene žrtve rata, 1994).

Berezin, M. and Schain, M. (eds), *Europe without Borders: Remapping Territory, Citizenship, and Identity in Transnational Age* (Baltimore and London: The Johns Hopkins University Press, 2003).

Berreby, D., *Us and Them: Understanding Your Tribal Mind* (New York & Boston: Little, Brown and Company, 2005).

Bey, H., *TAZ. Privremene autonomne zone, i drugi tekstovi* (Katarina Peović Vuković (eds)), (Zagreb: Jesenski i Turk, 2003).

Bhabha, H., 'Of Mimicry and Man', *Location of Culture* (London: Routledge, 1994).

Bogdanović, D., *The Kosovo Question Past and Present* (Belgrade: Serb Academy of Sciences and Arts) Monographs, VOl. DLXVI, Presidium No.2.

Bose S., *Bosnia after Dayton: Nationalist Partition and International Intervention* (London: Hurst, 2002).

Bošnjak, Dragica, *Pasti globalizacije v znanosti. / The Traps of Globalisation in Science*. In Delo, 3 (November 2005).

Bowman, G., 'Antagonism and Identity in Former Yugoslavia', *Journal of Area Studies*, 3, 1993.

Brudar, M., *Politički život Srba na Kosovu i Metohiji, 1987–1999* (Belgrade: Nova srpska politička misao, 2003).

Buden, B., 'Neću novi ni bolji svijet', interview with Nina Ožegović, *Vijanac* br. 75. 21 November 1996; at www.arkzin.com/bb/intervws/vijenac.htm.

Buturović, A., *Stone Speaker: Medieval Tombs and Bosnian Identity in the Poetry of Mak Dizdar* (Basingstoke: Palgrave Macmillan, 2002).

Carl Brown, L. (ed.), *Imperial Legacy: The Ottoman Imprint on the Balkans and the Middle East* (New York: Columbia University Press, 1996).

Cento Bull, A., *Social Identities and Political Cultures in Italy: Catholic, Communist and Leghist Communities between Civicness and Localism* (New York and Oxford: Berghahn Books, 2000).

Chirot, D. (ed.), *The Origins of Backwardness in Eastern Europe* (Berkeley, CA: University of California Press, 1989).

Clark, H., *Civil Resistance in Kosovo* (London: Pluto Press, 2000).

Codevilla, A. M., *The Character of Nations: How Politics Makes and Breaks Prosperity, Family, and Civility* (New York: Basic Books, 1997).

Čolović, I., *Bordel Ratnika: Folklor, Politika i Rat* (Belgrade: Biblioteka XX vek, 1994).

Čolović, I., *The Politics of Symbol in Serbia* (London Hurst, 2002).

Constitutions of Europe. Texts Collected by the Council of Europe Venice Commission (Leidon-Boston: Martinus Njihoff, 2004).

Čopič, S., 'Spomenik Franju Malgaju', in *Spomeniki v slovenskem kiparstvu prve polovice 20. Stolja*, Ljubljana, 2000, p. 17.

Čopič, Š., Prelovšek, D. and Žitko, S., *Outdoor Sculpture in Ljubljana* (Ljubljana: Državna založba Slovenije, 1991).

Crnković, G., 'Underground Anti-Nationalism in the Nationalist Era', in Pavlaković, V. (ed.), *Nationalism, Culture, and Religion in Croatia since 1990*. The Donald W. Treadgold Papers in Russian, East European and Central Asian Studies, No. 32, 2001.

Čuprić, Č. (ed.), *Duh vedrine, Kultura protesta – proteste kultura: gradanski i student-ski protest 96–97* (Belgrade: Faculty of Political Science, 1998).

Cvijetić, S., 'Red Carpet District', *Central Europe Review*, 2, 15; at www.ce-riew. org, 15 April 2000.

Cvijic, J., *La peninsule balkanique: geographie humaine* (Paris: A. Colin, 1918) Serbian translation: *Balkansko poluostrvo i juznoslovenske zemlje* (Beograd: SANU, 1922).

Cvijic, J., *Sabrana Dela* (Beograd: Srpska Akademija Nauka i Umetnosti, 1987).

Dahl, R. A., *On Democracy* (New Haven, CT and London: Yale University Press, 1998).

Dahrendorf, R. *After 1989: Morals, Revolution and Civil Society* (New York: St. Martins Press, 1997).

Dahrendorf, R., *After 1989* (London: Macmillan Press, 1999).

Dahrendorf, R., 'The Changing Quality of Citizenship', in Van Steenbergen, B. (ed.), *The Condition of Citizenship* (London: Sage, 1994).

Dallmayr, F., *Dialogue Among Civilizations: Some Exemplary Voice* (New York: Palgrave Macmillan, 2002).

Daskalovski, Ž., 'Five Flavours of Brain', *Central Europe Review*, 2, 5; at www.ceriew.org, 7 February 2000.

Debeljak, A., *The Hidden Handshake: National Identity and Europe in the Post-Communist World* (Oxford: Rowman and Littlefield Publishers, Inc., 2004).

Debeljak, A., *Twilight of the Idols: Recollections of a Lost Yugoslavia* (New York: White Wine Press, Fredonia, 1994).

Deklaracija OTPORA za budućnosti Srbije (Belgrade: Srpski Otporaš (pamphlet), 1999).

Diamond, L. 'Three Paradoxes of Democracy', in Diamond, L. and Plattner, M. F. (eds), *The Global Resurgence of Democracy* (Baltimore and London: The Johns Hopkins University Press, 1996).

Dieckhoff, A. (ed.), *The Politics of Belonging: Nationalism, Liberalism, and Pluralism* (Maryland: Lexington Books, 2004).

Dimitrijević, N., *Ustavna demokratija shvaćena kontekstualno* (Belgrade: Fabrika kniga, 2007).

Dimitrijević,V., 'Ethnonationalism and the Consititutions: The Apotheosis of the Nation State', *Journal of Area Studies*, 3, 1993, 50–56.

Dimitrijević,V., *The Insecurity of Human Rights after Communism* (Oslo: Norwegian Institute of Human Rights, 1993).

Dizdar, M., *Kameni spavač-stone sleeper*, prijevod/translation – Francis Jones; *pogovor*/afterword – Rusmir Mahmutčehajić (Sarajevo: 1999).

Djukić, S., *Milošević and Marković: A Lust for Power* (Montreal and Kingston: McGill and Queen's University Press, 2001).

Document of the European Commission for Democracy through Law (Venice Commission CDL, 2007).

Dolar, B. E., *Abortus – pravica do izbire?* (Ljubljana: SŽZP, 1991).

Duijzings, G., *Religion and the Politics of Identity in Kosovo* (London: Hurst, 2000).

Dukić, D. and Senjković, R., 'Virtual Homeland? Reading the Music of a Particular Web Page', *International Journal of Cultural Studies*, 8, 1, 2005: 45–63.

Đurković, M., 'Pop-politika i pop-ideologija. O (zlo)upotrebi masovne kulture i umetnosti u ideološke svrhe', *Republika*, br. 266–267, 2003, 1–31.

Eco, U., *The Limits of Interpretation* (Bloomington, IN: Indiana University Press, 1990).

Elaković, S., *Sociologija slobodnog vremena i turizma* (Belgrade: Savremena Administracija, 1989).

Eley, G., 'Culture, Nation and Gender', in Blom, I., Hagemann, K. and Hall, C. (eds), *Gendered Nations. Nationalism and Gender Order in the Long Nineteenth Century* (Oxford and New York: Berg, 1999).

Elias, N., *The Civilizing Process* (Oxford: Basil Blackwell, 1994).

Elias, N., *Involvement and Detachment* (Oxford: Basil Blackwell, 1987).

Ferro, M., *The Use and Abuse of History, or, How the Past is Taught* (London: Routledge & Kegan Paul, 1994).

Fetveit, A., 'Anti-Essentialism and Reception Studies. In Defence of the Text', *International Journal of Cultural Studies*, 4, 2, 2001, 173–199.

Firth, R., *Symbols. Public and Private* (London: George Allen & Unwin Ltd, 1973).

Flenley, P., Editorial, *Journal of Area Studies*, 3, 1993.

Fought, C., *Language and Ethnicity* (Cambridge: Cambridge University Press, 2006).

Frank, T., *One Market under God: Extreme Capitalism, Market Populism, and the End of Economic Democracy* (New York: Anchor Books, 2000).

Freud, S., 'Group Psychology and the Analysis of the Ego', *The Pelican Freud Library*, Vol. X (Harmondsworth: Penguin, 1985).

Fukuyama, F., *The End of History* (London: Hamish Hamilton, 1992).

Fukuyama, F., *The End of History and the Last Man* (New York: Avon, 1993).

Gaber, S., 'The Limits of Democracy: The Case of Slovenia', *Journal of Area Studies*, 3, 1993.

Gagnon, V. P. Jr, *The Myth of Ethnic War: Serbia and Croatia in the 1990s* (Ithaca, NY and London: Cornell University Press, 2004).

Galtung, J., and Ruge, M., 'The Structure of Foreign News', *Journal of Peace Research*, 1, 1965.

Gearing, F. O., *The Face of the Fox* (Chicago, IL: Aldine, 1970).

Geisler, M. E. (ed.), *National Symbols, Fractured Identities: Contesting the National Narrative* (Lebanon: University Press of New England, 2005).

Gellner, E., *Encounters with Nationalism* (Oxford: Blackwell, 1994).

Gellner, E., *Nationalism* (New York: New York University Press, 1997).

Giddens, A., *Europe in the Global Age* (Cambridge: Polity Press, 2007).

Gillis, C. (ed.), *The Political Papacy: John Paul II, Benedict XVI, and Their Influence* (London: Paradigm, 2006).

Goff, P. M. and Dunn, K. C. (eds), *Identity and Global Politics: Empirical and Theoretical Considerations* (New York: Palgrave Macmillan, 2004).

Golubović, Z., 'Nationalism and Democracy: The Yugoslav Case', *Journal of Area Studies*, 3, 1993.

Good, D., *The Economic Rise of the Habsburg Empire: 1750–1914* (Berkeley, CA: University of California Press, 1984).

Gordy, E., *The Culture of Power in Serbia: Nationalism and the Destruction of Alternatives* (University Park, TX: Penn State University Press, 1999).

Grazioli, E., 'Notizie di carattere politico; III verbale. L'anno 1941/XIX, il giorno 3 luglio, alle ore 10.30, nella sala delle riunioni dell'Alto Commissariato di Lubiana' (*Arhiv Republike Slovenije*, Collection Visokega komisarja za Ljubljansko pokrajino, Fascicle 1: Seje konzult, 1941).

Gross, D., *Lost Time* (Amherst: University of Massachusetts Press, 2000).

Gusfield, J. R. (ed.), *Kenneth Burke on Symbols and Society* (Chicago, IL: University of Chicago Press, 1989).

Habermas, J. (1994), 'Citizens and National Identity', in Van Steenbergen, B. (ed.), *The Condition of Citizenship* (London: Sage, 1994).

Halpern, J. M., *A Serbian Village* (New York: Colophon, 2nd edn, 1967).

Halpern, J. M. and Kerewsky-Halpern, B., *A Serbian Village in Historical Perspective* (Prospect Heights IL: Waveland Press, 2nd edn, 1972).

Harty, S., and Murphy, M., *In Defense of Multinational Citizenship* (Cardiff: UWP, 2005).

Hayden, R., *Blueprints for a House Divided: The Constitutional Logic of the Yugoslav Conflict* (Ann Arbor, MI: University of Michigan Press, 2000).

Hladnik Milharčič, Ervin, *Intervju: dr. Slavoj Žižek. Tisti z zunanjega minis-trstva, ki je dal dokument, bi moral biti razglašen za Slovenca leta/Interview:*

Dr Slavoj Žižek. *The Guy from the Foreign Ministry who Leaked the Document Should be Proclaimed Slovenian of the Year.* In Dnevnik, Objektiv (Saturday Supplement, 5 April 2008).

Hobsbawm, E., *Nations and Nationalism since 1789* (Cambridge: Cambridge University Press, 1995).

Hodge, C., *The Serb Lobby in the United Kingdom* (Seattle, WA: University of Washington, Donald Treadgold Papers in Russian, East European and Central Asian Studies, No. 22, September 1999).

Horowitz, D., *Ethnic Groups in Conflict* (Berkeley, CA: University of California Press, 1985).

Hribar, I., *Moji spomini* (Ljubljana: Slovenska matica, 1983/84).

Hribar, I., *Stavbnemu odseku in odseku za olepšavo mesta občinskega sveta v Ljubljani* (Manuscript in Zgodovinski arhiv Ljubljana, Reg. I., fascicle 2021 Spomenik Francu Jožefu, folia 397, 1903).

Hribar, Spomenka, 'Avantgardno sovrašto in sprava', *Nova Revija*, Ljubljana, 1987, pp. 74–103.

Hribar, Spomenka, *Krivda in greh/Guilt and Sin* (Maribor: ZAT, 1990).

Hribar, Spomenka, Zaustaviti desnico / To halt the rightists, in: *Delo*, 18 April 1992, y. 34, no. 91, 1992: 24–25.

Hriba, Tine, *Euroslovenstvo / Eurosloveniaess* (Ljubljani: Slovenska matica, 2004).

Hribar, Tine, *Slovenci kot nacija: soočanja s sodobniki / Slovenians as nation: confontations with contemporaries* (Ljubljana: Enotnost, 1995).

Hribar, T., 'Slovenska državnost', *Nova Revija*, 57, 1987.

Hudelist, D., *Kosovo: bitka bez iluzija* (Zagreb: Centar za informacije i publicitet, 1989).

Hudson, R., 'The Return of the Colonial Protectorate: Colonisation with Good Intent in the Western Balkans', in Aguirre, M., Ferrándiz, F. and Pureza, J.-M. (eds), *Before Emergency: Conflict Prevention and the Media* (Bilbao: University of Deusto Press, 2003).

Hudson, R. and Heintze, H.-J. (eds), *Different Approaches to Peace and Conflict Research* (Bilbao: University of Deusto Press, 2008).

Ignatieff, M., *Empire Lite: Nation-Building in Bosnia, Kosovo and Afghanistan* (London: Vintage, 2003).

Inalçik, H. and Quataert, D. (eds), *An Economic and Social History of the Ottoman Empire: 1300–1914* (Cambridge: Cambridge University Press, 1994).

Isaković, A., *Riječnik karakteristične Leksike u Bosanskom Jeziku* (Sarajevo: Svijetlost, 1993).

Ivanišević, Đ., 'Vodite stranke, ne zaboravite narod', *Fokus. Hrvatski tjednik*, 7 November 2003.

Jajčinović, M., 'Hrvatski bog Janus', *Večernji list*, 5 November 2007.

Janko Spreizer, A., 'Avtohtonost v slovenskem narod(nost)nem vprašanju in koncept staroselstva: nastavki za analizo ideologij primata / Autochtonism in the Slovenian national(ities) issue and the concept of indigenousness: elements for the analysis of primacy ideologies', *Razprave in gradivo / Treatises and Documents*, No. 50–51 (Ljubljana: Institute for Ethnic Studies, 2006): 236–271.

Jeglič, A. B., *Dnevnik. Nadškofijski arhiv Ljubljana* (Collection Škofijski arhiv Ljubljana, Diary of Bishop Jeglič 1908–1912, box 13/1c, 1908).

Josipovič, D., 'Declining Fertility and the Role of Immigration in Population Growth in Slovenia at the Dawn of the 21st Century', *Globalizirana Evropa* (Koper: Založba Annales, 2005).

Josipovič, D., 'Population Development of Slovenia from the Beginning of Counting to the Present Day', *Slovenia* (Ljubljana: Association of the Geographical Societies of Slovenia, Založba ZRC, 2004).

Judah, Tim, *Kosovo: War and Revenge* (New Haven, CT and London: Yale, 2000).

Judah, Tim, *Kosovo: What Everyone Needs to Know* (Oxford: Oxford University Press, 2008).

Kajzer, J., *S tramovi podprto mesto* (Ljubljana: Mihelač, 1995).

Kamnogorski, L. T., 'O Vodnikovem godu' (*Novice*, 27 January 1858, 29–30).

Kelmendi, Muhamet, *Realiteti dhe perspektivat e çështjes kombëtare* (Tirana: Albin, 1998).

Kelmendi, V., 'Kosovo Under the Burden of the Serbian Discriminatory Laws: Facts and Evidence' (1993).

Kelmendi, B. and Kelmendi, N., 'Dismantling and Serbianization of the Judicial System in Kosova', *Kosova Watch*, 1, 2, August 1992.

Kenny, M., *The Politics of Identity* (Cambridge: Polity Press, 2004).

Kerčov, S., Radoš J., and Raič, A., *Mitinzi u Vojvodini 1988. godine: radjanje političkog pluralizma* (Novi Sad: Dnevnik, 1990).

King, I. and Mason, W., *Peace at Any Price: How the World Failed Kosovo* (London: Hurst, 2006).

Klein, N., *No Logo* (London: Flamingo, 2001).

Knežević Hočevar, Duška (ed.), 'Talk About Fertility in Slovenia. Anthropological Notebooks', *Thematic Issue*, No. 2 (Ljubljana: Slovenian Anthropological Society, 2007).

Knežević Hočevar, Duška, 'The Vanishing Nation: Discussing Nation's Reproduction in Post-Socialist Slovenia', *Anthropology of East Europe Review*, 22, 2, Fall 2004: 22–30.

Kobašić, A., *Turizam u Jugoslaviji* (Zagreb: Informator, 1987).

Kola, P., *The Search for Greater Albania* (London: Hurst, 2003).

Kolbe, K. B., *Egejci* (Kultura: Skopje, 1999).

Kos, Janez, *Glejte ga, to je naš Prešeren!* (Ljubljana: Kiki Keram, 1997).

Kostovićova, D., 'Albanian Parallel Education System and Its Aftermath: Segregation, Identity and Governance', in Dimou, A. (ed.), *'Transition' and the Politics of History Education in Southeast Europe* (Göttingen: Vanderhoeck und Ruprecht, 2009).

Kostovicova, D., *Parallel Worlds: Response of Kosovo Albanians to loss of autonomy, 1986–1996* (Keele: Keele European Research Centre, Keele University, 1997).

Kostovicova, D., *Kosovo: The Politics of Identity and Space* (London: Routledge, 2005).

Kovačič, D., Del zgodovine sta Kardelj in Kidrič in ne njuna spomenika (*Slovenec*, 13 April 1996): 30–31.

Krasztev, P., 'Dvojni Pogled ili Kakve su Nevolje sa Istorijom Kulture Balkana?' (*Mostovi* 123/124, 2000).

Krenar, G., 'Kosovo Albanians Look beyond December Deadline', *Balkan Investigative Reporting Network*, 26 October 2007; at http://birn.eu.com/en/109/10/5399/.

Krenar, G., 'US Ponders Freezing Kosovo's Status Until 2020', *Balkan Investigative Reporting Network*, 29 October 2007; at www.birn.eu.com/en/110/10/5411/.

Kuci, H., *Independence of Kosova/o: Stabilizing or Destabilizing Factor in the Balkans?* (Houston, TX: Jalifat Group, 2005).

Kuljić, T., *Kulturna sećanja: teorijska objašnjenja upotrebne prošlosti* (Belgrade: Čigoja štampana, 2000).

Kymlicka, W., 'The Forms of Group-Differentiated Citizenship in Canada', in Seyla Benhabib (ed.), *Democracy and Difference* (Princeton, NJ: Princeton University Press, 1996).

Kymlicka, W., 'Multicultural Citizenship', in Shafir, G. (ed.), *The Citizenship Debates, A Reader* (Minneapolis, MN and London: UMP, 1998).

Kymlicka, W., *Multicultural Citizenship: A Liberal Theory of Minority Rights* (Oxford: Clarendon Press, 1995).

Kymlicka, W., 'Western Political Theory and Ethnic Relations in Eastern Europe', *Can Liberal Pluralism be Exported?* (Oxford: Oxford University Press, 2001).

Lampe, F., 'Grof Radecki, oče naših vojakov' (*Dom in Svet*, No. 6 in 7, 1892).

Lampe, J. R. and Mazower, M. (eds), *Ideologies and National Identities: The Case of Twentieth Century Southeastern Europe* (Budapest and New York: CEU Press, 2004).

Lazić, M., ed., *Society in Crisis: Yugoslavia in the Early Nineties* (Belgrade: Filip Višnjić, 1995).

Leader, D., *Why Do Women Write More Letters Than They Send? A Meditation on the Loneliness of the Sexes* (New York: Basic Books, 1997).

Lears, J., *Fables of Abundance: A Cultural History of Advertising in America* (New York: Basic Books, 1994).

Lehning, B. P., 'Towards a Multicultural Civic Society: The Role of Social Capital and Democratic Citizenship', *Government and Opposition*, 33, 2, Spring 1998.

Levec, F., Vodnikov spomenik v Ljubljani (*Ljubljanski Zvon*, 1888/89): 445, 765.

Lijphart, A., *Democracy in Plural Societies: A Comparative Exploration* (New Haven, CT: Yale University Press, 1977).

Likar, A., Prijazna beseda o spomenikih (*Novice*, 4 August 1858): 250.

Linz, J. J. and Stepan, A. (eds). *Problems of Democratic Transition and Consolidation: Southern Europe, South America and Post-Communist Europe* (Baltimore and London: The Johns Hopkins University Press, 1996).

Lovrić, J.,'Je li Račan predao izbore?', *Novi list*, 14 November 2003.

Lowenthal, D., *The Past is a Foreign Country* (Cambridge: Cambridge University Press, 1985).

Lowenthal, D., *Possessed by the Past* (New York and London: The Free Press, 1996).

Macdonald, S. and Fyfe, G. *Theorizing Museums* (Oxford and Cambridge, MA: Blackwell Publishers/The Sociological Review, 1996).

'Macedonian Security Council against Partitioning of Kosovo', *Balkan Investigative Reporting Network*, 24 August 2007; at http://birn.eu.com/en/100/15/3934/.

Mach, Z., *Symbols, Conflict, and Identity* (Albany: State University of New York Press, 1993).

Magas, B., *The Destruction of Yugoslavia: Tracking the Break-Up 1980–92* (London and New York: Verso Books, 1993).

Magaš, Branka and Žanić, Ivo, *Rat u Hrvatskoj i Bosni i Herzegovini, 1991–1995* (Sarajevo: Jesensk i Turk, Zagreb and Dani, 1999).

Malcolm, N., *Bosnia: A Short History* (Basingstoke: Palgrave Macmillan, 1994).

Malcolm, N., *Kosovo: A Short History* (Basingstoke: Palgrave Macmillan, 1998).

Maleš, M. (ed.) *Spomenik Viteškemu kralju Aleksandru I. Zedinitelju v Ljubljani.* (Ljubljana: Odbor za postavitev spomenika Viteškemu kralju Aleksandru I. Zedinitelju v Ljubljani, 1940).

Maliqi, S., 'The Albanian Movement in Kosova', in Dyker, D. and Vejvoda, I. (eds), *Yugoslavia and After: A Study in Fragmentation, Despair and Rebirth* (London: Longman, 1996).

Maliqi, S., 'Albanian Self-Understanding through Non-Violence: The Construction of National Identity in Opposition to Serbs', *Journal of Contemporary European Stuidies*, No. 3, 1993.

Maliqi, Shkëlzen, 'Kosovo kao katalizater juvoslovenske krize', *Kosovo-Srbija-Jugoslavija*, 1989: 69–80.

Maliqi, S., *Kosova. Separate Worlds. Reflections and Analyses, 1989–1998* (Prishtina, 1998).

Maliqi, S., 'Non-Violent Resistance of Albanians', in *Conflict or Dialogue: Serbian–Albanian relations and integration of the Balkans* (Subotica: Open University – European Civic Centre for Conflict Resolution, 1994).

Maliqi, S., *Nyja e Kosoves: as Vllasi as MIllosheviqi* (Knot of Kosova: neither Vllasi nor Milošević) (Ljubljana: Krt, 1990).

Marshall, T. H., *Citizenship and Social Class* (Cambridge: Cambridge University Press, 1950).

Masson, D., *L'Utilisation de la guerre dans la construction des systèmes politiques en Serbie et en Croatie, 1989–1995* (Paris: L'Harmattan, 2002).

McBride, K. D., *Collective Dreams: Political Imagination and Community* (Pennsylvania State University Press, 2005).

McGarry J. and O'Leary, B., *The Politics of Ethnic Conflict Regulation: Case Studies of Protracted Ethnic Conflicts* (London: Routledge, 1993).

Memorandum, OTPOR!, www.otpor.com.

'Memorandam SANU' (Belgrade: Duga, June 1989).

Memorandum SANU, SANU (Belgrade, 1986).

Mennell, S., *Norbert Elias: An Introduction* (Oxford: Basil Blackwell, 1992).

Mesić, Stipe, *The Demise of Yugoslavia: A political memoir*, Budapest and New York: Central European University Press, 2004).

Middleton, D. and Edwards, D. (eds), *Collective Remembering* (London: Sage, 1990).

Miheljak, Vlado, *Kdaj operacija Čista granata? / When Operation Clean Granate?* In Dnevnik, 16 April 2008.

Milanović, I., 'Studenski protest: Spontanost, organizacija i pare', *Vreme*, 830, 30 November 2006.

Milić, A. and Čičkarić, L., *Generacija u protestu: Sociološki portret učenska studenskog protesta 96/97 na Beogradskom univerzitetu* (Belgrade: The Institute for Sociological Research (*Institut za sociološka instraživanja*), Faculty of Philosophy, 1998).

Milinčević, V., 'Omladinska levica na Velikoj Školi (1863–1875)', *Ideje i pokreti na Beogradskom univerzitetu od osnivanja do danas*, Book 1 (Belgrade: Centar za Marksizam, University of Belgrade, 1989).

Mimica, A. and Grac, Z. (eds), *Visoko obrazovanje u Srbiji na putu ka Evropi četiri godine kasnije: Zbornik radova* (Belgrade: AAOM, 2005).

Močnik, R., *3 teorije: ideologija, nacija, institucija /3 Theories: Ideology, Nation, Institution* (Ljubljana: Založba, 1999).

Močnik, Rastko, *Postdemokracija?* / *Post-Democracy?* In Mladina, 20 November 2000, p. 18.

Močnik, Rastko, *Šestdesetletnica* / *The 60th Anniversary*. In Mladina, 30 April 2005.

Morris, M., 'Banality in Cultural Studies', in Mellencamp P. (ed.), *Logics of Television* (Bloomington, IN: Indiana University Press, 1990).

Muhić, F., 'Macedonia – an Island on the Balkan Mainland', in Deyker, D. A. and Vejvoda, I. (eds), *Yugoslavia and After: A Study in Fragmentation, Despair and Rebirth*, (London and New York: Longman, 1996).

Musil, R., *Posthumous Papers of a Living Author* (London: Penguin Books, 1995).

Navarro, V., 'The Worldwide Class Struggle', *Monthly Review*, LVIII, 4, September 2006; www.monthlyreview.org/0906navarro.htm.

Negt, O. and Kluge, A., *Maßverhältnisse des Politischen* (Frankfurt 1992).

'Ni studenti nisu neka bili', *Glas javnosti*, 17 November 2006.

Noel, M., *Kosovo: A Short History* (London: Papermac, 1999).

Norris, D. A., *In the Wake of the Balkan Myth: Questions of identity and Modernity* (London: Macmillan, 1999).

Novak, L., 'Ključne zablude koje ometaju reformu visokog školstva u Srbiji', in O'Donnell, G., Schmitter, P. and Whitehead, L. (eds), *Transitions from Authoritarian Rule: Southern Europe* (Baltimore: The Johns Hopkins University Press, 1986).

O'Leary, B., *Debating Partition: Justifications and Critiques*, Mapping Frontiers, Plotting Pathways, working paper, 28, 2006.

O'Leary, B., 'The Nature of the British–Irish Agreement', *New Left Review*, 233 (1999).

Orwell, G., *Nineteen Eighty-Four* (Harmondsworth: Penguin Books, 1984).

OSCE Report, *Human Rights in Kosovo: As Seen, As Told*, Volume I, October 1998–June 1999.

OSCE Report, *Human Rights in Kosovo: As Seen, As Told*, Volume II, 14 June–31 October 1999.

Pavičić, J., 'I Božić posta Nova godina' *Jutarnji list*, 3 January 2004.

Pečauer, M., 'Dr. Tine Hribar, filozof. 'Končni cilj je spremeniti Slovenijo v katoliško državo', *Delo, Sobotna priloga*, 15 December 2007, 4–6.

Pehar, D. 'Civic Elements of Compromise and the Crippling Of Dayton' (Sarajevo, *Forum Bosnae* 15/02, 2002).

Perica, V., *Balkan Idols: Religion and Nationalism in Yugoslav States* (Oxford: Oxford University Press, 2002).

Perović, L., 'Yugoslavia was Defeated from Inside', in Biserko, S. (ed.), *Yugoslavia: Collapse, War Crimes* (Belgrade: Centar for Anti-war Action and Belgrade Circle).

Perry, D. M., *The Politics of Terror: The Macedonian Revolutionary Movement* (Durham and London: Duke University Press, 1988).

Pesić, Vesna, *Serbian Nationalism and the Origins of the Yugoslav Crisis* (United States Institute of Peace, 1996).

Petrović, Vesna, *Human Rights in Serbia and Montenegro 2005: Legal Provisions Practices and Awareness in the State Union of Serbia and Montenegro Compared to International Human Rights Standards* (Belgrade: Beogradska Centar za Ljudska Prava, 2006).

Phillips, A., 'Dealing with Difference: A Politics of Ideas, or a Politics of Presence?', in van Steenbergen (ed.), *The Condition of Citizenship* (London: Sage, 1996).

Phillips, A., *The Politics of Presence* (Oxford: Oxford University Press, 1995).

Pierson Roach, R., 'Nations: Gendered. Racialized. Crossed with Empire', in Blom, I., Hagemann, K. and Hall, C. (eds), *Gendered Nations. Nationalism and Gender Order in the Long Nineteenth Century* (New York and Oxford: Berg, 1999).

Pittaway, M., *Eastern Europe 1939–2000* (London: Arnold, 2004).

Plumb, J. H., *The Death of the Past* (London: Macmillan and Co., 1969).

Popov, A., *Nationalities and Politics in the Post Soviet World* (Washington, DC: International Research and Exchanges Board, 1994).

Popović, S., Janča, D. and Petovar, T. (eds) *Kosovski čvor: drešiti ili seći* (Belgrade, 1990).

Popovović, S., Janča, D. and Petovar, T. (eds) Kosovski čvor: drešiti ili seći? (The Kosovo Knot: To untie or cut?) (Belgrade: 1990).

Popovski, V., *Makedonskoto nacionalno-oloboditelno dvizenje do TMORO* (Skopje: Makedonska Kniga, 1989).

Port, M. van de, *Gypsies, Wars and Other Instances of the Wild. Civilization and its Discontents in a Serbian Town* (Amsterdam University Press, 1998).

Preez, du, P., *The Politics of Identity: Ideology and the Human Image* (Oxford: Basil Blackwell, 1980).

Premdas, R. R., Samarasinghr, de A. SWR, Anderson, A. B (eds), *Secessionist Movements in Comparative Perspective* (New York: St Martin's Press, 1990).

Primoratz, I. and Pavkovic, A. (eds), *Identity, Self-Determination and Secession* (Burlington: Ashgate, 2006).

Pula, B., 'The Emergence of the Kosovo "Parallel State", 1988–1992', *Nationalities Papers* 32, 4, 2004: 797–826.

Pulig, Srećko, 'Mit o tranziciji' in Tranzicija koja teče. *Zarez*, no. 205, 3 May 2007; at www.zarez.hr/205/z_sadrzaj.htm.

Pupavac, Ozren, Springtime for Hegemony: Laclau and Mouffe with Janez Janša. In Prelom, No. 8, pp. 115–136 (2006).

Qosja, Rexhep, *The Albanian Question* (Prishtina: Albanološki institute u Prištiny, 1994).

Qosja, Rexhep, *Çështja shqiptare: historia dhe politika* (Botimet Toena: Tiranë, 1998).

Radics, Peter von, *Führer durch Krain. Die Landeshauptstadt Laibach und die schönsten Touren in Oberkrain, Innerkrain und Unterkrain für Reisende und Einheimische* (Laibach: Verlag von J. Giontini, 1885).

Radović, Bojana, 'Seksepil u službi politike', *Večernji list*, 15 November 2003.

Rady, M., 'Minorities and Minority Protection in Eastern Europe', in Hudson, R. and Réno, F. (eds), *Politics of Identity: Migrants and Minorities in Multicultural States*, Palgrave, 2000, pp. 205–222.

Rajić, L., 'Ostrvo usred stvarnosti', in Antić, Č. (ed.), *Decenija: spomenica studenskog protest 1996–2006* (Belgrade: Evoluta, 2006).

Ramet, S. P., *Balkan Babel* (Colorado: Westview Press, 1999).

Ramet, Sabrina, 'The Murky Legacy of Franjo Tuđman' in Pavlaković, V. (ed.), *Nationalism, Culture, and Religion in Croatia since 1990*, The Donald W. Treadgold Papers in Russian, East European and Central Asian Studies, No. 32, November 2001.

Rawls, J., *Political Liberalism* (New York: Cambridge University Press, 1993).

Report of the Security Council Mission to Kosovo and Belgrade, Federal Republic of Yugoslavia, 14–17 December 2002 (S/2002/1376).

Report of the Security-General on the UNMIK, United Nations, Security Council, S/2004/348.

Rifkin, J., *The Age of Access* (New York: J.P. Tarcher, 2000).

Robertson, J., *Discourses of Democracy and Exclusion in the Streets of Belgrade 1968–1997* (Sydney: University of Sydney Press, 2006).

Roško, Z., *Paranoidnije od ljubavi, zabavnije od zla. Rekreacijska teorija za unutarnja tijela* (Zagreb: Naklada MD, 2002).

Rubić, Vladimir, '*Studenski protest 1996/97*, između političke heterogenosti i strateškog konsenzusca', in Gormović, G. and Erdei, I. (eds), *O studentima I drugim demonima: etnografija studentskog protesta 1996/97* (Belgrade: Filozofski fakultet, 1997).

Rugova, Ibrahim, Allain, Marie-Françoise and Galmiche, Xavier, *Çështja e Kosovës* (Peje: Dukagjini, 1994).

Salecl, R., *On Anxiety* (London: Routledge, 2004).

Salecl, R., *The Spoils of Freedom: Psychoanalysis and Feminism after the Fall of Socialism* (London: Routledge, 1994).

Salomon, M. E. (ed.), *Economic, Social and Cultural Rights: A Guide for Minorities and Indigenous Peoples* (London: Minority Rights Group, 2005).

Sarat, A. and Kearns, T. R. (eds), *Identities, Politics, and Rights* (Ann Arbor, MI: The University of Michigan Press, 1995).

Sarkanjac, B., *Makedonski katahrezis: kako da se sburova za Makedonija* (Skopje: Forum, 2004).

Sarkanjac, B., 'Multiculturalism in Macedonia', in Dodovski, I., ed. *Multiculturalism in Macedonia: An Emerging Model* (Skopje: FIOOM, 2005).

Savić, M. 'Philosophiam Profiteri', *Filozofija i društvo* XXXI, 2002: 165–203.

Schierup, C. (ed.), *Scramble for the Balkans: Nationalism, Globalism and the Political Economy of Reconstruction* (London: Macmillan, 1999).

Schopflin, G., *Nations, Identity, Power: The New Politics of Europe* (London: Hurst & Co Ltd, 2000).

Schwartz, S., *Kosovo: Background to the War* (London: Anthem Press, 2000).

Shackel, Paul A., 'Public Memory and the Search for Power in American Historical Archaeology', *American Anthropologist*, 3, 2001: 655–670.

Shirer, W. L., *Berlin Diary* (Boston, MA: Little, Brown and Company, 1988).

Simms, B., *Unfinest Hour: Britain and the Destruction of Bosnia* (London: Allen Lane, 2001).

Smith, A., *Ethno-Symbolism and Nationalism: A Cultural Approach* (London: Routledge, 2009).

Smith, A., *National Identity* (Harmondsworth: Penguin, 1991).

Smith, G. and Margalit, A. (eds), *Amnestie oder Die Politik der Erinnerung* (Frankfurt, 1997).

Šnuderl, M., *Dnevnik 1941–1945* (Založba Obzorja, Maribor, 1993).

Spicer, R., *Conspiracy: Law, Class and Society* (London: Lawrence and Wishart, 1981).

Stahl, P., *Household, Village and Village Confederation in Southeastern Europe* (New York: Columbia University Press, 1986, East European Monographs CC).

Stanković, Đ., 'Revolucionarni studentski pokret i fašizam', *Beogradski univerzitet u predratnom periodu, narodnooslobidilačkom ratu i revoluciji* (Belgrade: Centar za Marksizam, University of Belgrade, 1983).

Starc, Gregor, *Šport kot socialna arena nacije v Sloveniji / Sports as the Social Arena of the Nation in Slovenia*. In Razprave in gradivo / Treatises and Documents, No. 50–51, pp. 272–84 (Ljubljana: Institute for ethnic studies, 2006).

Stefanovski, G., *Sobrani drami*, Vol. I. (Skopje: Tabernakul, 2002).

Stibrič, J., Zbiranje podpisov proti rušenju spomenikov (*Delo*, 6 July 1996): 16.

Šumi, Irena, *Etnično razlikovanje v Sloveniji: izbrane problematizacije. / Ethnic Differentiation in Slovenia: Selected Problems*. In Razprave in gradivo / Treatises and documents, No. 45, pp. 7–39 (Ljubljana: Institute for ethnic studies, 2004)

Šumi, I., 'The Slovenian "national question": An Academic Tradition or an Ideology?', in Podnar, G. (ed.). *Vulgata: Kunst aus Slowenien: 12. Mai–24. Juni 2001, Neuer Berliner Kunstverein* (Berlin: Neuer Berliner Kunstverein, 2001).

Šumi, I. and Josipovič, D., 'Avtohtonost kot resna grožnja manjšini /Autochtony a serious threat to minorities', *Večer*, y. 62, No. 7025, March 2006: 40–41.

Šumi, Irena and Duška Knežević Hočevar (forthcoming) *Anthropology in Slovenia. A Short History*. In History of Anthropology Newsletter (Chicago, IL: University of Chicago).

Šumi, Irena, Cirila Toplak, Damir Josipovič, *Devet tez o stanju slovenske znanosti / Nine Theses on the State of Slovenian Science*. In Dnevnik, Objektiv (Saturday Supplement), 9 February 2008.

The Independent International Commission on Kosovo, *The Kosovo Report* (Oxford: Oxford University Press, 2000).

Taševa, M., *Etnickite grupi vo Makedonija: istoriski kontekst* (Skopje: Filozofski Fakultet, 1997).

Tenth Assessment of the Situation of Ethnic Minorities in Kosovo (period covering May 2002 to December 2002), OSCE Mission in Kosovo, UNHCR, March 2003.

Teski, M. C. and Climo, J. J. (eds), *The Labyrinth of Memory. Ethnographic Journeys* (Westport and London: Bergin & Garvey, 1995).

Touraine, A, *Qu'est-ce que la démocratie?* (Paris: Fayard, 1994).

Troebst, S., *Conflict in Kosovo: Failure or Prevention? An Analytical Documentation, 1992–1998*, in Minority Issues (ECMI) Working Paper #1 (Flensburg: ECMI, 1998).

Tuma, H., *Iz mojega življenja* (Ljubljana: Naša založba, 1937).

Turajlić, S., 'Visoko obrazovanje u Srbiji između tradicije i realnosti' (Belgrade: AAOM, 2005).

Turton, D. and González, J. (eds), *Cultural Identities and Ethnic Minorities in Europe*, Humanitarian Net (Universidad de Deusto, Bilbao, Spain, 1999), pp. 71–79.

Urbanič, I., 'Jugoslovanska 'nacionalistična kriza in Slovenci v perspektivi konca nacije', *Nova Revija* 57/1987.

Urry, J., 'How Societies Remember the Past', in Macdonald, S. and Fyfe, G. (eds), *Theorizing Museums* (Oxford and Cambridge, MA: Blackwell/The Sociological Review, 1996): 45–65.

Ustav Republike Srbije (Belgrade: Službeni list, 2006).

Van Krieken, R., *Norbert Elias* (London: Routledge, 1998).

Vasovic, A., 'Serbs Mull over Partitioning of Kosovo', *Balkan Investigative Reporting Network*, 16 August 2007; at http://birn.eu.com/en/99/10/3863/.

Velikonja, M., 'Ex-Home: Balkan Culture in Slovenia after 1991', in Resic and Tornquist (eds), *The Balkans in Focus* (Nordic Academic Press, 2002).

Velikonja, M., *Religious Separation and Political Intolerance in Bosnia-Herzegovina* (College Station: Texas A&M University Press, 2003).

Verdery, K., 'From Parent-State to Family Patriarchs: Gender and Nation in Contemporary Eastern Europe', *East European Politics and Societies*, 8, 2, Spring 1994.

Verdery, K., *The Political Lives of Dead Bodies* (New York: Columbia University Press, 2000).

Verdery, K., *What Was Socialism and What Comes Next?* (Princeton, NJ: Princeton University Press, 1996).

Veselinovič, B. and Ali Ž., 'Intervju: dr. France Bučar. Politična elita nima odgovora, kako naj se obnaša v novi Evropi / Interview: Dr France Bučar. The political elite has now answer as to how to behave in the new Europe', *Dnevnik, Dnevnikov Objektiv* (Saturday Supplement), 17 November 2007.

Vezjak, B., *Sproščena ideologija Slovencev: o političnih implikacijah filozofema 'sproščenost'/ The relaxed ideology of the Slovenes: on the political implications of the philosopheme relaxedness* (Ljubljana: Mirovni inštitut, Inštitut za sodobne družbene in politične študije, 2007).

Vidojković, M., *Kandže*, 5th edn (Belgrade: Samizdat B92, 2005).

Vladisavljević, N., *Serbia's Antibureaucratic Revoluition: Milošević, the Fall of Communism and Nationalist Mobilization* (Basingstoke: Palgrave Macmillan, 2008).

Vladisavljević, N., 'Grass Roots Groups, Milošević or Dissident Intellectuals? A Controversy over the Origins and Dynamics of Mobilization of Kosovo Serbs in the 1980s', *Nationalities Papers*, 32, 4, 2004: 781–796.

Vodopivec, A., 'Marko Perković Thompson o ustaškoj ikonografiji na svojim koncertima' (*Novi list*, 15 June 2004).

Vojnić. D., 'Zemlje u tranziciji – od konca osamdesetih do konca devedesetih – s posebnim osvrtom na Hrvatsku', in *Hrvatsko gospodarstvo u tranziciji* (Zagreb: ekonomski institut, 1999): 363–397.

Vosnjak, B., *A Bulwark against German: The Fight of the Slovenes, the Western Branch of the Jugoslavs, for National Existence* (London: George Allen & Unwin, 1917).

Vujačić, Veljko Marko, *Communism and Nationalism in Russia and Serbia* (1995).

Wachtel, A., *Making a Nation, Breaking a Nation: Literature and Cultural Politics in Yugoslavia* (Stanford: Stanford University Press, 1998).

Waldron, J., *Liberal Rights, Collected papers 1981–1991* (Cambridge: Cambridge University Press, 1993).

Weber, M., *The Methodology of the Social Sciences* (New York: Free Press, 1949).

Wenham, J.W. *The Elements of New Testament Greek* (Cambridge: Cambridge University Press, 1977), p. 196.

Wenke, S, 'Gendered Representation of the Nation's Past and Future', in Blom, I., Hagemann, K. and Hall, C. (eds), *Gendered Nations. Nationalism and Gender Order in the Long Nineteenth Century* (New York and Oxford: Berg, 1999).

Williams, B., *Truth and Truthfulness* (Princeton, NJ: Princeton University Press, 2002).

Wilson, T. M. and Donnan, H. (eds), *Border Identities: Nation and State at International Frontiers* (Cambridge: Cambridge University Press, 1998).

Young, I. M., *Justice and the Politics of Difference* (Princeton, NJ: Princeton University Press, 1990).

Žagar, M., *Sodobni federalizem s posebnim poudarkom na asimetrični federaciji v večnacionalnih državah* (PhD thesis, Ljubljana, 1999).

Žagar, M., *Upliv encipo pri pranje: seminarsko diplomsko delo* (Ljubljan, 1990).

Zajedničko saopštenje povodim materijalnog polažaja studenata, 21 November 2006, Internet presentation of the Faculty of Philosophy, University of Belgrade, www.f.bg.ac.yu.

Zajc, Marko, *Problem, ki se veča z leti: Slovensko-hrvaška meja skozi zgodovino. / The Problem That Recurrs: Slovenian-Croatian Border through History.* In Delo (Ljubl.), 14 October 2006, y. 48, No. 239, pp. 22–3.

Žavčanin, F. K., 'O zadevi Vodnikovega spomenik' (*Novice*, 24 November 1858): 372.

Zimmermann, W., 'The Last Ambassador: A Memoir of the Collapse of Yugoslavia', in *Foreign Affairs*, March/April 1995.

Žolnir, N., 'Usoda spomenikov Kidriča in Kardelja skoraj odločena' (*Delo*, 31 January 1996): 6.

Žižek, S., *Jezik ideologija Slovenci* (Ljubljana: DE, 1987).

Žižek, S., *Kitajska dolina solz / The Chinese Valley of Tears. In Dnevnik*, Objektiv (Saturday Supplement), 15 December 2007, p. 7.

Index

CPI Antony Rowe
Eastbourne, UK
August 29, 2019